NO TIME FOR FEAR

No Time For Fear

Voices of American Military Nurses in World War II

Diane Burke Fessler

∞ The paper used in this publication meets the minimum requirements of ANSI/NISO
Z39.48-1992 (R 1997) (Permanence of Paper).

 Michigan State University Press
East Lansing, Michigan 48823-5245

13 12 11 10 09 08 07   3 4 5 6 7 8 9 10

LIBRARY OF CONGRESS CATALOGING-IN-PUBLICATION DATA

No time for fear : voices of American military nurses in World War II / Diane Burke
Fessler.
p. cm.
Includes bibliographical references and index.
ISBN-13: 978-0-87013-440-1 (pbk. : alk. paper)
ISBN-10: 0-87013-440-X (pbk. : alk. paper)
1. World War, 1939–1945—Medical care—United States. 2. World War, 1939–1945—
Personal narratives, American. 3. Nurses—United States—Biography. 4. United States—
Armed Forces—Nurses—Biography. I. Title.
D807.U6F47 1996
940.54'7573—dc20
95-26667

g **green** Michigan State University Press is a member of the Green Press Initiative
press and is committed to developing and encouraging ecologically responsible
INITIATIVE
publishing practices. For more information about the Green Press Initiative and the use
of recycled paper in book publishing, please visit *www.greenpressinitiative.org*.

Visit Michigan State University Press on the World Wide Web at
www.msupress.msu.edu

Nurses are grand people, human creatures who will go through pretty much anything to ease pain.

Congresswoman Frances Payne Bolton, 1943

Contents

Foreword by *Senator Daniel K. Inouye* ix

Foreword by *Colonel M. Irene Clark Woodman* xiii

Acknowledgments xv

Introduction 1

Chronology 9

Chapter 1. Pearl Harbor, Hawaii
"Like rats in a trap." 11

Chapter 2. Pacific Theater of War
*"You can see what men are made of when
you get them freshly wounded."* 29

Chapter 3. Japanese Internment Camps, Philippines
*"You don't know what freedom
is until you lose it."* 79

Chapter 4. China, Burma, and India
"Culture Shock" 105

Chapter 5. North Africa, Sicily, and Italy
*"90 mm shells would zoom right over
the hospital."* 123

Chapter 6. England
"Buzz bombs, blackouts, and barrage balloons" .151

Chapter 7. France
"Normandy, and the Battle of the Bulge" 167

Chapter 8. Germany
"V-E Day" 189

Chapter 9.   Russia
             "The Eastern Command" 193

Chapter 10. The 166th General Hospital
             "Raining again" 199

Chapter 11. Snap Shots
             "You never know what will happen when you
             join the service." 233

Chapter 12. The War Ends
             "I can't express how I felt when I heard it
             was over." 243

Further Reading 263

        Index 265

Foreword

This is an amazing story, and one that has been waiting to be told for nearly fifty years. Those of us who experienced the horrors of World War II on a first-hand basis, to a person, quickly developed a very deep appreciation for the dedication, compassion, and professionalism of our comrades who were serving in the military nurse corps. When we were wounded, *they* were ever present, taking care of our needs, listening to our inner thoughts and prayers and, if necessary, chiding us to regain independence. When we were under fire, *they* were often right there with us, often suffering the same wounds and "fears of the unknown" that we did.

And yet, as I reflect upon how much World War II has affected our nation and been described in the popular media, on our television and movie screens, and through a seemingly infinite number of publications, I realize that very few historians or producers have ever taken the time to listen to the nurses' story—to the thoughts and reflections of those women and their medical colleagues who gave so much of themselves to our nation and its warriors in their time of greatest need, while asking so little for themselves. This publication is the story of *their* experiences, *their* thoughts, and *their* remembrances. It is an imaginative collection of voices and sounds, of hopes and aspirations, of dreads and destruction. Here is a very personal view of a critical component of our Armed Forces that very few have ever thought about, let alone experienced. And yet, without these dedicated professionals, many of us simply would never have been able to return home to our loved ones, or return to the front line to continue to serve our nation. All of us who were in uniform, as well as those who were not, owe so much to those who were so few in number but so large in their impact upon our daily lives.

As Chairman of the Senate Appropriations Subcommittee which has jurisdiction over the Department of Defense, I was very pleased to annually receive testimony from each of the services' chief nurses. To put it mildly, the more tradition-oriented medical establishment simply does not know how to respond. Those of us who served and were wounded in World War II, and then came under military nursing care, know only too well that their clinical accomplishments, leadership, and dedication have always been there.

There are many individual stories to be told, from many different perspectives. And yet, taken together there really is only one voice, one vision, one mission: to serve our nation to the fullest extent of one's ability. *No Time For Fear* is a most appropriate title, a very timely story. Professional nursing was there when the bombs and strife first struck Pearl Harbor. Flight nurses flew under heavy fire onto the fields and beaches of France and Italy, and through the narrow gaps of the Himalayan Mountains; they ditched in the treacherous oceans of the Atlantic and Pacific. Hospital ships were chased by submarines, and nurses were captured in the Philippines, walking in the infamous marches behind enemy lines. They froze, starved, suffered segregation, and became ill with numerous unknown diseases. Many never returned. They also experienced the pleasures of learning new cultures and the joys of making lasting friendships. Nurses persevered and provided the highest quality of care under the most adverse conditions, often against the greatest odds. They made a real difference in the lives of their patients—I can assure you that no higher compliment can be paid. They are the future of their profession—a most glorious profession. *Their* story is our nation's story.

Daniel K. Inouye
United States Senator

While serving as a platoon commander in the 442nd Regimental Combat Team, Lieutenant Inouye was seriously wounded in action near Aulla, Italy, in April 1944. For heroism he was awarded the Distinguished Service Cross and three Purple Hearts. In his autobiography, Journey to Washington *(Prentice Hall, 1967), Senator Inouye gives tribute to an army nurse who helped him in Leghorn, Italy:*

I wish I could remember her name—I'll never forget her face—but all I remember is that she came from Eagle Pass, Texas, and as far as I was concerned she was the best damn nurse in the United States Army. In a single moment she had made me see the job that lay ahead of me, and in all the weeks that followed she found a thousand subtle ways to help me master it.

Foreword

To army and navy nurses *duty* is the most sublime word in the English language. During World War II nurses performed their duties under fire near the front lines throughout the world, in all theaters of war. We lived and worked under the same hardships as the men in battle in many areas overseas. Nurses lived in tents with shortages of heat, electricity, and water. Many ate field rations without complaint, bathed in their helmets, helped set up hospitals, and were on duty for double and triple shifts.

These are the nurses who came from across America and enjoyed dancing to the music of Glenn Miller and Guy Lombardo. We missed our families, got involved in sports, and watched romantic movies with the men we dated. Always, concern for the men in combat was first in mind, and duties were performed with courage and selfless devotion. Countless missions of mercy are well known to the soldier, sailor, marine, and airman, as well as the families of combat veterans. Indeed the nurses' contributions have earned many awards and decorations. Because of the success of procedures established during the early days of the war in the North African theater, the same were used in every theater of war to evacuate the sick and injured by train, hospital ship, and aircraft.

This book is about military nurses who served our nation and know first hand the many faces of war because of the duties they performed under combat conditions and the hardships some endured as prisoners of war.

M. Irene Clark Woodman
Colonel, U.S. Army, Retired

Stationed at Schofield Barracks, Territory of Hawaii, when Japanese bombs hit Pearl Harbor and the surrounding military bases in 1941, M. Irene Clark Woodman tells of that harrowing time in this book. She later served as the twelfth chief of the Army Nurse Corps from 1963 to 1967. Retiring after thirty years' service with the rank of colonel, she was awarded the Distinguished Service Medal and the Army Commendation Medal.

After retirement Colonel Clark married Professor Ernest A. H. Woodman. In 1993 she was inducted into the Michigan Women's Hall of Fame. That same year she received the University of Michigan School of Nursing Outstanding Alumni Achievement Award.

Acknowledgments

Gratitude to nurses who relived fifty years with photo albums, scrapbooks, and uniforms; Lorraine Taylor, my "Auntie Raine," who did the things that made me want to write this book; Charlotte Mallon and Helen Miller for their early help in locating others; my husband, Bob, and son, Bill, who were patient and helpful in countless ways; and Victor Howard of MSU Press with his encouraging words.

Introduction

The voices you hear in *No Time For Fear* speak proudly. Nothing prepared these nurses for the magnitude of a Pearl Harbor bombing or the sight of an overfilled ward of legless and armless young men fresh from battles in France or Iwo Jima. This oral history collection provides an important counterpoint to the strategy and planning of warfare so often chronicled by the male warrior. Women, moreover, take center stage. One smells, sees, and feels war through their senses.

"My parents took me to the train when I joined the army, and I remember Mom saying, 'You might accept sending your son to war, but not your daughter.'" As she remembers her mother's words, the graying grandmother becomes the twenty-one-year-old nurse, eager to meet the world in 1942.

Nurses served bravely under fire beginning with the first battle of World War II at Pearl Harbor in Hawaii. In the Philippines and Guam American military nurses were captured by the Japanese and continued to use their skills to aid other prisoners, despite having to endure devastating illnesses and extreme hardship.

World War II is recorded in books, films, awards, and ceremonies that deservedly commend the brave fighting men, strategies of the generals and admirals, as well as the ships, tanks, and planes used to carry out the battles. Consistently, there is a serious lack of recognition of nurses who were overseas with the soldiers, close to the fighting, and caring for wounded men brought straight from the battlefield. The nurses of the 1930s and 1940s who volunteered to join the army and navy have compelling stories that will now be recognized as an important part of that war's strategy.

American troops were not sent into battle in World War II without plans for medical care. When the invasion of the Nazi-held coast of

Normandy took place on 6 June 1944, thousands of nurses, doctors, corps-men, and supporting hospital staff had been waiting for months in Great Britain to cross the English Channel with the troops. They were prepared to set up Field Hospitals, Evacuation Hospitals, Station Hospitals, and General Hospitals as the battles moved across the Continent. Hospital ships waited offshore to receive the wounded and return them to the States for more care. Nurses flew in evacuation aircraft, caring for injured GIs on their way to treatment in hospitals back in England. They were on every continent by war's end, prepared to do their jobs under any circum-stances and conditions.

These nurses' war stories began as a tribute to my favorite aunt, and became this collection of precious memories told by more than a hundred aunts, mothers, and grandmothers. They personally relate the horrors, tri-umphs, romances, and frustrations of war. Each tells her own story as she remembers living it.

It never rained when I was growing up that I didn't hear my Aunt Lorraine say, "You should have seen the mud in France! It was up to our knees!" I watched her go off to war and return in her neat, olive-drab uni-form. A brown eyed redhead, she smiled at us from under a brimmed uni-form hat in the framed portrait in our living room. Her experiences in both Europe and Japan opened up the world to this little girl, who never tired of hearing about her trip across the oceans.

I had many criteria in mind while selecting the subjects for inter-views. First and foremost, I wished to document the lives and memories of the women who shared my aunt's adventurous and meaningful experi-ences. It was important to mention the varied locations, the crude living conditions, and the willingness to move frequently. Over and over I was told by these women, whose ages now range from seventy-two to ninety-five, how proud they were to know that the nurses of WWII were going to be remembered. They'd felt neglected as the years passed by. It was also important to show how thousands of young American women vol-unteered to forsake the safety of their own country to face known and unknown dangers, while forming bonds of friendship never to be bro-ken. Thousands of military nurses proudly cared for servicemen in the United States, but only those who served overseas during the years 1941 to 1946 were interviewed. At that time Hawaii and Alaska were consid-ered overseas, as they were not states, and each had been invaded by the enemy.

Numerous members of the hospital staffs were greatly appreciated and fondly remembered by these women, including the corpsmen, wardboys, doctors and Red Cross workers. Nothing should detract from the courageous medics who were side-by-side in battle with the American fighting men. They shared the hardships, anguish and rewards recounted by nurses in this book. A few women have written their own books, to be read by family and old friends at reunions. I have not taken from these books, but they are listed in the Further Reading section.

Interviews followed the same general outline of a questionnaire sent to approximately 300 nurses. With almost 200 responding, a recorded phone call or personal meeting followed. More often than not the direction struck its own course, depending on the interests of the woman being interviewed. A few preferred to write their experiences. Narratives were recorded, transcribed word for word, then edited for flow, continuity, and chronology. I retained all that was historical, anecdotal, and of human interest, including the stories of a few non-nurses. Repetitions were deleted, unless it was clear how these experiences affected different people, or unusual conditions were repeated throughout the world.

"My memory is, (pause) detained," explained a nurse when asked about a specific date. This book is about memory and the experiences of those who went to war more than fifty years ago. Age takes a toll in most people's memories, and it can be difficult for even younger veterans to recall exact dates and places. Taking this into account, many nurses gave me yellowed copies of their transfer orders and other official documents. Being specific about dates and places wasn't as important as hearing how they remembered the experiences military nurses shared overseas. I verified dates and locations when possible and deleted them when it wasn't vital to the story.

During an interview, one woman asked me to stop the recorder because she had something to relate that might embarrass a doctor should he be alive. She then told of "specialing" a young GI as he died (to stay at a patient's bedside until he dies), because a surgeon had left an instrument inside his wounded body. She's carried this memory for over fifty years, and still can't forget it. Following a telephone interview, another nurse wrote to ask that her story not be told, and it isn't. Though her war experience wasn't unusual, she wouldn't tell me why it bothered her. When asked about indiscretions on the part of nurses, a woman admitted they certainly happened, then added, "It was rare, but under the circumstances, we didn't judge each other." I was asked by some who'd remained in the service for careers, what was my purpose and what were my credentials as to understanding the military life. My aunt's service and my husband's twenty-five year military career opened the door with them, and they knew I would "understand the lingo."

Nurses died in the line of duty during the war, such as Wilma Vinsant Shea, killed in action over Germany while flying with the 806th Medical Air Evacuation Squadron. In her honor an award is given annually to an air force evacuation nurse. Six nurses were killed when the hospital ship USS *Comfort* was hit by a Japanese suicide plane on 28 April 1945. An explosion killed nurses during the battle of Anzio, Italy. In this book readers will learn about some nurses who returned to the States as patients because they suffered from shell shock. Several women discuss their personal challenges when the war ended, dealing with what is now referred to as "Veterans' Syndrome." Long after the Vietnam War ended in the 1970s, this term indicated the problems veterans had in leaving war behind, and nurses of World War II were no different.

Several groups of nurses gather frequently for reunions and are willing to have me attend their meetings, or at least search out members. It was through one of these contacts that I attempted to locate Jeannette "Tex" Gleason. Boy. She "hit the silk" during a routine evacuation flight over China, without prior parachute training, and landed safely on a mountaintop, scared but safe. Her exciting story is told in Esther Baer Moseley's autobiography, *Lady Don't Stop Here.* Though the brave and inspiring stories of army and navy nurses captured in the Philippines is recounted here, I regret not being able to contact any of the navy nurses captured by the Japanese on Guam at the beginning of the war. A chapter in *Navy Nurse* by Page Cooper tells of their internment and eventual liberation.

Officially noncombatant, some nurses were issued firearms to protect themselves and their patients. Nurses were awarded numerous medals and awards, including The Legion of Merit, Silver Star, Distinguished Flying Cross, Bronze Star, Air Medal, and Purple Heart.

Objections to nurses being close to the front lines, or performing duties that had only been done by doctors, were put aside as need overtook old-fashioned standards. However, racial segregation was official policy, and nurses were not immune. Mrs. Eleanor Roosevelt, and a few other prominent Americans, prevailed upon the army surgeon general to recruit African-American nurses into the Army Nurse Corps in 1941, prior to the attack on Pearl Harbor. A quota of forty-eight nurses was set. The attack on

Pearl Harbor eliminated the quota, increasing the number of African-American nurses accepted. Segregated in their living and working assignments, contingents of nurses were sent to various areas within the continental United States and overseas. During World War II, African-American nurses were assigned as segregated units with the army to Liberia, England, Burma, and the South Pacific, including Australia, New Guinea, and the Philippines. Their proud stories are told in this book. Within the United States, African-American nurses were assigned to hospitals holding German, Italian, and Japanese prisoners of war, as well as returning American servicemen. African-American women were not accepted as flight nurses or in the U.S. Navy Nurse Corps until 1945.

During the American Revolution and the Civil War, the government hired civilian women to work in military hospitals, on and off the battlefield. Many were relatives of the sick and wounded and helped others as the need arose. The lack of trained medical aid during the Civil War prompted nursing schools to spring up around the country between 1865 and the end of the 19th Century. When the Spanish-American War began in 1898, thousands of trained nurses answered the call for contract nurses with the army, some being assigned to overseas posts. The need for nurses was obvious, and the Army Nurse Corps was formally established in 1901, with the Navy Nurse Corps following in 1908.

The First World War saw over ten thousand nurses serving in Europe, in addition to those on duty in Puerto Rico, Hawaii, Philippines, and China. By 1920 the government recognized military nurses with relative rank, thus giving them most of the rights and privileges of officers, but more importantly defining their position in the military establishment. Soon to follow were retirement and disability benefits.

Military nurses were given little or no military training until 1943, when special training programs began. At first, nurses were sent overseas with inadequate clothing and unfamiliarity with their military relationship in the army. Uniforms for nurses were different almost every year of the war, and often from one location to another. Navy nurses received their first uniforms in 1942. The narratives in this book often recount the variety (or lack) of military training and uniforms that many of them experienced.

The American Red Cross recruited nurses for the military services before and after the beginning of World War II. Some tell how they signed a request to join the ARC upon graduation from nurses' training and soon afterward were surprised with orders to report to an army camp. Congress authorized actual commissioned rank for nurses during the war, when both the civilian and military need for nurses was great and recruiting was difficult. So desperate was the need for nurses in all theaters of operation and in military hospitals at home that a bill to draft graduate nurses was passed in the House of Representatives in March 1945. Because of the magnificent response by nurses and progress of the military campaigns, the bill was withdrawn before action was completed in the Senate.

Gathering these stories in person, by telephone, and through written records, has been immensely rewarding to me. I cried with "my nurses" as they remembered individual soldiers. Every nurse could recall at least one patient, usually referred to as a boy, who remains in her thoughts to this day. "I'll never forget . . . " or "I always wonder what happened to . . . " were phrases heard over and over again. "You can see what men are made of when you get them as fresh casualties," a navy nurse who served twenty-two years exclaimed, "and believe me ours are made of the best!" The nurses' laughter caught me also, and we would "howl" at a memory of an embarrassing moment or the experiences of all when they tried to live like soldiers in skirts and stockings. Patriotism was, and still is, extremely important to these adventurous women. Throughout the narratives, the word *we* is used to refer to "the United States," "our side," "the Allies," "our boys," or other nurses sharing the same experiences. Often it was difficult to coax a personal experience from them when they wanted to relate what the whole unit did.

The subject of romance was not difficult to recall, since many of the nurses married men they met during the war. At the beginning, military nurses had to be unmarried, and rules against dating enlisted men were to be strictly enforced. "But we liked them," I was informed several times, and marriages took place between nurse officers and men of all ranks. As the need for nurses grew, married women volunteered, often hoping to follow their husbands overseas.

During World War II, nurses were allotted trust and responsibility, which introduced a new era of professional growth. Techniques once performed only by physicians were done by nurses as doctors relied on them because of shortages. Having corpsmen perform non-nursing chores relieved nurses of many routine housekeeping duties and dignified their professional status. After the war, nurses were involved in health care with greater self-esteem and responsibility, which continues today.

Before World War II, nursing schools were connected to hospitals, and the women learned in classrooms as well as on-the-job. After a three-year program, they were graduated with the title of Registered Nurse (RN) and some would take specialized training with universities' hospitals. The military nurse at that time was required to be an RN, already trained at her own expense. As the need grew greater during wartime, the military services provided training in certain specialties, such as anesthesiology. After the war, the GI Bill (tuition for veterans) helped many go on to receive bachelor's and master's degrees at universities. Most of the nurses went back to civilian life after 1946, but a surprising number of them returned to active duty to serve again in the Korean War and even in Vietnam.

Nurses are trained to be selfless and not to despair. During interviews it became clear they didn't "talk shop" with each other in order to avoid becoming emotional at the expense of the patient. Morale of the overseas nurses was high when the patient loads were heaviest, and complaints of being overworked were never heard. "I hope your book won't be morbid," a nurse said as we parted. "We made sure we had a lot of fun when we had time." In this book, their lighthearted attitudes prevail because the memories of camaraderie and sisterhood during wartime are strong, even after fifty years.

Chronology

1901		Army Nurse Corps established.
1908		Navy Nurse Corps established.

World War II

1941	7 December	Japanese forces bomb Pearl Harbor, Hawaii.
	8 December	United States declares war on Japan.
		Japanese bomb Philippine Islands and Guam.
	11 December	United States declares war on Germany and Italy.
1942	January	U.S. Army and U.S. Navy nurses are taken prisoner in Philippines.
	February	Congress authorizes commissioned rank for military nurses.
		Military nurses are sent to England, North Africa, Australia, and India, and serve on hospital ships in war zones.
	25 December	First U.S. Army Air Force flight nurses depart for combat zones in North Africa and the Pacific.
1943	January	Medical air evacuation takes hold in North Africa, Europe, and the Pacific theater.
	July	Military nurses land in Sicily and Italy.

1944	6 June	D day invasion by Allied forces launched on the northern coast of France against the Germans.
	December	Battle of the Bulge
1945	10 January	First navy flight nurses graduate and depart for Pacific theater.
	February	Nurses rescued from Japanese prison camps in Philippines.
	8 May	V-E Day; war in Europe officially ended.
	2 September	V-J Day; victory over Japan.

PEARL HARBOR, HAWAII 7 DECEMBER 1941
7:55 A.M

"Like rats in a trap"

Agnes Shurr U.S. Navy   **USS Solace**

A native of North Dakota, Agnes joined the navy in the 1930s; it was the pay and the chance to see the world which attracted her. She retired thirty years later.

Before the war, we nurses were often invited to dinner on other ships in Pearl Harbor, and I remember one of the captains asking me something that I have remembered often over the years. He said, "What do you folks think of the situation? Do you think there is going to be a war?" He must have thought we had information he didn't.

I was asleep that Sunday morning on the hospital ship *Solace* out in the middle of Pearl Harbor, "in the stream," as we say. "COMMAND BATTLE STATIONS!" was the first thing I heard. Our sailors were in their dress whites waiting to go ashore on liberty, but when the explosions started, they went around in the liberty boats, picking up injured and wounded out of the water. We received casualties almost immediately. Our ship was painted white, had a red cross on each side, and must have stood out among the other ships in the harbor. But it was never hit. Later that morning the ship moved to a more secluded area in the harbor.

We worked all through the day without stopping. Late at night, I was sitting at the dinner table with other nurses when the executive officer came and talked to us for awhile. "Well," he said, "we don't know what's going to happen next. But we're all still here, kind of like rats in a trap! We're going to carry on the best we can." Because we were so busy, I hadn't been aware really of the seriousness of our own situation. I could see the ships in the water and the smoke rolling up and hear the sounds of ships firing at aircraft. But around the table, it began to dawn on me that we were really in a precarious and dangerous position in the harbor.

11

A few days later we were allowed to go ashore for the day, and the air raid siren sounded, so we had to return to the ship. Somehow that was more frightening to me because I didn't know if we would be able to get back on the ship or be stranded. The ship was my safe haven. In Honolulu one day, I was carrying a lot of art supplies and dropped them as I was crossing the street. A young American-Japanese boy stopped and picked them up for me. I remember thinking, "These are the people who just bombed us." Of course, he was probably a good American, but I couldn't help thinking that.

After all these years, I still recall one boy who was very badly burned. His mother wrote him a letter that I'm sure she meant to be encouraging, that said, "When you think your troubles are terrible, you need to put on a tight pair of shoes, and you'll forget about your other troubles." All I could think was that he couldn't even get shoes on. Of course, she didn't know how bad he was, but he did kind of smile.

Valera Vaubel Wiskerson U.S. Navy   Navy Hospital, Pearl Harbor

Val left a position with a Chicago hospital to join up in 1937. After a tour in San Diego, she arrived for duty in Hawaii in 1940.

I'd just served breakfast to the patients who couldn't go to the mess hall and was going across to get some food for myself, when I heard a horrible explosion. I looked across the water at the hangar on Ford Island. It looked like it was picked up into the air and dropped down—PLUNK! There was nothing but smoke where there had been that great big airplane hangar with all the planes sitting in a row.

A plane with a huge red circle came close enough to tell it was Japanese. It dived over the hospital, and if I'd had a gun I could have killed him. I was a sharpshooter at the time, because a fellow had been taking me with him to practice shooting.

They started bringing men in with burns and fractures by whatever means they could get there in. Patients had tags on them telling how much morphine or whatever had been done for them. Doctors decided who went to which ward or what treatment they needed. I was an acting dietitian but also worked in other wards for the next several days. The diets were mostly liquids because of so many burn cases.

Patients who'd been there before the bombing left to return to duty and didn't take their records with them, so we never knew what happened to them.

An experience I can't forget to this day was a patient who was in shock. When I went to get him a blanket, none were there, so I went upstairs to get one. A doctor called me over to help lift a patient in the burn ward. We'd lift a patient up and draw the sheet from underneath, and because the burned skin came off, fresh oil was put on the sheet. I was holding under the patients' thigh and lower leg to raise him when his leg separated from the knee in my hands. I turned white as the sheet, and the doctor looked at my face. I took deep breaths to keep from fainting. After the patient was put on the sheet, I found a blanket and took it downstairs. The patient who needed the blanket had died, and a new one was in his place, so I covered him with the blanket.

I remember the burn cases where eyelids and lashes were burned, and you couldn't see the nose. Burns smell horrible. Our chief nurse kept a perfumed handkerchief in her pocket, and while she was feeding a burn patient, she would sniff it. Once a patient asked if he could sniff it too, because he couldn't stand the smell. She thinks it saved his life because he ate better then.

Volunteers came to the hospital to help, such as service wives and friends. Prostitutes from Honolulu came too, but they weren't all helpful, because some tried to get a little business, and we had to throw them out.

Soon after the "blitz" I was assigned to the shipyard dispensary. Everyone on the base had to be given tetanus and other shots, and we were just changing needles and giving shots to civilians as well as military families by the hundreds. Then I set up a dispensary at the main gate so the families wouldn't have to go into the shipyard.

Phyllis Dana U.S. Navy   **Navy Hospital, Pearl Harbor**

Phyl had been at Pearl Harbor for six months; she was twenty-four years old when the war began.

Burn patients were the biggest challenge. We had eight wards for burn victims because men on the ships were thrown or jumped into the water where oil was burning. We used sulfa powder and mineral oil in treating them; today that is a really bad treatment as it isn't sterile. We relieved the pain with morphine and phenobarbital. The rate of survival was surprisingly good, considering what we can do now for burn victims.

The nurses slept in the wards so I wasn't aware of what was going on, even in the rest of the hospital, for several days. I can still hear the sounds of those men moaning. For the rest of my life I was aware that I could survive and function in emergencies and for the long term.

Lenore Terrell Rickert U.S. Navy   Navy Hospital, Pearl Harbor

Lenore became a Navy Nurse in 1939 and had just begun her second year at Hospital Point.

Everybody wants to know if we were afraid. Fear never entered into it. Most everyone who was there says the same thing. We never even gave it a thought, never worried about our personal safety.

I was making rounds with the Medical Officer of the Day at the Pearl Harbor naval hospital when we heard a plane right overhead. Because of the patients, our aircraft never flew over the hospital. Even though navy planes were right there at Ford Island, and Hickam Field was on the other side of us, it just never happened. We ran to look and the plane was coming in between the two wards. We knew right away what was happening.

I ran to the nurses' quarters to sound the alert, and that's when the actual bombing started. Then I could hear the bombing. I saw the planes up above, and I could see the bombs coming out six in a row. The first Japanese plane that was shot down crashed in the hospital yard, but there were only some minor fires from that.

The ambulatory patients immediately left the hospital to get back to their ships. One patient, whose eyes were both bandaged, got out of bed, crawled underneath, and pulled a

Lenore Terrell, U.S. Navy, survived the bombing of Pearl Harbor, 7 December 1941.

blanket down to lie on, so we could use the bed for the wounded. Everyone was worrying about the others and not themselves.

The hospital really surprised me, everything went so smoothly. Up until that time, if you sent your weekly supply request on Friday, you were lucky if you received fifty percent of it the next week. On that day you scribbled what you needed on a piece of paper and someone ran over to the supply room and brought it right back. It was unbelievable, the way the whole hospital was that day. The corpsmen were spectacular during it all.

Helen Entrikin U.S. Navy   **Navy Hospital, Pearl Harbor**

Helen, a 1936 graduate of the University of Pennsylvania, joined the navy because the pay was better than civilian nursing. In 1941 she was in Hawaii with her sister, Sara, who was in the army nurse detachment.

My twin sister was a U.S. Army nurse stationed in Hawaii and urged me to transfer there because it was so nice. Sara was at the hospital at Hickam Field, right across the fence from our navy base. We were both on duty that morning.

When the planes dropped their bombs, then strafed as they came back, I ran inside the hospital and gathered up the narcotics and everything we would need. A little dressing room became a mini-operating theater, because the regular operating rooms were so backlogged. The patients were scared, and when they died we received others right away in their place. We put mattresses on the hallway floor to rest a little at a time.

My sister and I were both worrying about each other, because we heard that each place was being bombed and leveled. A patient who had a leg cast stayed at the desk and tried to get on the phone to Hickam. The lines were down, but about 10:30 that night, Sara got through to tell me she was all right. Four days later I was able to send a telegram to our mother, who had the two of us to worry about. I finally saw my sister about two weeks after the raid.

Sara Entrikin U.S. Army   **Hickam Field**

"Sally" had applied to the two services but the army responded first. She had worked at Schofield Barracks first and then transferred to the army air base.

Hearing the explosions, I ran outside and saw the red sun on a plane that was coming in so close that I could see the faces of the pilots. One of them looked at us and smiled. I rushed to the hospital. Casualties were coming in fast and furious because the barracks were right along the runway and that's where the bombs hit first. Our hospital was close to the runway also, and we had a lot of noise and smoke from shells ricocheting over to it. There were only seven of us nurses, and we couldn't possibly begin to take care of all the wounded and dying men. The decision was made to treat patients with first-aid-type care and send them to Tripler General Hospital in ambulances. Soon there weren't enough ambulances, so the local people drove patients in their cars.

Not too far from the hospital there was an American flag flying, and after the Japs dropped their bombs, one plane came back and circled, shooting until the flag was torn to shreds. That night we put up blackout window covers; we were told that if captured, to only give our name, rank, and serial number. Hearing that was kind of scary.

I didn't know if Helen was dead or alive, everything was so hectic. My sister and I tried to call each other but couldn't get through. An ambulatory patient sat at the desk, trying to reach her all day, and finally did about 10:30 that night.

Mildred Irene Clark Woodman U.S. Army   **Schofield Barracks**

Irene had studied at Mayo Clinic at the army's request and became a pioneer in the application of intravenous (IV) anesthesia.

Loud explosions awakened me and I heard planes overhead. I opened the door and saw planes coming through the pass in the mountains between Honolulu and Schofield. The large bright insignia of the rising sun was boldly on the side of each plane. They flew so close I could hear the radio communications between the pilots. In one minute I dressed and ran to the hospital.

The hospital was hit, even though the hospital building had a large red cross painted on the roof, according to the provisions of the Geneva

Convention. Casualties were arriving on stretchers as I reported to the operating room, with ambulance sirens wailing in the background. In a short time, the nine operating rooms were extremely busy, while patients waited for care in the corridor. I kept hearing planes overhead, but we were too busy to be afraid or to ask what was happening. All day and into the evening I went from one patient to the next without sitting down or having a cup of coffee. Someone brought fried chicken in but few of us felt hungry, as we had seen too much death and were involved with the most serious wounds and bravest of men. Patients had arms and legs amputated, severe chest and spinal wounds, abdominal and cranial wounds. Many wanted to go out and fight back. Some wanted a prayer said or to hear the 23rd Psalm, and we obliged them along with the surgical procedures.

Two anesthetists slept in the hospital for over two weeks following the attack. Operating rooms and patient areas were blacked out with dark army blankets; it was like a steambath at night when we had to operate. Later, black paint was used on the windows.

Sometime near early morning following the attack, several of us had the opportunity for a quiet moment to talk to each other and exchange our limited knowledge of what happened. We talked quietly since there was a rumor that the Japanese had eighty transports off Diamond Head and were landing parachute troops in the nearby cane fields. The subject of being captured and becoming prisoners of war came up and each voiced her plan. Two indicated they would walk into the sea, others would hide in caves, some would go with their friends to prison, while others of us would fight to the death and never be captured alive.

The Prayer of an Army Nurse
by Mildred Irene Clark

Hear my prayer in silence before Thee
      as I ask for courage each day.
Grant that I may be worthy of the sacred
      pledge of my profession
and the lives of those entrusted to my care.
Help me to offer hope and cheer in the
      hearts of men and my country.
For their faith inspires me to give the world
      and nursing my best.
Instill in me the understanding and compassion
      of those who led the way.
For I am thankful to You for giving me
      this life to live.

Gelane Matthews Barron U.S. Army   **Tripler Hospital**

Having exchanged orders with a friend bound for the Philippines, "Jerry" felt safe for the moment; her friend became a prisoner of war.

The morning of December 7, 1941, I was on duty in the Emergency Room at Tripler Hospital and met the chief nurse walking up the ramp. She had a blank stare on her face, and I said a cheery, "Good morning," and got no response. Farther on up the ramp I met a corpsman who was covered with blood. I asked him what happened and he responded, "The Japs shot me." I'd heard shelling but thought the navy was practicing. It was just before 8:00 A.M.

I went to my duty station and saw all these litters in the hallway. "Where does one start?" I thought. But I guess God gives nurses strength to do what has to be done, although most nurses who have worked ER seem to have it in triplicate. Nurses and corpsmen, in teams, gave tetanus and morphine to the patients, marking *T* and *M* on foreheads because there wasn't time for paperwork. The least injured went back to duty. Then we evaluated those who needed surgery, sending them to the operating room, and those with no recovery possibility, or DOA, to the makeshift morgue. With less than sterile techniques, somehow we had no infection or gangrene among our patients, though many of the wounds were from shrapnel. There was a constant stream of injured being brought in, and we were still working the next morning. About 5:00 A.M., we all sat on the floor and cried.

Women and children patients in the hospital were sent across the street to a storage tunnel at Fort Shafter to be safe. Working everywhere I was needed, I wound up delivering two babies in the tunnel. Fortunately, the American Medical Association was holding a convention in Honolulu, and many of the doctors went to hospitals in the area to help. Inactive nurses showed up. Some prostitutes thought the hospital was a safe place, and we put them to work making bandages, and other supplies. They were a great help, but after a couple of days, they tried to make some money and we had to get rid of them.

Doris Francis Backinger U.S. Army   **Tripler Hospital**

"Fran" graduated from the University of Kansas Medical Center and joined up in 1940; she had been at Pearl for one month.

I was making a bed in the ward when I heard loud noises, like a Fourth of July celebration. Tripler was on the side of a hill, and from the second-story balcony, I saw explosions and ships burning in the harbor below. At Hickam Field I could see wounded soldiers lying on the tarmac. I went right to the operating room, where the injured and wounded were being brought in, mostly from Hickam Field. Windows in the operating room were damaged by the strafing, and later we heard the sound of boards being hammered in place to black them out. There was no panic, but everyone kept busy doing their jobs. Nobody talked. A radio was on. The first announcement of the raid was from the comedian, Jack Benny. He was eloquent as he described the beautiful, sunny morning in Hawaii, with the palm trees, and then how we were hit. After that there were speeches by FDR and Churchill. We all just went on with the operations.

I tried to take brief naps but couldn't sleep because of emotions and anger that I kept to myself. A patient I remember well, whose leg was dangling, wanted me to take care of his buddy first. The buddy was beyond hope. Wednesday morning I went off duty and finally saw the outdoors again.

One dark night during the blackout that followed, Nellie Osterlund and I were coming back from bowling at Fort Shafter, which was just across King's Highway. I heard a rustling noise from the grassy area, and automatically said, "Stop, who goes there? Halt!" A very young man's voice came back saying, "It's the guard, ma'am." Then he said, "Ma'am, would you please put out your cigarette." I told him I wasn't smoking, and we finally figured out the light was the radium dial on my watch. That's how spooky people were.

The week before the bombing we were put on alert until Friday, December 5th, when it was lifted. We were told it was because the Japanese ambassador was coming through on a ship on his way to the mainland. A lot of us now think an attack was expected and allowed to happen to get support to go to war.

Nellie Osterlund U.S. Army   **Tripler Hospital**

Nellie joined the army while on the staff of Iowa Lutheran Hospital in Des Moines and was on the island three weeks when the bombing began.

We didn't have enough sense to be afraid, but went right to the wards. That was a scene I'll never forget. The big, open ward had about forty beds, and these bloody patients were just put on the beds. Men were picked up where they were hit, put in the ambulance or whatever vehicle could be found, brought to the hospital, and put on a bed, with all the blood, gore, and everything. We were so busy taking care of the patients that I didn't think much about what else was happening outside as far as the bombs were concerned. It was quite an experience to have that many patients to take care of all at once.

Hospitals today have emergency rooms with "umpteen" people taking care of one injury. This was different. The doctor gave priorities to those who were to have immediate care or those that could be delayed. There were some burn cases that couldn't live, and we had to leave them. That really bothered me that we couldn't do anything for them.

Everything was blacked out so we were given flashlights to work with. The flashlights had blue filters that made all the patients look blue, which wasn't so good. After a couple of days the windows were boarded up so we could turn on the lights. By Wednesday all of our patients had been taken care of properly; the blood and gore was washed off and they had been treated. That night when I went off duty, I finally realized I was scared to death. I relaxed, and thought to myself, "Oh my God!" and about what had happened. I couldn't do anything but lie there and quiver.

There were all kinds of stories going around that the Japanese had landed. "Don't trust the ones who lived on the island as they were putting poison in the water." It turned out that the Japanese-Americans were very loyal. They were as mad as anyone else. After the Battle of Midway, in June 1942, we finally felt the Japanese wouldn't be coming back.

It's hard to find the words to describe how it felt to be awakened by the sound of bombing, and then seeing Japanese planes flying all around. I'll never forget the horror of seeing smoke and fire coming from Pearl Harbor and Hickam Field, picturesque places I'd looked at every day since coming to Hawaii.

Mary Catherine Babczak Croyle U.S. Army   **Honolulu**

As a Red Cross nurse, Mary was working in Honolulu; one of her brothers was stationed on the USS Nevada in Pearl Harbor.

For eighteen months I'd been an operating room nurse at Kauikeolani Children's Hospital. On December 7th I was at mass in the convent chapel, next door to the hospital, when a nun announced the Japanese were attacking Pearl Harbor. As I ran across the lawn to return to the hospital, loud explosions could be heard in the distance. The afternoon brought us several children, badly injured by fragments of falling bombs, and in the next few days, some of them died from their injuries.

My brother's ship was badly damaged during the bombing but not sunk, and fortunately, he wasn't injured. Two other brothers were already in the service also, and on December 12 I went to Fort Shafter and joined the Army Nurse Corps. Farrington High School was taken over by the army, and I was assigned to the operating room there.

Hawaii After the Bombing

Gelane Matthews Barron U.S. Army

Following the bombing of Pearl Harbor I set up a school for medical corpsmen, and life went back to somewhat of a routine. Then in February of '42 a Japanese plane snuck in and dropped bombs on Punchbowl several times. Finally the navy found out where he was refueling and bombed that atoll.

Phyllis Dana U.S. Navy

Several of us nurses who lived in Makalapa Housing after the attack formed a "Wonderful World Club." We'd been warned not to talk about anything sensitive, even among ourselves. So if one of us said something about a boyfriend's ship leaving or that we were expecting someone, one of the others would say "wonderful world," and the subject was changed. Going through such experiences together has kept us very close friends today.

Doris Francis Backinger U.S. Army

Life settled down eventually after Pearl Harbor was attacked and I set up surgical units on other islands. On Maui we used a school building, but on Kauai we were in a tent in the middle of a field. I was married April 1943 on Maui. Instead of the traditional sabers, six officers held tommy guns in an arch over the steps when we came out of the church, and we rode away in a flower-bedecked armored car. By then nurses had dress uniforms, which my attendant, Nellie Osterlund, and I wore for the ceremony. My husband left for the South Pacific in 1944, and I went back to the mainland to be discharged and have our first child.

Leaving the chapel in Maui after her wedding, Doris Francis Backinger and husband ride off in a decorated half-track.

Mary Catherine Babczak Croyle U.S. Army

The next four-and-a-half years in Hawaii I worked with and helped care for many wonderful, heroic people. Our hospital was a stepping-stone for those wounded in the Pacific battles, and as soon as their recovery permitted, they were sent stateside. Memories of those years are of the brighter side of life, because Hawaii was a wonderful place to live and work. After all this time, I hear from two men who were in the choir with me at the Fort Shafter chapel. Most of us learned to dance the hula, and I still have the cellophane and straw hula skirt. As a matter of fact, it's been used several times since then.

My wedding was ten days after V-J Day, and three days later my husband went to Japan with the Army of Occupation. I was sent stateside with other married nurses, and he returned a year later.

**Dorothy Carter Morris U.S. Army   148th General Hospital
147th and Twenty-second Station Hospitals**

"Jane" grew up on army bases, and her first assignment was to Hawaii where her father had been stationed years before.

The day of the attack on Pearl harbor, my family was very upset that anyone would bomb "our" Hawaii, because we'd lived there in 1933. I volunteered right away to go overseas and was sent to San Francisco, attached to the 148th. We sailed to Hawaii, thinking we would go on to Australia, but stopped there. The first few months we were at Mountain View on the island of Hawaii. It was early in the war so we didn't have battlefield patients. I remember a fellow who'd been injured during maneuvers and was in a body cast, which was different than casts are today. The plaster went all the way up the back behind the head and around the chest and hips. There was a hole carved in front of the belly. This guy was ambulatory and able to get around, especially to go to a fire station near the hospital where the patients went to play poker. This patient was a big, husky kid from New York, who played poker all the time and beat everyone. When he came back to the hospital, he would have a huge wad of money stuck right in front, in the belly hole in the front of the cast.

In December 1942 I was transferred to the 147th on Oahu. The hospital had taken over St. Louis College, located in a lovely section of Honolulu, and we could walk to Waikiki when we had free time. For a while there were more army nurses than needed, and the civilian hospitals were shorthanded, so we filled in around town until the army needed us.

I had four different uniforms during that time. Going on the ship we wore blue skirts with a blue blouse and a dark blue jacket. Then we changed to olive drab uniforms. The white uniform we wore on duty was changed to a brown-and-white seersucker wraparound uniform. It was

This familiar sign in Honolulu showed how many miles it was to world cities from Kau Kau Korners, a popular restaurant at the corner of Kapiolani and Kalakaua Avenues.

always breezy and we had to hold on to our hats, the skirt, a purse, and anything else we were carrying.

My future husband was transferred to Hawaii from Canton Island and was on the army baseball team. We nurses sat on the hill and watched games, and that's how we met. Nobody said anything about my dating an enlisted man until we wanted to get married. The chief nurse didn't like it, and two weeks before the wedding she had me transferred to the Twenty-second on Maui. That chief nurse was very understanding and cooperative, and we were married as planned in Honolulu in January 1944. The baseball coach reserved a room at the Halekulani Hotel on Waikiki Beach for a reception, and we spent our four-day honeymoon there. Eddie then hopped flights over to Maui to see me whenever he could get a pass, and we'd stay with some civilian friends who had an extra room.

Our first date had been to see the movie *Pride of the Yankees*, which was about baseball, of course. The song "Always" was played in the movie, and it became "our song." We wrote letters back and forth while I was on Maui and always expressed ourselves through the titles of songs. It was the way we told each other how we felt, and songs were all through our letters.

In November our Maui group was transferred back to Oahu, near Schofield Barracks. We called it Pineapple Plantation Gulch. Eddie and I rented a place in Waikiki.

When my father was stationed in Hawaii in 1933, I'd gone to school in Lelihua near Schofield. One day I was sitting outside with some patients and a man rode by on horseback, who turned out to be the father of a high school friend of mine. He invited Eddie and me to dinner for a nice reunion.

The day after V-J Day we went to Kau Kau Korners for breakfast, and it was packed. Kau Kau Korners, on Kalakaua Avenue, was everyone's favorite place. Every serviceman and woman who was in Hawaii the last couple of years of World War II will remember Kau Kau Korners. One thing it was known for were the signs pointing to cities all over the world.

It sounds like my time in the army was pretty nice, and it was. Though I cared for an awful lot of wounded men who passed through Hawaii, I prefer to remember and talk about the happy times.

Age of Innocence

(Dedicated to the nurses who were at Pearl Harbor on December 7, 1941)

On a heavenly day of peace and love,
Bombs rained panic from up above!
Paradise was a fright'ning place,
When chaos shattered the Navy Base.
No one felt that it could be true.
Couldn't be real!—with a sky so blue.
The nurses assembled and gave their best,
Responding to needs. They met the test!
They tirelessly served their fellowmen,
Hardly believing the happenings then . . .
But, oh, it was grim!—a man-made hell.
The suff'ring they saw, no words can tell.
They shall NOT forget that day of rage!—
That ending, for all, of an innocent age.

by Maude Smith, Col., USA (Ret.)
43rd and 114th Station Hospitals

Figure 1. Map of the Pacific Theater of War

THE PACIFIC THEATER

"You can see what men are made of
when you get them freshly wounded."

T hough many Americans had never heard of Pearl Harbor, by 8 December 1941 their first major reference point for the Second World War had become this military station on the "edge" of the Pacific Ocean. Soon other stations, like Wake, Midway, and Guam took on their own immortality. Again and again, Americans and their allies, the British, Australians, and New Zealanders, went ashore onto islands whose names were known only to traders, cartographers, and the agents of the empires that had owned them. The long, brutal trek to the Japanese home islands became known as "island hopping" with names such as New Guinea, Guadalcanal, Tarawa, Saipan, the Philippines, Iwo Jima, and Okinawa. Casualties on both sides were humbling, as men flung themselves off of small landing craft onto beaches that were mined and wired; to lose the beachhead was to fall back into the sea. None were lost and the islands were taken.

The final air, land, and sea combats of World War II took place in the Pacific. The Allies did not have to assault Japan; the atom bombs made that unnecessary. In one unforgettable, great moment on board the USS Missouri in Tokyo Bay, General Douglas MacArthur, in one last flourish, declared, "These proceedings are closed."

Agnes Shurr U.S. Navy   **USS *Solace***

Soon after the attack on Pearl Harbor the *Solace* went to the South Pacific, and when we were at an island called Tongatabu, an enormous number of warships appeared in the harbor. Everyone knew they were gathering for something, but we nurses were never told what. That was when the battles of the Coral Sea and Midway were being planned early in the war. We went on to Noumea, New Caledonia.

29

We took on casualties from the Coral Sea battle and from Guadalcanal and that area. Casualties were terribly high. We treated them and took them to hospitals in New Zealand; we made several trips like that. Sometimes we transferred patients from our ship to another at sea.

The time I was most frightened, we were traveling "blackout," with blackout curtains and red lights inside that allowed us to see. Hospital ships usually traveled alone, and at night turned lights on. This time our commanding officer felt that if we were lighted up, the Japanese would see the warships. We were fired on in the middle of the night, and it hit not far from where I was sleeping. I woke up to the sound of the explosion and the "call to stations." Earlier that day we took on a large load of casualties. My ward had litter patients so I prepared them to abandon ship. We waited, and I was sure we were going down. How could anyone fire on us, unless they intended to sink us? After a period of time, the all-clear sounded, and we were never told what happened. In those days everything was secret, and we accepted it.

It wasn't until 1991, when a book was published by one of our hospital men, that I found out the firing was from a "friendly" ship. The book, *The USS Solace Was There*, states that a U.S. ship asked for identification, then fired across our bow but hit us instead. Our lights were turned on, and it was all over.

Five of us left the ship in New Zealand to transfer back to the States, sailing under the Golden Gate Bridge in San Francisco on January 1, 1943. I worked in a hospital in San Diego that had 10,000 beds, and ships full of patients arrived, unloading long, long lines of casualties. After that I worked in Corona, California, where we had twelve wards of tuberculosis patients. In the South Pacific, tropical diseases were so common that the warning signs of TB went unnoticed.

After the war I stayed in the navy and became a flight nurse. When I first graduated from nurses' training in Rochester, Minnesota, I joined the navy because it offered more security than civilian nursing. After seeing the world and experiencing all that I had by the time the war was over, it was more than security that kept me in.

Margaret Richey Raffa U.S. Army Air Force
801st Medical Air Evacuation Squadron

A native Texan, Margaret was assigned to the new flight nurse program at Bowman Field, Kentucky, but was sent overseas before classes began.

Hospital ships, like the USS *Solace* shown here, were painted white with a five-foot green band painted on each side of the hull, the Geneva Red Cross on both sides, and crosses on the deck and stacks.

We were the first flight nurse squadron to go to the Pacific, landing in New Caledonia in February 1943. We enjoyed the temperature and flowers, which are equally beautiful there all year, but conditions were very primitive. The river behind our tents was our washing machine, and we hung clothes to dry from the trees. There were twenty-four nurses, and millions of mosquitoes, all living in one tent. One night during the first week, the tent blew down during a typhoon, and our foot lockers almost floated away.

C-47s flew to the front with cargo and ammunition, and the nurses rode on top of the cargo. We often had troops going to the forward areas, which was sad for us. They would get into long discussions, feeling that they would probably never come back. The worst part is, some of them didn't.

When we went to Guadalcanal, the plane wouldn't fly directly over the island but flew along the beach, staying low to avoid being spotted by the Japanese. This was emotionally trying for us, not knowing what the landing field would be like. There were no ambulances. The most seriously wounded patients would be on litters, with other wounded in different vehicles. We took off quickly because the Japanese were strafing the field. Our casualties were still in rather bad shape, having had only first aid treatment. They had shrapnel and bullet wounds and injuries from hand grenades, often of the chest, abdomen, or head. It presented quite a problem, since there were no doctors on board, and we had to rely on our own initiative. We always had to be alert for symptoms of shock and hemorrhage, and from the time we took off until we landed, we had our hands full with these mutilated bodies. One nurse might have twenty-four patients, most of them on litters, for a five hour flight, and in those days we didn't have the enlisted medical technicians. We felt a tremendous responsibility.

Some patients were taken to the hospital in New Hebrides and later evacuated back to the States, but there were general hospitals in New Caledonia where these patients received good enough care to be returned to duty. We took boys back up to the front lines a month or two after we'd brought them out wounded.

The problems were constant. For instance, after we reached 8,000 feet there was a lack of oxygen, and often we climbed to 10,000 feet because of weather conditions. Then we had to give oxygen to patients continuously. Small oxygen tanks were all we had room for, and patients shared them. We did use alcohol on the tanks between patients, but it wasn't very sanitary. A lot of the planes didn't have heaters, and at 10,000 feet, even in the South Pacific, it was cold.

Sometimes we had to make forced landings because of maintenance or weather or fuel shortages, and this caused big problems for the commanding officers of the airstrips where we landed. Most of the time these fields were under attack by the Japanese, and we'd often have to head for foxholes, with the war being fought right above us. One time I was going to stand at the edge of a foxhole to watch as they went after a Japanese plane. A GI decided to head for the same place and hit my feet, knocking me over. I decided to stay down after that.

We were moved to New Hebrides at the end of 1943, and I flew into Bougainville right after the Seabees put down the landing strip, within two miles of the front line. There were fighter escorts accompanying us into the field, and as we flew over the battle, we could see the mortars and firing. Smoke screens were visible, the artillery was a little too close for comfort, and it was raining. With all this going on, the troops heard that air evac was coming in that day, and those who weren't at the front line were down at the strip to watch us come in.

In addition to the wounded and injured, we had mental patients, who were emotionally shocked and upset. They came on the plane dazed. In handling these boys we had help from the ambulatory patients who knew the condition of these patients, their buddies.

Dorothy Shikoski McCarthy U.S. Army Air Force
801st Medical Air Evacuation Squadron

Joining the army in Wisconsin in 1942, "Shy" served in the Pacific as a flight nurse before getting air evacuation training.

Our flight had left a planeload of patients off and we were returning to Noumea, New Caledonia. It was evening, and there was dense fog. The pilot was circling and circling, trying to get close to the island and we almost crashed into the side of a mountain. I looked out the window and felt I could have touched the mountain, we were that close. It was really scary. We knew we were going to ditch in the water, so everyone was ready.

When the plane hit the water, we inflated the rafts and got out. The plane stayed afloat just a very few minutes, then sank. A spare engine was stowed in the back of the plane, and when we hit the water it came forward and crushed the navigator in his seat. He went down with the plane.

There was a New Zealander camp on top of the mountain, and they came to help. My leg was broken and I'd injured my back, so I had to be carried up the mountain, where we stayed the night. The next day an ambulance arrived and took us back to the base.

When we first arrived in New Caledonia, the "brass" didn't know what to do with us, until we convinced them we were there to fly. We were very eager. After the crash, when they asked me if I wanted to go back to the States to recuperate, I refused. They put a walking cast on me, and I was back at work in six weeks. I even went to dances in it.

Flying to the front lines, we had the most severely wounded patients; there are several I remember after all these years. One young man lost his arms, legs, and eyesight, and his cheeks were wired together. There were many patients whose minds had been affected by the strains of island fighting.

Natives were the only sign of civilization where we were, and when we first arrived, the river was the only place we could wash ourselves. At one time we all had diarrhea, and the latrine was several tents away. We had to run past all the other tents, maybe eight or nine times a day, and the guys would yell out, "There she goes again."

We'd been sent overseas with no flight training, so when we returned in April 1944, they made us take the course in Kentucky. The instructors became very tired of our correcting their lessons because we knew what it was really like.

Edith Vowell U.S. Army   153rd Station Hospital

After joining through the Red Cross in 1941, "Edie" remained an army nurse for a career that lasted twenty years.

We sailed from New York on March 4, 1942, and everyone thought we were going to Europe, but after we were at sea it was announced we were headed for the Pacific. When we reached the Panama Canal some chief nurses went ashore, under cover of darkness for security reasons, to buy summer clothes for some of the nurses. We didn't have uniforms that matched, but when we marched off the ship in Brisbane, we all wore suntan culottes, matching shirts, and helmets.

The 153rd may have been the first army hospital to operate in Australia. We arrived in Brisbane April 6, 1942, and the nurses were kept on the ship, out-of-sight until it was dark. When we debarked, we climbed into covered trucks and were driven to the hospital in Gatton, Queensland. Our first casualties were from the important Battle of the Coral Sea, which was fought in May. By October we had moved to New Guinea, near Port Moresby.

The nurses were first off the ship at Port Moresby, and the press was there. We made news because we were the first non-native women to arrive since the evacuation of the plantations. Pictures and articles about us appeared in papers all over the world, and many anonymous people sent copies to my parents. After six months, our hospital was back in Australia, where we were moved from one location to another during the next two years, until the war ended.

Audrey Lampier U.S. Army   119th and 362nd Station Hospitals
Second Field Hospital

Audrey was trained in Milwaukee and from there joined the army which sent her crisscrossing the Pacific.

We debarked at Milne Bay, New Guinea, going ashore on a barge with all our luggage on our backs. We were very envious of the navy nurses who were dressed more formally, wearing skirts and jackets. All they had to carry were their purses.

There are many memories of those two years that bring either a laugh or a lump to my throat. Atabrine was given to us at once, and soon everyone looked yellow. Later when our tans deepened it looked worse, and some would stop taking it until we'd have a patient with brain malaria, and that would scare everyone. Milne Bay was a staging area, and we heard about nurses who staged there for a year without ever working in a hospital. We were only there about five weeks and considered ourselves lucky. We all fell in love at least once, and I had many good times. The navy men had real liquor, whereas our medical men just had plain alcohol. The enlisted men made a very good brew.

Large lizards lived in the thatched roofs over our huts. Thirteen nurses lived in my hut, and we called ourselves "Barracks Bags." Often we had to wash with only the water in our helmets, with three sometimes using the water from one helmet.

There were several "singsings," where the natives came from one hundred miles away to put on these events. They made elaborate hats and danced in the middle of a circle and chanted. The women danced on the outside of the circle, as the men were the main stars. We asked why they had such red teeth and found it was from beetlejuice, a form of narcotic that they chewed constantly. Occasionally we treated native children and tried to teach them to brush their teeth. Some of us had brought evening gowns, and we wore them on Christmas Eve, intriguing the natives. On days off, our chaplain took us to some local villages where there were only women and children. The men were off to the war.

While we were at Oro Bay, I was temporarily assigned to the 362nd while our hospital (the 119th) was under construction. Tropical storms hit often, and rats were everywhere. Many nights I stood on top of the desk, to the amusement of the patients. We had mosquito nets over our beds, and one of the girls in my tent wouldn't use hers. One night I heard her screaming because the rats had gotten into her bed. She used the net after that. There were some nurses who "cracked up" and were sent home, but most of us could handle it.

At Oro Bay one ward had a lot of IVs. We set up the apparatus, then a doctor would come and start it. One time I looked up from the desk and saw a patient drinking the IV through the tubing. I guess he was tired of waiting, or else didn't like the idea of the needle.

In May 1944 we went to Finschafen, where mud was everywhere and we referred to our quarters as "Tobacco Road." The hospital was completed soon, and we moved to its permanent location twelve miles north of Finschafen, on the ocean. It began to look like real civilization because our tents were built on wooden platforms, had canvas roofs, and there were actual buildings, made of plywood.

After a few months, another nurse and I were transferred to the 2nd Field Hospital in Zamboanga, Mindanao, Philippines. Our chief nurse there

While with the 362nd SH, Audrey Lampier (front row) and Mary Robertson treated Japanese prisoners, communicating with a lot of gestures.

was Captain Catherine Acorn, nicknamed "Bataan Maizie." She had escaped with General Douglas MacArthur when the Japanese took over in 1942 but came back to the Philippines, like he did. Whenever she made rounds in our wards, she'd have a list of party invitations and would ask if we wished to sign up for one. We usually did.

General MacArthur was coming to visit our unit once, so we had to learn to salute better. Everything was all cleaned and polished. There was great anticipation of his visit, and we finally were ready for him. When he came he stayed in the jeep, and when he drove past the hospital, he saluted. We never saw him any closer. Years later, I was watching the television show "M*A*S*H," and there was a scene that was exactly like our experience with MacArthur. I called one of the nurses from that hospital, and we had a good laugh, because that's how it really happened.

A lot of celebrities came to put on shows. Kay Kyser was pretty raunchy, and every time he told a dirty joke, every eye in the audience would turn and look at us. The high-ranking officers fell all over themselves for the women entertainers, much to the amusement of everyone else. When Martha Tilton was visiting, the officer escorting her took her through a lab, and she asked to look into a microscope. She said, "Aren't they cute!" All the nurses howled because we knew she was looking at a syphilis specimen.

Prudence Burns Burrell U.S. Army   268th Station Hospital

Prudence was one of the first African-American nurses to join the army in World War II.

As a member of the American Red Cross in Kansas City, Missouri, I was asked to recruit African-American nurses for the Army Nurse Corps. Thus, in October 1942, I recruited myself and was assigned to Fort Huachuca, Arizona. My three brothers were in the service, and I had a reunion with one of them there. Two combat divisions made up of African-American troops, the Ninety-second and Ninety-third Infantry, were in training. Due to segregation policies, there was a separate hospital for African-American personnel and dependents, and another hospital for other military and civilian personnel.

I was at Fort Huachuca a year, during which the 268th Station Hospital was formed. Fifteen nurses were assigned to the all African-American unit for service in the southwest Pacific. We sailed from San Francisco on the

**llustration of Milne Bay, New Guinea—Audrey Lampier sketched
this scene inside the Second FH in Zamboanga, Phillippines.**

The 119th SH at Finschafen, New Guinea, looked like this to Audrey Lampier. The movie theater was located among coconut trees, where there was the risk of coconuts falling on someone's head.

USS *Monterey* in October 1943. Protected by a navy blimp and destroyer escorts for two days, the ship then zigzagged unescorted across the Pacific and arrived in Sidney, Australia, eighteen days later. The nurses went by train from Sidney to Brisbane to await the completion of our hospital being built in Milne Bay, New Guinea. We were in a staging area with white nurses but remained segregated for sleeping and eating.

The Brisbane newspaper featured each of us fifteen nurses shortly after we arrived. I had attended the University of Minnesota School of Public Health prior to my army service. While I was there Sister Elizabeth Kenny, an Australian, was teaching her method of wet-pack treatment for polio victims, now known the world over as the 'Kenny Treatment'. Her relatives assumed that I had known her, and they came out to the staging area to meet me. After that I had a merry time, as they took me every place, along with some of the other nurses from our group. That contact continues today with some of her cousins.

There were embarrassing occasions because of segregation. A white lieutenant colonel made a very loud statement to a group of Australians who had us as guests at the zoo, that he resented our being served before

**Mail call in Australia for Prudence Burns (3rd from right) and nurses of
the 268th SH.**

him at the restaurant because where he came from, "niggers" were not
allowed into the white facilities. They told him to wait or leave.

Several of us joined the Australian YWCA and Crafts Club. It was
through these organizations that we were able to get the Non-
Commissioned-Officer Club location moved out of a dangerous "red-light"
district. We obtained lists of restaurants that refused to serve the African-
American soldiers, and as officers we visited these places to dine. The
Australians came to know us and began to treat our soldiers as human
beings, and restaurants were opened to them.

Some Yanks told the Australians that we had tails. I remember being
invited to dinner at a home, and noticed there were pillows on all the
chairs, except the one for the hostess. So I sat there, and she became
upset, and I said a few words and left. The nurses with me teased that I
should have waited until we had eaten!

One Sunday at church, a young girl invited me to her home for dinner
after the service. Rose Hosier said it was customary to ask all persons in
uniform to dinner at the family home. The Hosier family entertained all
nationalities every Sunday, and I was there often, along with white officers

and enlisted men. The four Hosier daughters and I are still very much in contact, and we have visited each other since then.

Soldiers from other countries invited some of us to their affairs and mess halls for dining. One Javanese soldier asked me to marry him and go to his parents until the war ended. He even sent letters to my Detroit address.

Our hospital in Milne Bay, New Guinea, was finished in April 1944, and we sailed from Brisbane on a hospital ship. The 268th Station Hospital, for African-American servicemen only, was constructed on a hill, overlooking the bay. No white soldiers were to be admitted. I was head nurse in the surgical ward where we had to use blood that was designated by the letter "A" for African American. That was devastating, and showed scientific ignorance.

We weren't to give it to any white soldiers. There is one white guy walking around with that blood in his system. He was in an accident near our hospital and needed blood. He said, "I don't give a damn what kind of blood it is, save my life!"

In May 1945, we received orders to close our hospital and prepare to move to the Philippines. We were given Spanish classes in order to communicate with the Filipinos, but they weren't too helpful because the language of the country was Tagalog. Luckily, most of the Filipinos were fluent in English. However, to greet a person in Spanish paved the way for further conversation. We were sent to Manila in order to connect up with General MacArthur for the invasion of Japan. Manila was practically destroyed, with homeless children roaming the streets. We did what we could for them.

Phyllis Simpson McGlory U.S. Army   Thirty-third Surgical Hospital Fifth, Thirteenth, and 362nd Station Hospitals

Phyllis joined in 1942 inspired by the film So Proudly We Hail, about American nurses in the Philippines.

I was on the Pacific Ocean on the USS *Lurline* on the Fourth of July 1943. Everyone had to muster on deck to salute the flag and sing the "Star Spangled Banner." Each night the ship was blacked out, and we had a few scares from submarines. As soon as we were out of bed, we had to put on the kapok life vest, and wristwatches that had luminous dials were to be worn inward.

I was a "casual" nurse, assigned to the Thirty-third Surgical Hospital but on duty with the Fifth Station Hospital in Rockhampton, Queensland, Australia. The men in our unit were sent to an island near Guadalcanal to work, but without nurses. Of all the casualties I cared for, there was a young, eighteen-year-old marine from Ohio that I cried my heart out for. He was badly wounded from throwing himself on a grenade, lost a leg, and the other leg was in a stryker cast. We could only put a needle in his right arm, because his left arm was mangled. Oh, God, he was pathetic. He died on me. I can never forget that handsome boy.

In October 1943 we boarded a ship by climbing up the cargo net, went to Port Moresby, New Guinea, then flew to Oro Bay, where we were put on temporary duty with the 362nd Station Hospital. For two weeks, I worked nights in a Japanese prison ward. They were the scrawniest, skinniest, sickest patients. Of course, they couldn't speak English, and they loved paregoric. The only way they could tell me they wanted it was to pantomime that their bowels were loose, and then they pantomimed taking medicine. There was only a piece of canvas separating them from the Americans on the other side of the ward. We had three MPs guarding about twenty Japanese patients.

A year later we were sent to Noemfoor, Dutch East Indies, near Biak. The enlisted men and officers of the Thirty-third were there, and this was the first time we joined them. I remember the chaplain who gave me an awful scolding for allowing gambling on my ward. This was a tent ward with twenty beds on each side and the nurses station in the center. I was busy and thought the GIs were just playing cards. He was kind of a stuffed shirt.

I recall a Military Policeman who was my patient. Some GIs had been picked up when they got in trouble, and the MPs didn't frisk them. One of the GIs had a pistol. He shot the MP from temple to temple, right behind the eyes. He was blind the rest of his life.

In February 1945 we nurses went on detached service again, to Mindoro, Philippines, with the Thirteenth Station Hospital, and were there until the bomb was dropped. Right after V-J Day I went home.

Clara Wynick White U.S. Army   **Thirty-fifth General Hospital**

Determined to be an army nurse, Clara twice rode a train 200 miles from home in West Virginia to take the physical exam, which she passed on the second attempt.

Most of us had never heard of such a place as New Guinea when we were told at sea that was our destination. Our hospital was at Lae, where we had the luxury of living in barracks.

There were earthquakes and a typhoon, but mostly I remember the mosquitoes and rats. The rats were almost as large as rabbits, and we could hear them scurrying over the tops of our mosquito nets. We wore long-sleeved shirts, and each evening tucked our trouser legs into leggings as added protection against the mosquitoes. Mosquito nets had to be securely tucked in over our cots at 5:30 P.M. Besides malaria, hepatitis, and fungus killed some of our staff.

One night I was awakened by the sound of people running past the tent and thought it was Japanese troops invading. I grabbed my mess kit knife, woke up the other girls, and we waited. Then we found out it was a psychiatric patient from the hospital being chased through our area. I guess I was a little "spooked." Our food supply was cut off by the Japanese once, and we ate canned chili and canned spinach for a month.

The Christmas we spent in New Guinea comes back to my mind every time I hear Christmas carols. We had a thatched roof chapel, and I sang in the choir. Our robes were white surgical gowns with red crepe paper collars. The officers and nurses acted out the nativity, and one of the men sang "O Holy Night" in his beautiful tenor voice. It sent chills through everyone there.

After a year I was sent to Biak, a coral island in the Dutch East Indies, then to Leyte, Philippines, when the Americans landed there. Dysentery and skin problems were really taking their toll. Penicillin was a new drug and we had to keep a record of every drop.

Althea Williams U.S. Army   Ninety-second Evacuation Hospital

A civilian nurse in Fort Collins, Colorado, "Willie" was commissioned shortly after Pearl Harbor was bombed.

Thinking we were going to the African desert, we sailed on the *Lurline*, in June 1943. We wound up in Australia, setting up a tent hospital at Rockhampton, where we were with the Forty-first Infantry Division.

Patients I remember were a boy who lost his hearing and another who lost his eyesight, so I put them together. The blind boy thought girls wouldn't like him, but he wrote me from home later that he wasn't having any problems. I still hear from the other one.

A sickness called 'scrub typhus' was killing soldiers in the South Pacific, and they flew some of us to the islands of Owi and Biak, in the Dutch East Indies, to care for them. It was constant nursing care, where we gave sponge baths all day to try to bring the patients' temperatures down. When you finished with them, you just started all over. In four weeks men were going from 180 pounds to 140, and fifty percent were dying. We finally licked it.

I was moved from Owi to Biak on a Dutch schooner that had been converted to a little teeny hospital ship. During the trip we heard a lot of gobbledy-gook coming over the loudspeaker, and once I understood something like, "Three unidentified planes coming." I thought the Japs were coming to bomb and was really scared. We ran to the side of the ship, ready to jump and swim. No one had a life vest on. Funny things people do when panicked; for instance, one girl ran back to get her cold cream. Eventually we were told the planes were friendly. I felt a little foolish.

Verna Loomis Rodd U.S. Army   Ninety-second Evacuation Hospital
132nd General Hospital

Verna joined in 1942 with the express intention of being assigned to the Ninety-second because of the caliber of doctors already in the unit.

We had foxholes for protection on Owi, an island off the coast of New Guinea. Every moonlit night one Japanese plane flew over. We heard it coming and called it "Washing-machine Charlie" because it had a different sound than our planes. One night, after these flights became routine, "Charlie" dropped bombs on the enlisted men's area and hit the latrine. No one was hurt, thankfully.

Different units invited us to parties, and one time we were flown to Biak, an island a short distance from Owi, for a party. When it was time to come back, my date didn't get me to the plane on time and it left without me, so I had to stay overnight. Another plane took me back the next day, but I was restricted to quarters for a month as a result.

In January 1945, the nurses were transferred to the 132nd on Biak. The airstrip was right behind the nurses' quarters, and one day a Japanese plane followed the American planes back to the base and bombed the runway. That was a close call for me; we had a lot of wounded from that attack.

Verna Loomis (2nd from right) sitting atop a foxhole near the Ninety-second EH nurse's quarters on the island of Owi.

Rosanna Comes Jones U.S. Navy   Fleet Hospitals 103, 111

When Rosanna and her colleagues arrived to set up the hospitals on Guam in August 1944, the island had just been secured by American troops.

We were sailing from Hawaii to Guam when some troops on board our ship mutinied because they found out we weren't headed to the States, but back to the battlefield. Until everything was brought under control, we nurses had to be escorted everywhere on the ship because the mutineers resented us as officers, among their other gripes.

We arrived in Guam shortly after the island was secured by the Americans in 1944. Our base hospital was a permanent structure, but the other three fleet hospitals were constructed of one of the war's more popular materials: tin. First erected in Samoa, one of the tin hospitals was reconstructed on Guam and was the cause of an inspection by Secretary of War James Forrestal to see how it held up. Whenever we had visiting dignitaries such as Eleanor Roosevelt or Secretary Forrestal, everything had to be whitewashed and polished. To polish chrome we made a paste out of lemon crystals, which were supposed to be used for drinks.

Visitors didn't come during the rainy season and missed seeing the top of the tin hospitals covered with rubber sheets. Rain came in anyway, and we waded in two inches of water inside the wards.

On his way back from the invasion of Iwo Jima, my brother was able to visit me in Guam. He'd escaped injury, but casualties were so high, only seventy men from his battalion could walk afterward. There were five hundred Purple Hearts awarded one Sunday. They just went from ward to ward, pinning them on the patients. At other times we had close to five hundred patients whose injuries were the result of the suicide planes. We applied oil on stocking net and wrapped these patients to the point that they couldn't feed themselves. Everyone came to help feed them, including our Red Cross girls and anyone off-duty.

One fellow I'll never forget was awarded the Congressional Medal of Honor while he was our patient. They didn't think he would make it, so Admiral Nimitz had the award flown to Guam and presented it to him at his bed. This brave man carried a phosphorous bomb through a plane full of troops after it came loose and threw it out. I remember he was so badly burned that his ears had to be reconstructed.

We didn't have hot water to take care of the patients from Iwo Jima. I know that would have helped their recovery. The recuperation rate might have been higher if they could have shaved, or we could have given them a bath to lift their spirits and morale. There were a lot of belly and chest wounds, and we ran out of dressings because of the number of patients that came all at once. We had to improvise quickly, and wrapped the packing from dishes around rags, with a piece of gauze around that, and used it for dressings to stuff in the wounds.

Admiral Nimitz's headquarters were on Guam, and he came for the opening ceremony of one of the tin hospitals. I never saw so much crystal, china dishes, silver sets, and linens. He left that afternoon quickly to announce to the United States that we had just invaded Okinawa. One thousand patients came from Okinawa, after we had the silver and everything put away.

When we weren't swamped with patients and had leisure time on our hands, most talk turned to food. Everyone griped about what we had, and no wonder! There was always a big can of oleo that tasted like grease and looked like melted cheese. Spam with raisin sauce and mutton from Australia were always cooking, and I can still smell it. Every week we had the same thing on the same day, like beans on Fridays.

I kept a diary, though cameras and diaries were not allowed in case information fell into the wrong hands. I used a writing tablet as a diary, and it would have been destroyed if they found it during an inspection. Luckily, it was never opened.

USS Refuge

Helen Wentz Miller *joined the Navy Nurse Corps in her home state of Pennsylvania in 1942.* **Ernestine Hess "Hessie" Davey** *went to sea from West Virginia.* **Esther "Wally" Wallenga** *spent twenty-two years with the navy, retiring as a lieutenant commander.* **Elizabeth "Betty" Torrance Staats** *had been a navy nurse since 1939 and found young patients on board who were from her hometown, Kearny, New Jersey.* **Bessie Glembocki Daniels** *from Sag Harbor, New York, received her nursing degree at Georgetown University.*

Playful activities of King Neptune's Court is an old tradition on ships when crossing the equator. During wartime, military hospital ships and troop transports continued the ceremonies whenever possible, as the following account will testify.

Helen: After serving in European waters and crossing the Atlantic several times, our hospital ship was sent to the Pacific. We sailed from Virginia to the Philippines on a forty-two day trip that was like a cruise for us. There were twenty navy doctors and twenty-nine nurses, plus the crew, and no patients. The chief nurse had a meeting as soon as we were on board and announced, "I want you to know that all the doctors are married!" She had an active imagination but nothing to worry about.

Wally: Crossing the equator for the first time was an experience I'll never forget. For several days the loudspeaker announced, "Polliwogs, beware!"

When I was put in "stocks" and a fire hose was turned on us, the force was so strong, I thought I was going to be washed overboard. Next we were dunked in a tank of water, and when I climbed out and started to walk away, my knees gave way, and I couldn't stand up. One of the sailors

Crossing the equator was a time for the Shellbacks aboard the USS *Refuge* to have fun with the Polliwogs. The first crossing for the nurses included dancing in celebration.

King Neptune's court was run by Davey Jones and Peg Leg during ceremonies aboard the USS *Refuge.*

was touching the back of my knees with an electrified pitchfork. After that, I was put in a barber's chair and the barber snipped all around my head. He held out a handful of dark hair, and I nearly cried. It was faked but very realistic. I know it sounds pretty rough, but it was all in fun, and we took it that way.

Betty: Our first crossing was such a memorable occasion that I wrote up this account. There were no patients on board, and we could wholeheartedly enjoy the fun.

King Neptune's Court, USS Refuge, 1944

"Polliwogs Beware!" We, the lowly polliwogs, are about to be initiated into King Neptune's Court. The shellbacks in their glory let imagination run riot. The nurses' wardroom is Polliwog Hotel, for not one of our twenty-seven can claim to be a shellback.

"Polliwogs Beware!" We live with this constant din in our ears from the loud speaker, the phone, the passerby. One finds signs hanging on the washing machine. The equator comes closer and closer and closer.

"All polliwogs fall in at quarters. Davey Jones and his retinue are coming aboard. All officers and nurses up to the signal bridge."

There we lowly scum stood at attention while Davey and his cohorts passed in review, and some of us were marked with X in red paint. Our initiation began. The Royal Court posted a "watch" list. Some had the fo'c'sle watch, some the crow's nest, some the life boat and the radio. The first watch was piped and the fun began. The ladies of the scarlet X were the ballet of the day, joined by the chaplain. After being reviewed by King Neptune, his family of Queen and Baby, a bouncing, burly beauty, Davey Jones and his gang, and the Royal Court, we were herded to the court.

The luckless polliwogs were put in stocks. Then the Royal Barber had to wreak havoc. As each nurse sat in the barber's chair, the barbers would grab a handful of hair and snip busily. Then to our horror they would shake before our eyes a handful of hacked-off hair. It was purely a scare, but the men fared not so well. To even out the wreckage, many bald heads were seen, making us look like a convict ship.

Led to the Royal Ducking Tub, we ascended a platform leveled about two feet above a tankful of water. Two shellbacks were advantageously placed to help reticent jumpers. As we rose to the surface, one was grabbed by three shellbacks and after remarks such as "What? Still breathing?" down we'd go again.

As we left the tank we faced a double row of persuaders enhanced by the Devil in long purple underwear. He had an electrically-sparked pitchfork which he applied to our backs. Then he'd double up with laughter, always recovering in time to catch the next victim.

The end of the road was in sight, with only one obstacle. A net was strung up to block escape. As we crawled under and became entangled in the mesh, fire hoses were played up and down our struggling figures.

Thus, the Refuge, *with a crew of trusty, new and aching shellbacks, crossed the equator. We all await the day when we can terrorize the unwary traveler—Polliwogs Beware!*

Helen: With no patients, we had a lot of leisure time to sunbathe. I'll never forget the captain coming up to the sundeck once and saying, "Oh, my nurses, my nurses, if you only knew how dangerous it is, you wouldn't be up here taking a sunbath." We never thought of danger.

Ernestine Hess was photographed aboard the USS *Refuge* and found her picture used as a recruiting poster.

Hessie: I was photographed aboard ship by a navy photographer, and my picture wound up being used on posters throughout the country for recruiting.

Helen: After the *Refuge* arrived in the Philippines, we shuttled back and forth between Leyte and Hollandia, New Guinea, picking up wounded and bringing them to the hospital in New Guinea. I made five trips. Most of our patients came off ships that were bombed.

We had "basket cases," men whose arms and legs were gone. Some would be naked, having been blown out of a ship and surviving in the water until we rescued them.

Wally: We picked up patients from the fierce battles at Leyte, Philippines, and when they were brought in, they'd just lie there, staring. They couldn't believe it. Everything was so clean, and they had white sheets for the first time in ages. Sometimes, though, there weren't enough beds, and sacks would be lined up along the deck for the men who weren't too badly wounded.

These casualties were the worst. You can see what men are made of when you get them freshly wounded. Believe me, our boys were made of the best!

Bessie: There were two burials at sea. They always played the song, "Nearer My God To Thee," and I still get goose bumps when I hear it today.

Helen: The heat in the South Pacific was incredible. We had to wear duty uniforms, which were cotton dresses with long sleeves and a big wide belt. The chief nurse came around to see if we were dressed properly, but when she wasn't there we hung our belts up near a fan to dry them out. There were always creases at our elbows, and our backs were always wet. Next to the engine room was a ward that was used for burns, but it had to close sometimes because it was too hot. It was below the water line with no portholes, no air conditioning, just little fans. The thermometers would rise to the top.

I recall making rounds in that ward when the strong odor of the burns and dressings was so pungent, and I had to get out because I was going to get sick. I pitied the corpsmen who worked there all the time. Today, I can still smell those burns.

Wally: The *Refuge* made several trips back to Hollandia and the Admiralty Islands, always traveling alone. At sea, the ship was lighted up at night to identify it as an unarmed hospital ship, but in a harbor, it had to be blacked out to protect the ships around it.

Helen: The ship had a red cross on it, and some of the line officers said they would rather be on a combat ship because they felt we were a target and had nothing to fight with. We weren't allowed to be near a convoy of ships, and if a convoy was passing by we had to go all the way around so

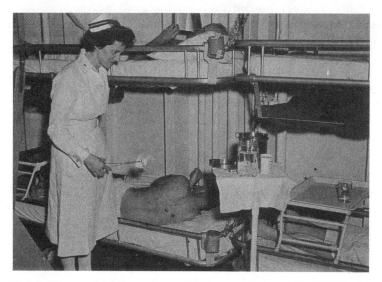

Helen Wentz cares for a wounded patient aboard the USS *Refuge*.

that we weren't in sight of it. One bright, moonlit night we were in the Hollandia harbor, and they put a smoke screen around our ship because we stuck out like a sore thumb. In the morning we could see that right next to us was an oil tanker being refueled.

Betty: We didn't only treat casualties, because I was assigned to the EENT (eye, ear, nose, throat) ward on the ship. Every time we dropped anchor there were hundreds of requests to replace glasses and have eye check-ups. We must have repaired every pair of eyeglasses that ever went to that war.

Helen: I remember little, strange experiences, like a soldier who wanted me to put powder on his pillowcase because he wanted to smell a woman's powder. One day in a triple-deck-bed ward, a soldier reached out and touched me on the shoulder, and I turned around thinking he wanted to tell me something. He said, "Excuse me, lady, I just wanted to touch a woman again."

Helen Wentz wrote to her parents on 27 December 1944:
    "Christmas was really something—never were so busy since we've been on the ship. I'm fine and enjoying my work. It's wonderful to take care of these boys after they have been through so much."

Margaret Carlson Larson U.S. Army   USS *Dogwood/*
                                                     218TH Hospital Ship

After basic training in Massachusetts, "Carley" was surprised to be
assigned to a hospital ship, making seven trips across the Atlantic to the
European theater, before heading off for the other war.

Our eighth trip out of Charleston, South Carolina, was to the Pacific. We
were being sent to replace a hospital ship that the Japanese had bombed.
This order wasn't revealed to us until we'd left Charleston, because the
captain feared that some of the Merchant Marine crew members would
"jump ship" rather than go to the Pacific theater.

We went through the
Panama Canal and
straight to Manila, arriving right after it was liberated. Then we began
transporting wounded
patients from island to
island. We operated on
the ship, then took the
patients to hospitals on
shore. We did this for
several months, stopping
everywhere.

The funny things that
happened are what I
want to remember,
instead of the war.
Mailcall was the best part
of any day, and if some-
one didn't get a letter,
we shared our's with
them. We couldn't tell
anyone where we were,
and used codes when
writing to our families.
Nel, my cabinmate,
informed her family that
she was now in a new

**"Heads down!" the captain ordered to the
men below, as nurses climbed down the ladder
in skirts.**

theater of operation. Her grandfather asked the family, "What in the world is she doing on the stage?" We always teased her about being our "leading lady" in the Pacific.

There was little time or opportunity for romance on the ship, as we were guarded by military police at all times. Lo and behold, when our ship returned to the States, one of our nurses and a Merchant Marine officer announced their engagement and immediate wedding plans.

Rosedith Van Hoorebeck Hawkins U.S. Army
Thirty-fifth General Hospital

Inevitably called "Sadie" after the Lil Abner cartoon figure, she joined the army on a dare from a friend.

I was injured in an accident while on night maneuvers at Camp Polk, Louisiana, and wound up spending six months recovering in the hospital. They gave me a choice then of being discharged or working in a hospital in New Orleans. I was having a pretty good time by then and went to work at LaGarde General Hospital, where Cliff Hawkins was one of my patients. When Cliff and I married, my chief nurse, who was "old army" and went strictly by the book, immediately transferred me overseas. She told me I was guilty of fraternizing with an enlisted man, and I told her I never heard of marriage being called fraternizing.

So I wound up on Biak, Dutch East Indies, on detached service with a unit from Harvard. My husband was soon sent to the Pacific also, hitched a ride to Biak, and we were able to take three days off for a honeymoon on Owi. It was great, on one army cot with a carbine between us! We didn't see each other for two years after that, until it was all over.

One of our nurses married in New Guinea, and I was happy to plan her wedding. Mortar shells became vases, holding beautiful island flowers. We bleached mosquito netting white for the bride's veil and used laundry bluing to dye some for the bridesmaids' headdresses. A master sergeant who had been a civilian cook made a gorgeous cake. The spiked punch was in a mixing bowl on top of a keg of nails draped with a sheet.

A patient I'll never forget was a sixteen-year-old boy who had lied about his age. He lost both legs and worried that his girlfriend wouldn't want him without legs. He wrote to me later to say she still loved him and as soon as possible they were to be married. I received many sad letters from parents of boys who died on my ward. I always wrote to them.

About eight months before the war was over, I went to San Fernando North in the Philippines. The boys who'd been in the Bataan Death March came to us, and I'm telling you, they were a mess. It would take us days and days and days just to get their heads clean. They couldn't eat so we just gave them liquids and soft foods. The first time they could really eat anything we asked what they wanted and tried to get whatever it was. About 99 percent of them wanted a hamburger. Almost all of them had lost a foot or arm or leg. They'd had no medical treatment and had healed very badly. They stayed with us until they were able to go back by boat, and some were airlifted. When I look back, we did things I never knew I could do and had experiences I never expected to have. Our training never included that kind of treatment. I wouldn't want to do that over again.

Dorothy Wood Angerer U.S. Army   Fifty-eighth Evacuation Hospital

After desert training in Arizona for service in North Africa, Dorothy was deployed to the South Pacific.

We arrived at a train station in Arizona that said "Hyder" on the sign, but there were no other buildings in sight. Trucks took us out into the desert, where we lived in tents through the heat of the summer. Our training included ten-mile hikes in that heat. After a while we moved to the desert near Indio, California, for more training, such as crawling under barbed wire with bullets whizzing over us. From there we went to Camp Stoneman and sailed out into the Pacific Ocean. Our desert training was all but forgotten in the jungles of New Guinea, as our patients were mostly suffering from malaria.

One night my roommate and I were sitting on our cots, talking, and she lit up a cigarette. All of a sudden she said, "Oh my God, there's a snake on my table!" We didn't have bedside tables but used bomb racks. It was a small snake, so I hit it with a hammer we just happened to have, and killed it. Then I said, "I've heard that when there's one, there's two." The next day I had to work, but she didn't. When I came off duty, she had moved everything, washed all the bedding, and cleaned the whole place. That night we went out again, and when we returned and were sitting there, she said, "There's another snake in the same place." She killed that one herself.

A few months later we were sent to Los Negros, in the Admiralty Islands. We were living in a coconut grove, but the natives had to cut

Crawling under low-to-the-ground barbed wire with bullets whizzing overhead was part of training for some nurses.

down the coconuts so they wouldn't fall on our heads. Again, our patients were mostly malaria cases. One of my patients asked me for a spade or hoe one day, and when I asked him why, he said there was a snake coiled up in his bedside table. We didn't have tables there either, but boxes to keep things on. Another time I found a lizard in the glass with my toothbrush, and I washed off the toothbrush and used it again, since we couldn't get another.

This was our life, and we just worked along with it. I was always grateful for our mosquito netting, which we thought helped keep critters out of our beds. One roommate was lying on her cot and saw a snake up above, so we found a native who had a long pole with a leather loop on the end, and he brought it down. The Seabees built shacks up on stilts for us on Los Negros, and they installed a wringer-type washing machine in one of the shacks. A girl went in to do her laundry, and found a coral snake. There were some cases of beer stored in there, so she picked up a case of beer and dropped it on the snake. By this time we were so used to these things, she just took care of the problem!

We were in the Admiralty Islands for about six months. One morning in October 1944, we looked out across the water and saw the whole Seventh

Fleet. All the aircraft carriers, battleships, and everything that makes up a fleet were there, as far as we could see. I get choked up remembering that sight. We knew it meant something big was coming up; right after that our men left for the invasion on Leyte in the Philippines. It was said that General MacArthur was on our island, but I didn't see him. Soon the nurses were taken by ship to Leyte Harbor, and we went in on landing craft, getting off in the water and wading ashore.

It was really hell on Leyte, with mud, snakes, and all that goes with the tropics. The tent hospital just had cots and no floor and snakes everywhere. One morning when we went on duty, there was a fifteen-foot-long boa constrictor mounted on a piece of wood right outside the hospital.

The nurses landed on Leyte right behind the invasion. As we moved up north, the casualties were extremely heavy. I usually worked in medical units, but they were so busy in surgery I often helped there. I had to start blood, even though I'd never done an IV. I just did it. Fortunately, these kids had good veins so we could get in.

I remember one boy who was only about nineteen. He'd been shot and kept saying, "I'm gonna die, I'm gonna die." I said, "Oh no, they are going to get you into surgery and fix you up." Then I noticed he had his rosary, and I took mine out of my pocket. I said, "Let's say the rosary together," and we did. I still think about him. He was right; he didn't live.

There was always shooting, but I never felt personally afraid. I remember one day being taken out to learn how to shoot carbines. We were taught to lie on the ground and shoot, I guess to protect ourselves. An area was cleared of coconut trees so we could sit on logs and watch movies. Three Japs were caught there, watching the movies.

One evening the men were on their cots and I was sitting on a box, with a bigger box for a desk. I was trying to do some charting, and all of a sudden I felt like I was falling over. I must have looked like a fool, and one of the patients said, "It's all right, Lieutenant, it's just an earthquake." I had no idea what was happening.

It rained almost every day, with mud, mud, and more mud. Japs were all around, and there was a lot of shooting. We had blackout all the time. As the fighting moved forward, the men in our hospital went along, and we nurses were sent back to a station hospital.

There was time for a little social life as things were calming down, and a nightspot had been built right on Leyte Harbor. On August 6, 1945 I was there and was dancing. All of a sudden the band started to play the song, "When the Lights Go On Again All Over the World." All the ships in the harbor put their lights on. They had heard about the dropping of the bomb. It wasn't really over, but they felt the Japs couldn't take too much of this. This was it. I can't tell that story without tears.

We stayed at the station hospital for a few weeks, and some of us went to Tacloban, the capitol of Leyte, to see civilization. Meat was hanging out on strings with flies all over, so we couldn't see ourselves eating anything but K rations. My favorite K ration breakfast was corn fritters with syrup.

One thing that was exciting was the birth of a baby while I was at the station hospital. An American army major, who had been on Bataan, escaped and hid out in a village during the war and married a Spanish girl. He brought her in to have the baby, and we all enjoyed that change.

Toward the end, I was assigned to open a ward for ambulatory patients, who had to do a lot for themselves. One patient was very sick, needed a lot of help, and I gave him baths. The others gave me a bad time for being so good to him. So I said to them, "All you guys have is syphilis, and you can take care of yourselves." He had leukemia. I don't think penicillin was in use in the States yet when we first had it. A shot was given every four hours, and these guys would just turn over, butt up, barely waking up. Once I had impetigo in my armpits and was given a shot of penicillin, and it disappeared right away.

When I came back, I went to school for a master's degree in microbiology. I think all the malaria and worms and all we had to put up with whetted my interest in the subject.

Julia Polchlopek Scott U.S. Army   **369th Station Hospital**

"Judy" was from Hoboken, New Jersey and had joined in 1943, right from nursing school.

The marines secured Saipan in early July 1944 after very intense fighting. When eighteen of us nurses went in soon after, everything was pretty primitive. It was the rainy season, and the tents were put up on bare ground. Surgery took place under a single lightbulb. Air raids and blackouts were common. When the siren went off, I'd put mattresses over the bedframes of patients who couldn't be moved. Then I'd get under a cot and wait. There was strafing and bombing on the island and some Japanese troops hiding out in the hills. We had to have armed guards accompany us when we went off the base, and I kept a gun under my pillow.

We treated the wounded from the battles on Iwo Jima and other islands. They came in such terrible shape, we just worked until we couldn't move, took a rest somewhere, then went back and worked some more. One day a doctor asked, "Can you give IV?" I thought he was crazy because none of the nurses had. He gave me five minutes of instruction so he could go on with other things, and I learned to do intravenous anesthe-

Nurses of the 369th SH went through basic training in Hawaii before shipping out to Saipan.

Occasional breaks were welcome during ten-mile hikes in the mountains for 369th SH nurses.

**Before leaving Hawaii for Saipan, nurses from the 369 SH received
flower leis from local people during "Lei Day" (1 May) celebration. Julia
Polchlopek is third from the right, in the front row.**

sia on-the-job. It was scary. I stopped breathing with every one of them,
then took a deep breath when they did.

Off-duty we played a lot of poker, even during the blackouts. We'd put
a blanket on the tent floor, place flashlights turned toward the center, and
put another blanket over us. Then we'd deal.

We did everything in fatigue uniforms, and the heat caused perspiration
which soaked through the heavy shirts. There was also a wraparound
dress and a shirt and slacks uniform made out of tan and white seersucker,
which we wore on duty. The first uniform I was issued when I joined was
navy blue. Then we were issued the olive drab wool uniform. There was a
suit and a dress in that color and the same thing in "dress pink." Most of us
had something personal tucked away, and mine was a long black skirt and
white blouse.

The U.S. Navy often invited us on board ships anchored off the coast.
We loved to go because they had "real food," white tablecloths, china
dishes, and silverware, including sterling silver demitasse spoons. One
time I was feeling feisty and took the silverware I'd used, putting it in my
pants pocket. We climbed over the side and down a rope ladder to get off
the ship, and as I did, the silverware fell out of my pocket, clattering

across the deck. With hundreds of sailors watching, I couldn't ignore it, so I gave it back. But, the demitasse spoon stayed in my pocket and I have it still today. "USN" is engraved on it.

I was married there, and my wedding gown was made out of a "target sleeve." Target sleeves were made of silk, like parachutes, and were pulled behind trucks for target practice. A flight nurse brought the veil and shoes back from a trip to Hawaii. Soon I was pregnant and left for the States. Not leaving with the other nurses a few months later, I didn't get to keep in touch with them, and now I miss that.

When the bomb was dropped on Hiroshima, I

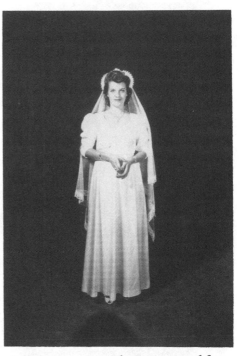

Silk from a target sleeve was used for Julia Polcholpek's wedding dress when she married on Saipan. (369 SH)

recall the rumors, then the reports, then the realization that the war was over. We were ecstatic but sad. We paid a lot for that victory.

Ellen Green Dellane   369th Station Hospital

Ellen joined the army in 1942 after graduating from nurse's training in Michigan.

When we first had patients in Saipan, we really had nothing to work with. Our supply ship had gone aground on a coral reef, and some supplies had to be flown in. I remember having only one thermometer to share for a group of diphtheria patients. At first we worked and lived in tents, but eventually Quonset huts were put up. The toilet was just two holes in the ground, but later they dug an "8-holer" for us. They didn't fill in the other one for a while, and one night a girl fell into it coming

**Using helmets for laundry was just one of many uses for this handy item
in Saipan.**

back from the Officers Club after dark. I was glad she didn't share my
tent.

When the wounded came, there wasn't enough room for all of them.
Sometimes even the chapel had beds in it. We worked fast and furious
then, shipped them out, and waited for the next group to come. Between
the battles raging on the different islands, we had a lot of waiting time. We
cleaned everything and socialized a lot. That's when a lot of songs were

The 369th Station Hospital on Saipan was one of many using portable Quonset huts made of corrugated metal.

Nurses of the 369th SH on Saipan line up in the mud for announcements. Headwear seems optional.

put together, and anyone contributed words or phrases as they thought them up.

Every moonlit night, two or three Japanese planes flew over, low enough to get under the radar. They didn't shoot, so everyone, including patients, went out to watch them. Then one day we had a daylight raid. It caught us all unaware, because the air raid siren was tested everyday at noon, and we came to ignore it. When it went off for real, I was in my tent, waiting to go back to work after lunch; I just thought it was the noon siren. My roommate was out in the open, and when the plane started strafing, she fell in the grass and stayed there for a couple of hours.

One young soldier from Hawaii was ready to leave the hospital and go home the next day. When the strafing began, he went out to look and was cut in half. Those planes strafed right over the hospital. It was our only daylight raid.

The Officers Club was the center of activity for us, since there were no towns, and the natives lived in a separate compound. The club faced the bay, and we watched the planes take off on missions, including the Tokyo bombing raids. They just skimmed over the water in front of us, and we watched, wondering who was on each plane. They flew overhead all the time, and when some didn't return after a mission, the girls who dated the pilots would be all shook up. One night I watched as a plane didn't rise enough and exploded while it was skimming over the water. The explosion shook the club, but in just a short time, there wasn't even a ripple on the water.

Commando Song

tune: Glory Glory Halleluja

When they took us out to KOKO Head and put us in a tent
Forty dollars once a month was far too much for rent
And our cold showers and latrines were far from heaven sent
When they tried to make commandos out of us.
Chorus: Glory Glory what a helluva time we had
      Glory Glory what a helluva time we had
      Glory Glory what a helluva time we had
When they tried to make commandos out of us.
They took us down to QM and they dressed us up like men
Complete with GI spats to our helmets made of tin
And what it did to glamour was actually a sin
When they tried to make commandos out of us. **Chorus**
They took us out to Bellows Field and made us dig fox holes
We dug and dug until we felt just like a little mole
The dynamite exploded and it nearly knocked us cold
When they tried to make commandos out of us. **Chorus**
They told us we'd have inspections and they told us what to wear
They told us this they told us that, we nearly tore our hair
And when we had inspection then the colonel wasn't there
When they tried to make commandos out of us. **Chorus**

Smile the While

tune: Till We Meet Again

Smile the while we bid you sad adieu
When our ship comes in we'll be with you
Then the skies will seem more blue
Back in the USA with you

All the crowd will drink so merrily
And Saipan will be a memory
We'll wait and pray each night and day
Till we meet again

Beer, Beer For 369th

Notre Dame Fight Song

Beer, beer for 369th
Come all you sots and have a good time
Send a shavetail out for gin
And don't let a sober person in
We never stagger we never fall
We sober up on GI alcohol
All you sots of the 369
We're out on a binge again

Pearl Will Haugland Bach U.S. Army   133rd General Hospital

Having grown up in Tacoma, Washington, Pearl had already served in Alaska and Canada by 1944.

There were about forty nurses with me on a big ocean liner that had been transformed into a troop ship, the *Willard A. Holbrook*. It was bulging with many, many troops as we zigged and zagged across the Pacific. We debarked at Hollandia, New Guinea, then went on to Leyte, Philippine Islands, on a hospital ship.

Our destination was the 133rd General Hospital, a big tent hospital way back in the jungle. The GIs who were there as patients greeted us with, "You'll be sorry!" Several of the nurses with my group were taken immediately to Manila to help the army nurses who were being liberated from Santo Tomás prison. We all felt such compassion for these ladies and donated lipsticks, shoes, and clothes.

The first three months were really lonesome and trying. It took that long before I received mail from my husband; conditions in the camp were so primitive. We lived out of boxes and suitcases and had to use helmets to wash in. Our patients were the wounded from battles on Samar and Sabo, and they came to us after having been just patched up in the field. Some had grass in their casts and bandages. More wards were built on to the hospital as battlefield wounded were brought to us. We worked twenty-four-hour shifts.

These GIs were sure glad to see women and be away from the battle-fields. Treatment often meant getting the "new stuff" called penicillin. I remember the first time I ever gave it to patients was when I worked night duty on a gunshot wound and fracture ward in July 1945.

Hazel Johnson Barton U.S. Army   156th Station Hospital

"Johnny" expected to serve for one year when she joined in July 1941, but she stayed for the duration and was discharged in October 1945.

When we reached Hawaii in November 1943, after zigzagging across the ocean, I was assigned to Tripler General Hospital, working in what had been Farrington High School. At first I was assigned to a neurosurgical ward, where many of the patients had been picked up from the beaches during the first wave of island offensives in the Pacific. There were many spinal cord injuries as well as head wounds. I remember one patient in particular who had a head wound with exposed brain tissue. Penicillin was just being introduced and the patient improved enough to be trans-ferred to the mainland.

I volunteered for forward-area duty later in 1944, was assigned to the 156th Station Hospital, and went to Schofield Barracks to await shipment with the unit. We sent some personal belongings ahead with the medical equipment, but a Kamikaze pilot hit the ship. My things were lost, along with some of the medical supplies, but no men were hurt.

In April 1945 we nurses boarded a Dutch ship, the SS *Tabinta*. We were quartered way below deck and were very cramped for space. The "head" was a makeshift deal at the end of the corridor with only four accommodations. I remember waiting in line when the first in line opened the door and said, "Oh, Oh, Full House!" The next gal said, "Yeah, Four Of A Kind!" The next one said, "If you ask me, it's a Royal Flush!"

We zigzagged our way westward and anchored for a while at Ulithi, a group of islands used by the U.S. Navy to repair ships. One night some navy officers blinked their signal lights to our ship, inviting four nurses to share a steak dinner with them on the beach. I was quite surprised to find my escort was FDRs son, who was a naval officer with the fleet on Ulithi.

Another night we returned to the *Tabinta* after "lights out" to find the stairs had been pulled up. We had to climb up the side of the ship on Jacob's ladder in a blinding rainstorm. I can still hear the troops on topside urging us onward and upward, singing these words from an old song, "She'll climb the rigging like her daddy used to do."

On the 18th of June 1945, we reached our destination, Okinawa. We disembarked using Jacob's ladder to get into an LST to go ashore. We spent our first night in tents and had an air raid alert. The next day we flew to Ie Shima, where we were quartered in tents with a high fence around the compound, covered with camouflage material, and a sentry standing guard at the gate. We were told not to leave the area unless accompanied by two armed officers.

Our patients were in tents and the operating rooms in Quonset huts. Almost every night there were air raids, and we had to get up and head for our foxholes. Drinking water was distilled in a lister bag outside the tent, and having been in the sun it was always over 100 degrees. Food was served from a mess hall—powdered eggs, milk, and potatoes, along with canned fruit, vegetables, and Spam. We always talked about what we would like to eat, if we ever got home again.

On August 19 the Japs landed on Ie Shima, on their way to the battle-ship *Missouri* for the signing of the peace treaty. My unit was sent to Korea, but I had enough points to go home. My chief nurse and I went to Okinawa to await transportation. A typhoon hit the first night there, and all the tents were leveled, except the one we were in. She rated a sturdy one with a floor, and I was lucky to share it with her. The mess hall was also gone. On October 19, I boarded the USS *General Bundy* for my trip home. I was on deck when told I had a visitor, who turned out to be Pat Barton, a fellow I'd first met in Hawaii. We had about an hour's visit before he had to leave. After five years in the army, I was discharged back home, and Pat and I were married in January 1946.

Kathleen Dial Coile U.S. Army Air Force
804th Medical Air Evacuation Squadron

Katie joined the army before the war, received flight nurse training in 1943, and arrived in New Guinea in 1944.

When my plane crash-landed, there were eighteen psychotic patients on board who were being sent back to the States. I had belly-landed on another flight, so when the pilot told us he didn't know where we were going down, that's what I expected to happen again.

I wasn't worried, and the sergeant and I made sure the patients were all restrained so they wouldn't bounce out of the litters. We had no place to sit, so the sergeant, who was about 6'6", sat down in the companionway, and I sat between his legs, with him holding me tight around the waist. We bounced once, and then on the second bounce I said, "Thank God!" But then the plane broke up. No one was killed, and I was hurt the worst, with a head injury, and my right shoulder was broken.

Prior to the crash the flight had been about three hours long, and when I was making rounds on the plane, I picked up the tag on one litter patient that read, "Homicidal Toward Women." He was just a youngster, and I said, "Are you really?" He answered, "Just let me loose and I'll show you." I told him I would be nice to him but would let him stay tied up. He was the only one who seemed sort of belligerent, but they were all restrained. Some were sedated, and some were in fitted litters to keep them in place. Most of them were depressed, having received "Dear John" letters and had gone off the deep end.

After we crashed I was able to help them get out of the plane. The weather was terrible, and when I was lying on the ground in the pouring rain, this patient, who was "Homicidal Toward Women," stood by my side to keep the rain off me. I said, "You are getting wet," and he said, "But you aren't."

That whole group was supposed to be sent back to the States, and the shock of the crash was treatment enough that they were all sent back to their units.

About three weeks before this happened, I had gotten married to the pilot I met on my first flight. We started to date as soon as we met and were married in a Baptist church in Townsville, Australia, with a female minister who also played the organ. We had a big reception with about forty-five GIs, then flew to Sydney for a two-week honeymoon. Right after we crashed my husband received a message that I was dead. He started checking and found me alive in the hospital at Port Moresby.

After the crash, when the weather cleared, I was flown to the hospital in Townsville where I had surgery. They wanted to send me back to the States for more surgery, and when I found out they were waiting for a hospital ship, I protested. They thought I would be afraid to fly again. So I flew back, spending the next five months in a hospital in Mississippi, near my home in Alabama.

My mother always worried, so I didn't tell her I was coming home, just like when I went overseas. Then I let my letters get farther apart, and after about five weeks she received a letter from a center in Australia saying that I had safely landed in Brisbane, Australia. She probably didn't even know where that was.

We were the first air evac nurses to land in Australia. A nurse who had been in the army for one-hundred years came on the ship to talk to us before we went ashore. She said, "I didn't send for you, and now that you are here, I don't know what I'm going to do with you." We sat around for about two months until General Kenney, who was in New Guinea, asked for us. He said, "Bring them up here, and let them do what they are supposed to do."

I've never been sorry about any of that time and was proud to receive the Distinguished Flying Cross and Purple Heart. Everyone wants to know if I was scared, but I don't think I had sense enough to get scared. It never entered my mind that everything wouldn't turn out all right.

Charlotte McFall Mallon U.S. Army Air Force
828th Medical Air Evacuation Squadron

In 1942 Charlotte joined the army in Michigan, entered the flight training program, and served on domestic military flights until her departure for the Pacific in October 1944.

The first time I flew across the International Date Line, the pilot asked for a dollar bill from everyone. He and the crew signed them and gave them back. This was called a "Short Snorter Bill." They told us whenever we went to a new country, we should pick up a local bill of currency and have it signed. We taped them together in a long strip; I had six by the time the war was over.

I flew all over the Pacific: Biak, New Guinea; Tarawa, Gilbert Islands; Leyte and Luzon, Philippines; Saipan; Tinian; Okinawa; Iwo Jima; Kwajalein and Eniwetok, Marshall Islands; Johnson Island; and Hawaii. Forget it if you had a boyfriend who hoped to see you, because you couldn't tell when you would get back.

Most people don't know that many of the flight nurses carried sidearms. I was in the fourth class at Bowman Field, Kentucky, and we all had to qualify on the firing range, learning to use a .45-caliber revolver. We were told it was against the Geneva Convention, but the reason was that flight nurses were in the forward areas, sometimes picking up patients within hours of the actual fighting. Our planes weren't marked by a red cross, and we could have been shot down and had to protect the patients. Weapons were issued after arriving overseas, depending on the situation, so not all flight nurses carried them.

Our planes carried twenty-four litters, twelve on each side, and six bucket seats in the tail section for the walking wounded. They were so thankful to receive their "going-home wound." There was a large station hospital on Saipan, for instance, and if we picked them up in the Philippines,

Flight nurse uniforms were practical for their active work in planes. Charlotte McFall wore the short jacket before assignment to the Pacific.

it was an eight-hour flight to Saipan. They were often in pain, and morphine was used to keep them out of shock. Flying at 10,000 feet helped also, because they would get sleepy with less oxygen.

My plane crashed on Eniwetok. Bulldozers would scrape rock and coral off to one end so we could have a landing area, however short it was. They'd just finished the airstrip, and the pilot braked as soon as the wheels were on the runway. The nose wheel of the C-54 hit the pile of coral, flipped us over on one wing, spinning us around, and the plane burst into flames. Another nurse, Mary Creel, and I jumped out through the flames. I escaped burns, but sprained my ankle, while the other nurses, crew, and some of the passengers were injured worse. Mary and Georgia Dixen suffered burns. I'd been asked to carry some secret papers to Tinian on that flight, which we weren't supposed to do, and had to be concerned about that, as well as helping the people who were injured.

Charlotte McFall (center) survived this crash on Eniwetok with only a sprained ankle. Others suffered worse injuries and burns when the plane in the background broke in half and burst into flames.

The barracks we stayed in usually had barbed wire around them. There was a nine o'clock curfew, but sometimes we heard rustling around outside and knew it was a Japanese soldier looking for food. They hid out in caves on the islands after they were overrun.

Commercial airline pilots flew our evacuation planes sometimes, and I remember island-hopping with one in particular. We had several patients, and he was making the roughest landings each time. I asked him to take it easy so the patients wouldn't be jostled around so much. When we got to the end he must have reported me, and I was "grounded" for about two weeks.

The men in these remote airfields were always so glad to see American girls. We had to wear the khaki men's uniform for flying, and they didn't fit too well. We would land at a pickup point, which was always some darn, hot, sweaty island, the door of the plane would open, and there we stood, looking like a million dollars to them. Some of these troops had been in the Pacific, fighting from island to island, for years.

When the navy flight nurses came into the war, there was some jealousy in the Pacific. We had been flying there for a long time, proving that

**Flight nurse Charlotte McFall (828 MAES) was awarded the Air Medal
while serving in the Pacific.**

air evacuation was the efficient way to take care of patients; we broke
ground in every way for nurses in combat zones. When they came over in
early 1945, they had nice-fitting uniforms to fly in, while we wore men's
khakis, and it seemed that they were getting all the glory.

One day I was in Saipan, waiting for patients to come in from various
places, when the chief nurse came into the barracks and asked us to get all
the fresh food, fruit, or anything we could find. She told us we were going
to put on a buffet, and we couldn't imagine what could be happening
because our food was so awful. She wouldn't tell us why, so we guessed
that some VIP was coming from Washington. All kinds of food was
brought together, because everyone had been getting it sent from home.
We took it to the hangar, where the mess sergeants had made potato salad,

and put out all the food. We waited for the planes, and pretty soon, two of them landed and taxied up to the hangars. They were not the usual evacuation planes, either, but the "plush" ones that VIPs traveled in.

When the doors opened, the stairs were wheeled to the planes, and the girls who had been prisoners in the Philippines came out. I can never tell this without crying. We knew immediately who they were. They were thin as rails. They had been given uniforms, which didn't fit, and their hats were down over their noses. The band struck up the "Star Spangled Banner," and there wasn't a dry eye anywhere, everybody was crying. We all greeted them, and ushered them to the buffet. The centerpiece was a sheetcake that was decorated red, white, and blue, and read, "Welcome Home To The Good Old USA." They were thrilled to pieces.

When I went through flight training in 1943, some of the girls in my class had escaped from Corregidor by submarine, just before the Japanese captured the nurses who were left behind. This had been in the back of my mind ever since.

Soon after that we flew into Manila to pick up American prisoners of war. I was at the airfield loading patients on the plane, and the pilot said we were getting three walking wounded, carrying their own records. We were all loaded and waiting when the three men came on board, quietly taking their seats. After they were settled, I went to the front of the plane and used the microphone. I announced to the other patients, who were on litters, "We are honored today to have three of our prisoners of war who survived the death march." Everyone applauded and shouted. It was wonderful.

Jane Simons Silva U.S. Army Air Force
829th Medical Air Evacuation Squadron

Having failed the navy's eye test, rather than return home she tried the army and passed.

I can still picture the air battle we watched between American and Japanese fighter planes as we circled over Okinawa, waiting to land and pick up wounded men. We couldn't land until the Japanese planes had been shot down, and watched from the air as the fighting continued on the ground as well. When it was clear enough for us to land, the patients we got were bloody and had barely been bandaged, they were so fresh from battle.

On another flight, I and everyone else felt so much pride when we picked up several former prisoners of war in the Philippines. These men were skeletons with swollen legs and feet, and they insisted on walking on the plane.

Jeanne Doll Dolan U.S. Navy Flight Nurse   VE 2/VRE 1 Squadrons

From Wisconsin, Jeanne was among the first two dozen women selected for navy flight training.

I was in the first class of nurses to graduate from the U.S. Navy's flight evacuation school in Alameda, California, and in the first group of twelve to go to Guam in February 1945. The island was barely secure, with fires still burning, when we landed. I'll never forget how hot and muggy it seemed when we arrived, because we'd been traveling in heavy, navy blue, wool uniforms, and stepped out of the plane into about a foot of red clay mud. No one was expecting us, but tents were quickly put up, and the area was put under armed guard. We lived that way for a while, with outdoor showers, until some Quonset huts were built.

On March 1 we made our first evacuation flights in DC-3s to Iwo Jima. During the six-hour flight, the nurse and a corpsman set up about twenty litters for the return trip. We landed amid anti-aircraft firing, and the patients, mostly marines right from the battlefield, were often just lying on the ground, waiting for us. The flight doctor evaluated the wounded; there were always a lot of abdomen wounds from hand grenades and shrapnel. There were no pressurized cabins, so we couldn't bring back those with head injuries.

In April we began going to Okinawa, which was about eight-hours flying time from Guam in a C-54, always leaving about midnight to arrive by dawn.

The first time we went there, I was on the second plane in and the weather was terrible. We didn't have radar in those days, and the pilot had to choose between two airstrips, which we could hardly see. The one he picked was the wrong one, because it wasn't completed. There was a big pile of coral rock at the end, and we nosed right into it. The tail stuck up thirty feet in the air, and the corpsman and I had to push the door out and jump to the ground. The pilot and crew escaped out the front hatch, just as the fuselage exploded and burned. We were all shook up, but no one was seriously hurt. I wasn't afraid while it was happening, but just did what I had to do to get out.

Planes were coming in at one-hour intervals, and all the rest found the right airstrip. It was pouring rain, but since we couldn't go back on that plane, the corpsman and I walked into the village of Naha and picked up souvenirs. When we went back to the airstrip, we were told it was too dangerous to go to Naha. I still have some utensils with bullet marks in them, which I treasure.

We could see the battles when landing, and when there was a delay for something like a blown tire, we knew we were in danger. The nurse was always responsible for "the box," which we guarded with our lives, because it contained morphine vials. Often we had to scrounge for places to stay on these islands, and I just dearly loved the army flight nurses we met. On Kwajelein we stayed at their quarters, and over the entrance a sign read, "Hell's Angels."

One of my most vivid memories was watching hundreds of B-29 bombers take off from the army airfield on Guam for the seventeen-hour flight to bomb Tokyo. We watched tensely as they returned, and hoped all were accounted for.

Stella Makar Smith U.S. Navy Flight Nurse   VE 2/VRE 1 Squadrons

"Stash" was promoted to lieutenant commander by the close of her four years with the navy.

When you are young, you're not afraid of anything, and we never hesitated about flying into Iwo Jima during the battles. Marine fighters circled overhead while we were on the ground to pick up patients, but there was still a lot of danger. We just always felt we had to do whatever needed to be done.

There was one brave young lad I'll always remember, who was probably only 18 years old. The doctor asked me if I wanted to chance taking him on the flight. How could I say no? He had shrapnel in his jaw and it was wired closed. He let me know he'd never flown before, so I told him, "You're going to make it," and he nodded his head, looking me right in the eye. On the long six-hour flight back to Guam, his eyes never left my face, and I never left his side. And he made it.

Norma Harrison Crotty U.S. Navy Flight Nurse
VE 2/VRE 1 Squadrons

After completing nursing school in Cleveland in 1943, Norma felt it was just natural to go into the navy.

Today people talk about women in combat, but we never thought of it that way. Our planes weren't armed, nor were we. When we were twenty-two years old, we thought we were invincible. I didn't get very upset until it was all over with. Now I get to remembering patients, and, well, I think if I had known more, maybe I could have done more.

Our flights always arrived in Iwo Jima right at daybreak, and the first sight was awesome. Sometimes we had to circle the island, while battleships fired over the airstrip. It is difficult to describe my feelings as we waited to land. Ships surrounded Iwo as far as you could see on the horizon, firing on the little island. I felt like I was living in a newsreel at the movies.

As soon as we landed, we ran to the aid station where patients were waiting, all very recently wounded. The sounds and smells of war were all around us. From the airstrip we could see Mt. Suribachi and the sea. The litters were loaded on the plane and we took off for Guam, with only a very young nurse and a corpsman to care for these severely wounded marines. We worked so well with the corpsmen, I can't praise them enough.

We were too busy to realize what we had seen, checking vital signs, changing and reinforcing battle dressings, always watching for bleeding. We fed those who were able to eat, using our sheath knives to open cans of boned turkey, sliced peaches, and grapefruit juice. There was oxygen for the pilots, but since we seldom flew above 5,000 feet, there was no need to have it for patients.

I remember that the patients used to like to see us put lipstick on, and they would say, "Do that again." Most of them were so very young and wanted their moms.

When we first arrived in Guam, we lived in a large tent and used an outdoor latrine, with sheets hung around for privacy. Things were pretty primitive so adversity led to close friendships, which we keep to this day. We lived in Quonset huts later and enjoyed first-class living, like mechanical whizzers [flush toilets], showers, a washing machine, and the greatest treasure, a refrigerator. There were other nurses on Guam, but we didn't mix with them and felt they resented us. Because we lived on the airbase, under the command of a naval aviator instead of a medical officer, we seemed to have more freedom.

With so few women and so very many men, our social life was out-standing with dances and parties. There was also a 10:00 P.M. curfew, and when we were out at night, there had to be two officers with us, one wearing a sidearm. So many of the nurses married fellows they met over-seas, and they didn't know very much about each other. Surprisingly, most of the marriages have worked out fine.

We often took patients to Honolulu and stopped on Kwajelein Atoll to stay overnight. That's where I had my only contact with Japanese. Some prisoners were kept in a fenced area near the flightline, and they always stood at the fence, watching us. We took their pictures, and they would say things to us, which we thought were kind of sassy. I was on Okinawa when President Franklin Roosevelt died in April 1945, and no one knew who the vice president was. Everyone was saying, "What will we do now?"

Japanese Internment Camps Philippines 1941-1945
Prisoners of War

"You don't know what freedom is until you lose it"

Margaret Nash U.S. Navy   **Cañacao Hospital, Cavite Navy Yard**

Peggy had been in the navy since 1936 with a specialization in tuberculosis treatment.

This experience was unique and I hope there will never be anything like it again.

My uncle was a U.S. Congressman from Pennsylvania, and in 1936 he suggested I join the navy as a nurse. Three weeks later I did, and there were only about three hundred of us in those days. I was sent to Guam and loved it because I met my fiancé, and planned to marry. Suddenly, in September 1941, two other nurses and I were transferred to the Philippines, with only two hours' notice to pack.

We traveled on ships painted black, under secret orders, not knowing where we were headed. After three weeks we dropped anchor in Zamboanga, where the navy was having maneuvers, then went on to Manila, where everyone asked why we were late. We were too naive to ask questions, but now I know they were expecting a Japanese attack.

Japan had moved troops into several areas of that part of the world, and civilians were being evacuated, including from the Philippines. In those days, I didn't realize the seriousness of these events, but we weren't informed about everything that was happening either.

On December 8, 1941, (December 7th in Hawaii) the loudspeaker came on and announced that Pearl Harbor had been bombed. I thought, "Where is Pearl Harbor?" Another nurse said, "I think it's the Japanese again. There's something going on. But they won't get across Manila Bay." All of a sudden it dawned on me that this was war. It was serious.

It had been two months since I arrived in the Philippines, and it would be more than three years before I was able to leave. Within one month I became a prisoner of the Japanese.

The day after the announcement about Pearl Harbor, we were told to evacuate our patients from the Canacao Navy Hospital, because the navy yard was a military target. Our patients were sent to Sternberg Army Hospital in Manila. Two of our nurses stayed at Sternberg, which left nine nurses at Cañacao. On Tuesday Clark Field was hit, and the next day the navy yard was flattened. It wasn't too long before the casualties started coming in.

Believe me, if I live to be one hundred, I could still see those men. They came in every type of conveyance you can imagine, four or five in a car and some on the roof. We sent corpsmen out in ambulances, and many of them did not return. We worked feverishly all day, taking care of the casualties, trying to save the ones that we could. All of our doctors were in the operating room doing surgery. There were two nurses on each ward, and we had to use our own judgment because there were no doctors to give orders. Knowing they would need tetanus, one nurse would fill up a 20cc syringe with tetanus vaccine. The next nurse followed with morphine, then started all over again. Everybody was screaming with pain. Every time I think about it, I wonder, "How did we ever get through the ward?"

The next time I looked out the window it was dark. There was fire all around, and the sky was red with flames and smoke. Manila was burning, and also the Cavite Navy Yard.

It was amazing how cool the nurses were. I never thought I could be like that. Two or three in a bed, on chairs between the beds, patients screamed, "Help me!" I can still hear the voice of one young man desperately repeating a plea for water. As we readied patients for surgery, sometimes we came to a bed and the patient was dead.

Once I ran to the operating room and saw the doctors operating on the steps and on the floor. It was like a nightmare there, but I couldn't stop to help because I had to get back to the ward. We worked like that into the night. Corpses filled the morgue. There was no time for fear.

The chief nurse then told us our orders were to evacuate the patients and leave the hospital, and we started getting the patients into little PT boats. We went back and forth, making many trips the ten miles across Manila Bay, a nurse on each boat, taking patients to the army hospital. The Filipinos were so helpful to us, and I'll never forget them. Of course, many of them were also patients.

The next day, at Sternberg Army Hospital, we were getting something to eat and the Japanese started bombing again. The army nurses thought we were crazy as we jumped under the tables.

From then on we were really on the go. All over the city, hospitals were filled. We set up small dispensaries in various places, even in nightclubs. I went to Philippine Union College, where we stayed in tents and slept on cots. Ants crawled up the legs of the cots, so the corpsmen had the idea to wrap strips with vaseline around the legs of the cots to keep the bugs from getting to us.

When I was in training, I'll never forget Sister Regina telling us, "You'll never have everything, and you'll have to improvise." That was the first time it came back to me, and believe me, we really had to improvise.

We were there until December 26, when the radio announced that Manila was declared an open city. Though we had no orders, our commander decided we should move back into Manila. The next day, we packed up the patients and took ambulances back into the city. We had to go over many makeshift bridges, and a corpsman said to me, "Peg, you're the religious one. Say a Hail Mary that this bridge will hold us up."

As we drove into Manila, the Japanese bombed the city. We pulled up close to fences, getting patients up close, until the bombing was over. Then we would just jump up and get back to work again. We headed for Santa Scholastica College, where the army had set up a hospital, before they pulled out to Corregidor.

A lot of people from all nations, all professions, and all walks of life had been accumulating, having been stranded in Manila. On January 2, 1942, the Japanese moved into the city, and we became their prisoners. A young priest, on his way to his first assignment in India, wound up with us, and I remember his spirit and humor. The day the Japanese came, he said, "We aren't going to let it bother us. We are going to have a spelling bee!"

A swarm of Japanese appeared outside Santa Scholastica and came into the hospital. They insisted on an inspection tour, with the chief nurse accompanying them through the wards. Several of them spoke English and let us know we could remain and take care of the patients. Then they left, leaving guards with rifles behind to watch our every move.

Our chief nurse made out schedules, and we just went on treating the many patients with a regular routine. We did this until March 12, having no idea what was going on outside the gate. We heard that as patients recuperated they were sent to prisoner camps. The Japanese didn't know what to do with us nurses and finally put us in Santo Tomás University, where all civilians were interned.

In Santo Tomás, we navy nurses were put in a room with fifty other women. They were from all over the world, speaking every language, the wealthy, and the prostitutes. By this time, we were adjusted to making the best of bad situations, but many of these women were troublesome and made life difficult for others and themselves. We offered to work in the hospital, which was formerly the carpenter shop at the university. Again, our chief nurse made out schedules and we returned to regular duties, such as they were. She always said that we should carry on as navy nurses, to be proud and do what we could in any situation.

Food was scarce and we were always hungry. After about eight months, two nurses were requested to go to Holy Ghost College to help with some children and their mothers, so I volunteered because I thought they might have more food. We were there about ten days, and not only were the children sick, but the mothers became sick as well. They didn't have any more food than we did, and we worked around the clock, twelve-hour duty each. Thank God we were young!

We were sent back to Santo Tomás, and pretty soon I came down with dengue fever, and boy was I ever sick. This fever is common in the tropics. It is carried by mosquitoes, causing very high temperatures, body aches, chills, and a measles-like rash. Eventually I became well enough to go back to work with the regular routine. In July, army nurses were brought to Santo Tomás.

In May 1943, the Japanese decided to open another prison camp at Los Baños College in Luzon, and we navy nurses were asked to go. Eight hundred able-bodied men were selected to work at Los Baños, to set up the camp. As we were piled into trucks by the Japanese, the internees of Santo Tomás serenaded us with "Anchors Aweigh." That moment is something I'll never forget.

We arrived at a railroad station filled with boxcars. In the navy, we'd been accustomed to traveling first class. They put sixty-eight men and two nurses in each boxcar. Before we left Santo Tomás, our meal consisted of a duck egg and a piece of bread. Thank God, they had boiled the egg. It took five hours to chug along, and as we stopped at different stations, they would open the doors to let just a little air in. It was suffocating, and maliciously inhuman.

When we got off the train, the men were forced to walk and the nurses rode in trucks. The college was abandoned with nothing but empty cottages, stripped bare. We hadn't had anything to eat but that duck egg and piece of bread. Someone saw a chicken, caught it, killed it, and found a way to boil it so we had that to eat.

We started improvising, as we had become used to doing. There was an operating room, and I was in charge of the dispensary. People confiscated things and everyone was turning up with all sorts of surprises, like cold cream jars to hold things. One guy made ointment and adhesive tape. The tape came from rubber trees. It was all makeshift, but very good, if I say so myself.

A wonderful Australian fellow walked me to the dispensary every morning at five o'clock. He asked me why I had to be there so early, and I told him I had to sterilize the instruments and get the clinic ready by seven o'clock. Doctors in the group had come up with some instruments. He asked what we used in the States, and I explained what a sterilizer was. I had been using a hot plate. A few days later he appeared with a sterilizer. I asked him where he ever found it, and he said, "Peggy, don't ask." From then on I never asked about anything that appeared.

After we were there about a year, I told my Australian that I needed a dressing carriage, which was a cart with wheels to take from bed to bed. He asked me to draw a picture. After a little while he appeared with a dressing carriage. One day someone told me my friend was on trial. I asked why and was told it was probably because the wheels on the commandant's bicycle were missing. I thought he had stolen the wheels for my cart, and that we all would suffer for it. But, he talked himself out of everything. I still hear from him to this day.

Life went on, with all our diseases. Everyone had jungle rot, a fungus, and I still have it. I'd have fifteen people soaking their feet in a solution that turned their feet purple. In September 1944, I became seriously ill. My legs and arms were swollen, and I had nodules all over them, along with a high fever. They decided to give me crude typhoid vaccine, to try to arrest the infection. I had two injections but nearly died. Evidently it helped, because I recovered. I did come back with the plague, tuberculosis, and beriberi, a disease caused by severe malnutrition.

Christmas day 1944, a Spanish bishop who was in the camp gave a homily that I remember well. He said, "One thing's for sure, we won't be here this time next year." We all understood the message. Either we would be rescued or we would all be dead, and we all knew it. A lot was happening, but we didn't know what it was. Planes began to fly over. The men had a radio somehow, and we'd get messages.

Imprisoned by the Japanese in the Philippines for more than three years, Margaret Nash and ten other U.S. Navy nurses were rescued from Los Baños in February 1945. Sixty-eight U.S. Army nurses survived internment near Manila at Santo Tomás.

In January 1945, we were living from day to day. One day we awoke and there were no guards in the camp at all. Filipinos were bringing in food, and we had no idea what happened. The rumor was that our forces were getting closer and that the Japs were leaving while they had time. But in a week they were back, and meaner than ever.

I'll never forget George. The basement where we slept was right next to a ravine, and we could hear the men slide down to escape. One day I was sitting in the shanty and heard a guard shout, "Halt!" Then I heard a rustle, looked out, and saw it was George. I headed for the hospital, and heard the guard say again, "Halt." I turned around, and George was lying on the ground, helpless. I wanted to get to him, but they would have shot me, so I headed for the nurses' quarters. Our chief nurse said she would never forget the look on my face. They left him lying there for hours in the hot sun. One of the doctors went out and begged them to let us bring him into the hospital, but they just left him there. They left him for five or six hours and then they shot and killed him.

Everyone had a shanty built out of bamboo, so we could have a little privacy. Soon after George's death, one of the guards stopped by my little shanty, and in his broken English and with the help of a dictionary, he asked if I was lonesome for America. Then he told me that he too had a family that he would never see again, and that he'd been fighting in China and now the Philippines. It was hard for me to hear this from him.

We were at the stage where we could hardly walk. The shanty that my chum built for me was on an incline, and when I had to go up to roll call, I could hardly make it there. But there was always some internee humor. Someone would say to another, "If you're going to die, dig your own grave because we're too tired to dig one for you." And when I said I couldn't eat something, like the stuff that tasted like wallpaper paste, another nurse would tease, "You're such a spoiled brat."

Carrie Edwina Todd U.S. Navy   Cañacao Hospital, Cavite Navy Yard

When Edwina was released, her new brother-in-law was part of the liberation forces.

I felt my religious upbringing helped me through some unusual situations during the internment. My father was a minister, and of course, taught to love your enemy, not knowing what that would mean to me one day. Rather than be defiant, I sort of treated the guards respectfully, as I had been taught. One day a man dashed into my cubicle and told me to hide a radio, because the guards were searching the camp. I drew a blank what to do but since it was on the bed I threw a blanket over it, leaving a lump on the bed.

Soon a Japanese soldier stepped in and asked if I had the radio, and since I could never lie, I said, "See for yourself." He stood there, looked around, and then left. He must have trusted me enough not to search. The radio was important because its news provided hope for us, and I believe that God knew how important the radio was to the camp and used my room to help sustain the hope.

Dorothy Still Danner U.S. Navy   Cañacao Hospital, Cavite Navy Yard

Dorothy joined the navy in 1937 from her home town, Long Beach, California, and had almost completed a two-year tour in the Philippines.

Transports left for the States every three months, and I was due to leave in January 1942. I was a prisoner by then, but my personal items had been sent ahead, and four years later when I did get home, my photo albums and everything were waiting for me.

The army had set up a small hospital at Santa Scholastica College after the bombings, but when Manila was declared an open city on December 26, 1941, the army left for Bataan. Orders to leave Manila with General MacArthur and the other military didn't come for the navy nurses, and we've never known what happened. We were still in Manila waiting for orders when the Japanese took over in January. The men in our unit, mostly corpsmen, were taken to an elementary school and then to Bilibid Prison, and we were sent to Santo Tomás. We didn't like being separated from them.

For the next three years, both in Santo Tomás and Los Baños, living conditions became worse and worse, as food became scarce and disease took over. We started out with two meals a day, which dwindled to less along with everything else. We ran out of dressings and used anything, like our white uniforms, to make dressings. Fortunately there was an autoclave to sterilize dressings and whatever instruments we had. Through the grace of God I didn't get an infection when I had my appendix removed in camp. We had dysentery and dengue fever all the time.

We were aware of some of the war action because people set up little handmade radios. The Japanese had taken over a newspaper, and the information they printed gave us an idea where fighting was going on.

Mary Rose Harrington Nelson U.S. Navy
                              Cañacao Hospital, Cavite Navy Yard

Born in South Dakota, educated in Iowa, Mary Rose joined the navy in 1936 "to get a better job."

When the Japanese army entered Manila, I went up to the third floor tower at Santa Scholastica to watch their "triumphal march" down the street. Leading the troops was a general riding in an open car, with flags and all. It was an eerie feeling to see this parade. Japanese civilians had taken refuge in their embassy, which was a block away from where we were. They'd made sort of an internment camp for themselves since they weren't safe on the streets, and were very glad to see the troops finally come into the city.

A few days later, some of the Japanese came over to look at the hospital we'd set up. They really didn't believe we had patients, and we had to take the dressings off to show them the wounds.

When we were moved to Los Baños Agricultural College, I thought it was nicer to be out in the country. I didn't feel so confined, as there was more space, at least at first. There was barbed wire, but it just seemed more open. New internees were isolated for a while and kept in a walled-off section. Because of all the missionaries that were brought in, that section was called "Vatican City," and we were in "Hell's Half Acre." A large barracks became a chapel because there were lots of different religions to be accommodated.

The Japanese only had a medical sergeant for their own care, but his knowledge was very limited and he came to us to ask about everything, like medicinal dosage. Our surgeon performed three appendectomies on Japanese soldiers. When they brought in the first one, the doctor told them the appendix would probably rupture and he would die if they took him to Manila. During the operation there were armed Japanese in the operating room with fixed bayonets, and if somebody had slipped, hard telling what they would have done. A guard stayed with that patient, and he recovered nicely. So they brought some presents of sugar and a few eggs.

I met my husband at Los Baños. Before the war, he'd been working as a civilian in Manila for the U.S. Treasury Department. When he broke his foot in the camp, the doctor put him to bed for a week, and that's how we met. He was one of the men we trained to be hospital corpsmen, so we worked together after that. He gave me his ring, and we became engaged in camp.

After all these years I get a little tired of people only talking about the horrors of the camps. That didn't happen every day. I know people were brutalized and beaten and even killed. Garrison guards weren't too bad. I had conversations with a sergeant who was on duty watching the patient. He told me he had two daughters, and I asked when he was going back home. He said in effect, "Who knows?" There are plenty of atrocity stories, but mostly they were just doing their jobs. Most of the time we were fighting boredom. We stood in line to go to the bathroom. We stood in line to get food. We stood in line for everything. Edwina Todd gathered books from everyone and started a lending library. Most of us tried to keep a good mental outlook.

Internees who worked and kept busy were better off mentally and, to a degree, physically than those who gave up. Even when we were in rather poor shape at the end, we plodded along and did what we could. I was lucky with my health, but all the nurses weren't so lucky. We worried that we wouldn't bring back one nurse, who had a heart condition, but we did. Our head nurse, Laura Cobb, was very good and really "mother-henned" us well. I had known her in the States and have great respect for her.

A lot of civilian internees who had lived in Manila had servants, and for a while at least, had good connections with the outside when they were at Santo Tomás. They sent out their laundry and even had food brought in. Some of them were wealthy people and did pretty well in camp.

When they first set up the camp at Santo Tomás, the Japanese offered to set up one part for husbands and wives to use for conjugal meetings. The Americans said, "No, we don't do such a thing." A communication problem there. So the Japanese said, "All right, it's a crime." For a while, if a woman became pregnant, the husband was put in jail. After a while, things changed.

In the camp there were professors, engineers, and many people who started teaching classes in anything you wanted to take. It depended on whether you wanted to keep an upbeat attitude because there was more boredom than anything. We dressed for dinner, so to speak, and there was music on the loudspeaker. Food was the main subject of conversation. A notorious saying went, "A woman could walk naked through the camp and no one would look up unless she had a ham sandwich in each hand!"

Madeline Ullom U.S. Army   **Sternberg Hospital, Manila**

"Madge" made a career of the army after the war, retiring at the rank of colonel.

I thought I knew what freedom was, but you don't know what freedom is until you lose it, and the little everyday things you take for granted are no longer yours.

Sternberg General Hospital started receiving wounded from all over the Manila area when the Japanese attacked. We had so many patients that warehouses were turned into wards. Fort Stotsenberg, which was at Clark Field, called for help, and we sent doctors and nurses to them. They soon had to evacuate and put their casualties on trains, buses, and whatever they could find to bring them to Sternberg. Hospitals were set up all over Manila, in schools, universities, even nightclubs.

When the Japanese troops landed on Luzon, the island where Manila is located, General Douglas MacArthur declared Manila an open city and withdrew troops to Corregidor and Bataan Peninsula. We were told to prepare to evacuate the night before the Japanese were supposed to come into the city. During the middle of the night I heard tanks rumbling by, and when I went out to look the chief nurse told me to get inside, because we didn't know whose tanks they were. We rode in ambulances through the dark streets of Manila with no headlights, dodging bomb craters.

A small boat was waiting for us at the harbor, and about five minutes later, the dock we had just left blew up. Our mood was lightened when someone made the remark, "Nothing like burning your bridges after you cross them." All over Manila harbor we could see sunken vessels. We transferred to an interisland boat, and the Japanese strafed it. The boat went on, dodging around mines, as we hid in the hold until early morning. When we docked at Corregidor, an air raid warning went off. A truck appeared and, not really stopping, sort of scooped us up and took us to the Malinta Tunnel.

Corregidor means "correction" in Spanish, and in the early days it was a Spanish penal colony. General MacArthur and Manuel Quezon, president of the Philippines, set up headquarters there. When the headquarters and hospital were heavily bombed, everything moved into the Malinta Tunnel. It was a massive tunnel, with railroad tracks and trains running through it. A lot of supplies were stored there.

President Quezon was reinaugurated on December 31, 1941, and I attended the ceremony in the tunnel. The army band marched, though their instruments had been blown up.

I went right to work in the operating room in the tunnel. We received casualties constantly, plus a lot of people with dengue fever and malaria. The Japanese never stopped bombing. Our patients were from all the services, and since the laundries were bombed out, they had to wear whatever they could find. Sometimes they wore an army shirt and navy trousers. They joined up with each other as their outfits were attacked, and we couldn't tell what branch anyone belonged to. Before too long, malnutrition was prevalent. We were cut off from land, sea, and air. Every day we went up to the top of Malinta Hill to see if the American fleet was coming in to rescue us.

There was a radio station, called the Voice of Freedom, that broadcast the news daily and always ended with "Corregidor still stands." After the Japanese took over, one day a voice said, "Corregidor still stands, under new management."

The fighting men were really brave. They fought against all odds, with little ammunition, medicine, food, or supplies. We were getting destitute, but the men kept on, sometimes with sheer will power, fighting day and night. I remember a fellow with a leg blown off and a big abdominal wound, and he said, "After they hit me, I got two of them." Or, they would insist you take care of someone else first. Malaria added to the problems, and some of the nurses were getting sick from it and malnutrition, but we tried to keep on doing what we could. The men called us "angels" and would say, "If you angels can take it, we can take it."

Early in May 1942 the Japanese pounded the tunnel with bombing and air raids. It went on and on. In the operating room, the dust was intense because the walls were just unfinished rock, and they shook with the bombing. We put wet gauze over the patients mouths so they wouldn't breathe dust. Everything fell from the shelves, and beds shook, but we had to go on operating.

The surrender took place May 6, 1942. The next morning the Japanese took ten of us, doctors and nurses, outside the tunnel. We were lined up, with a guard at each end, and didn't know what was going to happen. The Japanese officer in charge said in English, "Don't be afraid. I am a graduate of one of your universities. I know how you feel. We want to take your picture." So they did, and we went back inside the tunnel, a little shaken, I'll admit.

They kept us there about six more weeks. It was so hot. The smell was horrible with all the sick people, and they wouldn't allow dead bodies to be moved for several days. There were great big green flies, and everyone had terrible dysentery. The Japanese made rounds through the tunnel, and when they walked, their swords dragged on the ground. With the swords, and their big, heavy boots, the sound would wake up the patients at night.

The nurses slept in a lateral tunnel, with a sheet drawn across the entrance for privacy. The chief nurse, Maude Davidson, had a bed right at the entrance and a little table there. About twenty very high-ranking Japanese officers came to inspect one day, and the one leading them pulled the sheet down and started to enter. Maude was on her feet right away and said, "Halt! You cannot enter here without permission." The generals were all so surprised they stepped back and went the other way. Then Maude realized what she had done. Since we were their captives, the death penalty could be given for much less than ordering generals not to do something. She went to our commanding officer and told him what had happened. He talked to the Japanese, and about three hours later a big sign was put up, in Japanese, saying, "No one is to enter here without permission."

When patients' temperatures dropped to 100 degrees, they had to be discharged from the hospital, regardless of what the wounds or illnesses were. We could only guess what happened to them. We had little food, and an army veterinarian asked the Japanese if we could have more. They became irritated and took him out of the tunnel. We heard two shots, and never saw him again.

In July, the nurses were taken out of the tunnel and put in a boat, which was to take us to Manila. We were quite weak and had to climb up a rope ladder, which wasn't easy. More than 2,000 patients were put in the bottom of the ship. An officer, who spoke English, explained to us that there was a school outside of Manila all set up as a hospital. All we had to do was walk in and take care of the patients.

When we arrived at Santo Tomás University, the nurses were taken to a room and searched. They considered us dangerous because we took care of the military. For seven weeks, we were locked in two rooms in a dormitory. One room was for eating, and the other small room was for sleeping. We were very crowded, doubled up on little beds made of raffia (palm tree fiber), with no mattresses. We were all pretty thin by then, and in the morning there were patterns on our skin.

The university had become an internment camp, and eventually we took care of patients. The camp was organized into a small city. The first year we had a very good school system. There were many educated people from all over the world, and classes in just about every subject were offered. I took classes in landscape architecture, geology, English litera-ture, and anthropology. It gave us something to think about and kept our minds off our problems.

Every year it became worse. Our rations were cut back whenever the U.S. took over another island. We had to bow to the Japanese every time we passed one of them. We had classes on how to bow, and it had to be done correctly, or it would have to be done a second time. Twice a day there was roll call, when everyone had to stand at attention while the numbers were reconciled. And sometimes we had five or six roll calls a day, even during the night. There were inspections also, where about 100 Japanese swarmed all over with their guns and bayonets. If they came into the room and you had one foot on one step and one foot on another, you had to stay as you were.

We received mail three or four times during those years. The Japanese gave it out when they felt like it, often months after it arrived. We were only allowed to send letters twice, and didn't know if they were actually sent.

Japanese planes were always flying around, practicing dogfights. One day, an internee said to me, "You'd think this was for real!" We watched a Japanese plane drop from the sky and realized there were American bombers up there. On September 21, 1944, our bombers hit the port in Manila and shot Japanese planes out of the sky. We could see it happening and felt the buildings shake like an earthquake. The ships in the harbor had been loaded with ammunition, and they were all being blown up. This bat-tle lasted for three days, and the Japanese punished anyone they caught looking at the planes flying overhead. They made us stand at attention in the hot sun, all day, with no food or water. We were already so weak.

On Christmas Day leaflets were dropped that read, "Peoples of the Philippines: the Commanding Officer and the troops of the South Pacific wish their gallant allies their fondest wishes for the New Year." We were elated and knew they were coming to rescue us.

Many people were dying of malnutrition and starvation. I remember one twenty-four hour period when we had seven deaths. A civilian doctor was head of the camp medical department, and he wrote on death certifi-cates, "Cause of death: Starvation." The Japanese tried to get him to change it, and he wouldn't, so they put him in the camp jail until we were released. Dead bodies piled up for days, and footlong rats ate their toes off. The cemetery in camp grew bigger and bigger. Food was so scarce, the last ration we received in the camp was two bags of moldy rice for over four thousand people.

One day a plane flew over the camp, and the pilot dropped his goggles with a note that read, "Roll out the barrel! We'll be in today or tomorrow!" The night of February 3, 1945, we saw lights and then there was a battle at the gate. Six hundred men of the U.S. First Cavalry burst through the gate, and we all ran to them. The commander of the Japanese guards was very mean, and he came over to the crowd. He reached into his shirt and was going to throw a grenade into all of us, when an American saw him and put a bullet right through his neck. Never a dull moment.

We always knew the Americans would come and free us. One of the American officers was injured so I went right to work, and it took so much bandage to go around him. The Americans seemed so big, compared to the Filipinos or the starving internees. It turned out that this officer's father was on the board in Philadelphia when I took my physical to join the army. It was like old home week.

The Japanese wouldn't surrender and stationed themselves in a building where some of our male internees were. They wouldn't leave without their weapons, so negotiations began. Rather than risk more lives, the Americans agreed, and in the morning the Japanese were all lined up, ready to march out the gate. We had several hundred children in camp, and they started shouting, "Make them bow!" The American troops didn't know about the bowing, so they tried to distract the kids by saying, "How would you like an ice cream cone?" I heard one of the children say, "What's that?"

Beatrice Chambers U.S. Army   **Camp John Hay, Baguio**

Beatrice won a Bronze Star for her conduct in the camps, but her personal hero is still Douglas MacArthur.

My father was in the Spanish-American War and then became a prospector for the mining industry in the Philippines. My mother was a British citizen. I was born in Manila but went to nursing school in the States. After I returned to Manila in 1940, I joined the U.S. Army and was stationed at Camp John Hay in Baguio, a summer resort in the mountains. I was there when the war began.

Baguio was the first place the Japanese bombs hit in the Philippines. I'd just taken a man in a wheelchair outside and saw some planes swooping down, and thought they were wonderful flyers. All of a sudden, WHAM! came the bombs.

We stayed in Baguio until General MacArthur told us to evacuate. We put the patients in Santa Rosa Hospital, which was bombed too, and left with the military. Horse cavalry was all the army had there, and the Japanese came in with tanks. We were trying to go down the Balete Pass to Bataan and couldn't get past the tanks. Can you imagine sending horse cavalry against tanks? They killed all the horses and men.

There were only two nurses and a doctor, and the three of us stayed together the best we could after we were told to scatter. We became guerillas, hiding whenever we saw something. There were sawmills in the mountains and we tried to hide in them, but the Japanese were like ants up there, and after four days, they found us. The doctor ran away but was caught later. They took us on a three-day march, back to Camp John Hay, without food or water. It was terrible.

They put us in a school, lined us up to execute us, then changed their minds. A Jap officer wanted to march us through Baguio to show how invincible they were and how weak the Americans were. We were lined up with missionaries and other people from Baguio. Women were in one line, men in another, and children in another. They made us walk in three columns through the streets, and then drove their motorcycles through the columns. A little child was in the way and was killed.

The first two weeks we were given one cup of water a day, but no food. I found a ham once and put it under my shirt to hide it, but another nurse gave it to a woman who was pregnant. Everyone was starving. We squatted over slit trenches for toilets. There was no water or paper. Women had babies on the ground.

We were kept there about a year, then taken to a camp outside of Baguio. It was a terrible place, but we cleaned it up and made it into a model hospital, with four missionary nurses and the two of us. Malnutrition was unbelievable, and we had some terribly sick patients. We ate fish heads and tails and watery rice. I won't eat fish to this day. There were brutal beatings. I'm glad to tell this because no one knows the half of it.

After being there about a year and a half, they put us in some old trucks, and we didn't know where we were going. We were taken to the Bilibid Prison near Manila, where there were military prisoners on one side of a wall and we were on the other side.

Some emergency appendectomies were performed in the most primitive conditions. For skin sutures we unraveled rope, boiled it, and it worked fine! There were some cans of ether but no medicine.

Not having food was the hardest part. Watery rice was the mainstay of our diet for three-and-a-half years. Toothbrushes weren't available either.

Bilibid was an old Spanish prison, and I could climb up on top of a turret and look over Manila. What a wonderful sight it was when I saw Americans fighting the Japs! The Buckeyes took us out of that place to Santo Tomás, which had already been liberated. When they took that damn Jap flag down and put up Old Glory, we sang the "Star Spangled Banner." I'll never get over it.

Imogene Kennedy Schmidt U.S. Army   Fort McKinley

"Jeannie" joined the army in Mississippi right after graduation in 1941 and sailed for the Philippines in September.

For two months I'd been stationed at Fort McKinley, just outside of Manila, when we suddenly received a load of wounded patients. We hadn't heard any bombs or shooting, but that let us know something was happening. I was soon sent to Sternberg Hospital in Manila, and when Manila was declared an open city, I was transferred to Bataan.

Our nurses' training taught us to improvise and to be innovative, and that came in very handy on Bataan. We had few medications but did have a limited supply of quinine and Atabrine. Bamboo poles were used to make stretchers. Water came from a lister bag hung in the bamboo trees.

Bataan fell to the enemy, and we were ordered to leave our patients behind and go to Corregidor, where we worked in the tunnel. General MacArthur left just before the fall of Corregidor and some nurses went too. Because they did, we always thought we'd be going also, until the Japanese came into the tunnel. I thought they looked like animals. We heard they had been in Manchuria and were wild. Our chief doctor was strong, and he let them know what was what, though we did have to bow to them. When they took us by boat from Corregidor to Santo Tomás, they offered us tea, but we wouldn't drink because we thought they were trying to poison us.

In camp, we heard a lot of rumors about the Americans coming for us but were still surprised when they did come in 1945. I had begun to feel that the Americans thought we weren't worth saving, and to look at how scrawny we were, we probably weren't.

Dorothy Scholl Armold U.S. Army   **Sternberg Hospital**

From Independence, Missouri, Dorothy joined the army in 1936.

When the Japanese started bombing Manila, I went with several other nurses from Sternberg General Hospital to Bataan, where the fighting troops needed medical care. There were two hospitals set up in the jungle, just open tents, and the conditions were horrible. Supplies and food ran out, nurses and doctors became sick, the hospital was bombed, but there was not much time to think about what was happening. As the Japanese moved in, the nurses were ordered to leave for Corregidor. Getting there was a real adventure. Bombs exploded all over as we rode in trucks along bombed-out roads.

Starvation was the worst part of the internment. At Santo Tomás most parents gave all rations to their children, and many died from malnutrition. To keep our spirits up, the internees put on shows. The Japanese stopped them when our master of ceremonies gave us news of the first landing on Leyte by saying, "Better Leyte than never." When the Americans first bombed Manila, one of the men put on an old record, "Pennies From Heaven." That's how our news was delivered.

Evelyn Whitlow Greenfield U.S. Army   **Sternberg Hospital**

Having joined in 1940 "to see the world," Evelyn arrived in the Philippines three weeks before the attack.

The hunger! My God, the hunger was the worst part! We couldn't do anything about it. I just wished for a spoonful of sugar, or something. When I see hungry people on television today, it really bothers me. It's really terrible to be hungry, and it bothers me so much. I grew up in a family of twelve children, in North Carolina, and we were hungry at home, but nothing compared to what it was like in that camp.

The conditions on Bataan were the worst you could imagine. There were no supplies to speak of, and everyone was very sick. We all had dysentery and malaria. There was no medicine to treat the patients.

When the nurses were sent to Corregidor in April, ten of us were put on a plane for Australia. Engine trouble caused us to crashland on Mindanao, and the Japanese found us right away. The nurses were separated from the men and taken to a military hospital where we took care of patients, though by then we were sick ourselves. In September, we were put on a Japanese ship and sent to Manila to join the other army nurses at Santo Tomás.

Most of us were sick with malaria and dysentery and lived in a crowded room where our beds were about two inches apart. We just worked and did the best we could, day by day. It was the food. We had some kind of cereal in the morning and some rice for dinner and once in a while caribou or horsemeat, but not often. Everyone was always hungry. I saw so many people die.

Although we had patients who were beaten, the guards were not physically cruel to the nurses. Once a Japanese soldier tried to attack a nurse, so she lifted her skirt to show him that she was menstruating, and he left her alone.

Liberation

Beatrice Chambers U.S. Army

After I was rescued and taken to Santo Tomás, I was given food but couldn't keep it down. We were bombed there. Once I was standing in line to go to the toilet—the damn toilet was always broken—and someone was trying to fix it. I was tired of standing in line—there were always lines—and sat down on the ground in an alcove. I had just sat down when the Japanese bombs came and killed the people in line.

I think the world of General MacArthur. He was a good man who thought of his troops, and he shook hands with each of us nurses, saluted, and said, "Well done."

Madeline Ullom U.S. Army

The rescue didn't mean safety yet, because two days later the Japanese started shelling the camp, and seventeen people were killed. American reinforcements arrived soon after, and on February 11, 1945, all sixty-eight army nurses who had accumulated at Santo Tomás were able to leave the camp. Our plane was fired on as we flew in an overloaded plane to Leyte, to an army hospital.

Physical exams and interviews began then. Seventeen nurses who were quite ill went home in a hospital plane. The rest of us flew home, stopping at Pacific islands where we were treated royally by the troops, and especially the nurses. In Hawaii we stayed long enough to have haircuts, permanents, and have our fingernails polished.

Imogene Kennedy Schmidt U.S. Army

On the way home we were treated so well, given food and clothes, but we were surprised to receive swimsuits. Someone thought it would bolster our spirits, I suppose. In San Francisco the phone company let us call our families, and for the first time, my family knew that I was alive. They had been sending letters, which I received, but they didn't know it.

Before the war, I dated an American fellow who worked in Manila for a steamship company, and he was taken prisoner also. He was sent to Los Baños, and we didn't get to see each other until after the war. It's been a long, happy marriage.

Dorothy Scholl Armold U.S. Army

My husband and I met on the ship going to the Philippines. After he was captured, he was lucky to be sent to Japan with the first group. Some of the ships that took prisoners later were bombed by the Americans. He came through the three-and-a-half years pretty well, and we married when he came back home, several months after I did. I knew he was alive because his sister heard from him while he was in Japan, and I received a letter from her in Santo Tomás.

Bowing to the Japanese guards was one thing that always bothered me when I was in camp. In 1980 I visited the Philippines and ate in a restaurant where there were some people from Japan. I enjoyed it when they bowed to me as I was leaving.

Evelyn Whitlow Greenfield U.S. Army

My mother was notified that I was dead, but she told me later that she said, "She's not dead, and she'll be home." We were able to send a few postcards through the Red Cross, and eventually, she received one. Four out of the six girls in our family became nurses, and one of them [Elizabeth Whitlow Price] was stationed in Italy with the army during the war, though I didn't know it at the time.

I married a man who was at the camp. He'd been in the Philippines as a manufacturer of baby clothes. We were just friends in the camp, playing cards and talking. When I was on the bus, ready to leave with the other nurses after the rescue, he asked me to give him something to remember. I gave him a handkerchief, on which he wrote my name and address, and he looked me up when he returned to the States.

Margaret Nash U.S. Navy

On February 23, 1945, planes came flying over Los Baños. I saw something white and thought they were dropping leaflets, but then I noticed they were parachutes. In the meantime firing started, and amtracs [amphibious tractors] crashed through the gates. It was like something out of Hollywood! It was the Eleventh Airborne, and these men had been coming through the jungle for weeks. No one had known we were there until some of our internees snuck out of camp, went to MacArthur's headquarters in Leyte, and told them there were over two thousand people in Los Baños. They thought everyone was at Santo Tomás. We didn't know at the time, but it had been liberated three weeks before we were.

Everything about the rescue was well-timed. They knew we were up for roll call at seven o'clock, and that's when they came through the gates. The first thing we worried about was the safety of the patients, and we put them under the beds to protect them from stray bullets. When I looked out, the barracks were on fire. I thought to myself, "They finally found us!" I didn't know it was a rescue, and that we had to get out as fast as we could. Running up to a paratrooper who had just hit the ground, I said, "Do you have any food?" He had a chocolate bar, and gave me half of it. I put it in my pocket to save.

There were two newborn babies, and Edwina Todd took Ann, three days old, and I took Elizabeth, who was nine days old. Our chief nurse said, "Protect the babies with your life." The mothers were put on stretchers, and we all crawled into an amtrac. It was about two miles to the beach, and we were surrounded by Japanese firing at us. The bullets were flying all around when we climbed out on the beach, so I put myself on top of the baby to protect her. One of the men crawled up to me and said, "When they stop shooting, with all the strength God gave you, grab the baby and try to make one of the amtracs." Holding the baby close, I ran to the one where the mothers were.

While they were trying to close the door, someone yelled to push off, and water came in through the door. We held the babies over our heads until they closed the door, wondering after all this if we were going to drown. The firing continued, and it took us about an hour to get across the bay. The army was waiting with ambulances and jeeps, and it was the first time I had seen a jeep. A hospital had been set up at the Bilibid Prison, and that was where we were taken.

I took Elizabeth to one of the doctors and told him she was very, very sick. He took her and said she needed penicillin. I looked at him and asked, "What's that?"

I always wore my anchors on my collar. The Japanese used to point to them, and I was determined that they would never get me to take them off. When the army doctor saw the anchors, he wanted to know if I was a navy nurse. When I said I was, he wanted to know where I came from, and I told him I was from the prison camp. Then he asked if we could help, because they were really swamped. Casualties were lying all over. We asked if we could have something to eat first, and he sent us to the chow line.

Our first meal was beans and graham crackers. My chocolate bar had melted in my pocket by then. There was still so much fighting, and corpsmen were bringing casualties in with blood transfusions and intravenous everywhere. I was worried that it could be our last meal, because of all the fighting, and told another nurse we ought to save some of the graham crackers because we may not be getting anymore food. She said the army would drop food in by parachute, and that is what happened.

For ten days we worked, before they were able to bring in some army nurses. How well-fed those girls looked! Their chief nurse wanted us to continue working, but our chief nurse, Laura Cobb, protested, "My nurses are almost dead, and we have orders to go back to the States." She was terrific right to the end. They drove us in trucks back to Santo Tomás, and I'll never forget seeing bodies all over the place as we came down into Manila again. It was just terrible. It was a massacre, as the Japanese pulled out and the Americans came in.

After we were rescued, we found out that the Japanese had planned to execute everyone in our camp the morning we were rescued. When we were gone, they went to the villages around the camp and burned the bamboo houses and slaughtered the people. I have such affection for the Filipino people and can still get very weepy.

We remained at Santo Tomás awhile and then flew to Leyte. We had to stay in tents there, and the Japanese bombed us again. A few days later,

Admiral Kinkaid had a small plane fly us out, island hopping, to Samar. Our dramatic rescue didn't make the front page because, at the same time, the battle of Iwo Jima was raging. When we left they were still firing at us, and I said to one of the men in the plane, "Somebody is shooting at us." He insisted they were hailstones. How could it have been hailing in the South Pacific? That's how naive I was. When we stopped in Guam, we began to find out what had happened to our families.

A strange thing had happened to me the first time we were in Santo Tomás. One of the Japanese had followed me around all the time, and it worried me. One day I was in the hospital at a patient's bedside and I heard a click. The Japanese man had taken my picture, and when I looked at him, he bowed and walked away, and I never saw him again. The next day my picture appeared in a Japanese paper. It told about the internees and how well they were being taken care of.

The interesting part of this story is that in 1943, a commander I had known on Guam saw this picture in a paper that had been taken from a dead Japanese soldier. He identified me, and that was when my family knew I was alive, and that any of us were living. The navy had said we were missing in action and might be prisoners of war. That picture was in every magazine, and my mother received copies from everywhere, even places as distant as the Netherlands.

We had never seen the navy nurse uniforms, and on our way home, we saw them being worn in Honolulu. The nurses had rank instead of relative rank. We had lost out on all those years, like in a time warp. When we flew into San Francisco, there were ceremonies for us with all the food in the world, but we couldn't eat it. Everything I ate, I would throw up. We were given physical examinations, and I had it all. I was still swollen from the beriberi, and they discovered I had tuberculosis. I can remember someone saying that I didn't have long to live, as though I couldn't hear. I went across the country to recuperate at St. Albans, New York.

Uncle Murray was still in the congress, and my mother wouldn't let him near the house because she held him responsible for the whole thing.

A sad postscript to this is, because of my poor health, which lasted several years, I never tried to get in touch with my fiancé. We never knew if each other was alive.

A nice postscript to the whole story is that baby Elizabeth grew up to be a medical doctor, married, and had two children. She has kept in touch all these years and recently contacted me to see if there was some way she could get a birth record. She had nothing.

I know what helped me through that ordeal: my religion, my family, my profession, and my sense of humor.

Carrie Edwina Todd U.S. Navy

After we were rescued, an army lieutenant called me by name when I was walking up the steps at Bilibid Prison. When I asked who he was, he introduced himself as my brother-in-law, my sister Margaret's husband. I asked him, "Which one are you, Tom or Dave?" He said, "Who are they? I'm Al." My sister had written about some fellows she knew, but that was before the war started. So we talked a while and, when he left, he gave me all the money he had. I asked why I would need that, and he told me, "You'll see." After three years' internment, I had lost track of the reality of money.

Baby Ann, the three-day-old infant I took out of the camp when we were rescued, contacted me years later and let me know she had become a nurse. I remained a navy nurse until I retired at age fifty-five.

Mary Rose Harrington Nelson U.S. Navy

The morning we were rescued, I was working in the clinic, hanging up bandages. We boiled old dressings, if they weren't completely useless, and used them over again. I'll always remember the low, rumbling noise that we heard very early. It turned out to be the amtracs. When I heard airplanes, I looked up and saw parachutes. Then the Eleventh Airborne burst through the front gate. When we first saw them coming through the gate, we weren't sure who they were and waited until they came closer.

One paratrooper was shot in the shoulder, and we gave him first aid in the clinic. I didn't realize we were being rescued and would have to leave immediately, so I continued my regular duties and boiled the instruments. The troops got everybody out as fast as they could in jeeps, trucks, and trailers, but most were walking. One young woman was hit in the crossfire, so they put her on a bed and carried her along. The GIs had IVs with them and set them up right away. I rode on a tank but the men, including my poor fiancé, walked the two or three miles to the edge of the bay. Everyone was so weak. We were then taken across the bay to Bilibid Prison, which the U.S. Army had turned into a hospital after they captured it.

I went right to work and set up a night mess, because they had been cooking food on the wards. Everyone laughed because they were all sick and tired of Spam, and we ate it like it was caviar.

That night the Japanese massacred Filipinos in the village near Los Baños in retaliation for helping us.

My mother was in San Diego during the war, and at first heard that the Cañacao Hospital was hit and we all were killed. Then she received a few cards from me and sent me a couple of letters. We didn't receive mail or packages often, but the Red Cross handled it and some came through.

When we were able to leave Bilibid prison, I flew back to the States with the nurses. I met my fiancé's ship when he came into San Francisco and took him to meet my mother in San Diego. We visited the parish priest, who said he could marry us that Friday, and it's lasted all these years.

Dorothy Still Danner U.S. Navy

After being released, I came back to a very different world, having been gone five years. Of course we received a lot of attention, with flashbulbs like you wouldn't believe. After a ninety-day recuperation, I was assigned to Bethesda, Maryland, and was sent all over on U.S. Savings Bond Drives, giving talks. I began to feel like an object after awhile, sort of a freak. I didn"t feel like a heroine, as I was being called, because we thought the army nurses had endured so much more on Bataan and Corregidor.

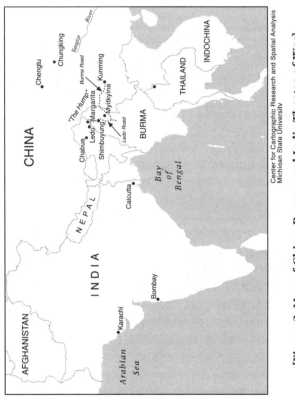

Center for Cartographic Research and Spatial Analysis
Michigan State University

[Figure 2. Map of China, Burma, and India Theater of War]

CHINA, BURMA, AND INDIA THEATER

"Culture shock"

Campaigns of the CBI [China Burma India theater] may not be as well known as those of the Pacific and Europe, but Americans will remember Joe Stillwell, the Flying Tigers, Merrill's Marauders, the Ledo Road, the Burma Road, Flying the Hump, and Orde Wingate. This was a theater of war that ranged from the fabled Himalaya Mountains to suffocating jungles, across subcontinents, and into the most densely populated regions of the world.

Burma had been lost to the Japanese, and its recovery was critical to the survival of British India. The fight for Burma was as mean as any encountered in the war, with British, American, and Chinese forces against the Japanese. Moreover, the weather and terrain could kill as surely as any human opponent. By early 1945 the Japanese had been destroyed, partly because a magnificent feat of engineering had created the Ledo and Burma Roads by which Allied troops and supplies could move.

Nationalist Armies of Chiang Kai-shek fought two wars in China. The one against the Japanese had been more or less continuous since the early 1930s, unrelenting in ferocity. In time, the United States provided armaments for Chiang's forces and he, in turn, ordered thousands of laborers to prepare air bases for B-29s to raid Japan. The other war was with Mao Tse-tung, leader of the Communist Party and eventual victor over Chiang.

Elsie Sours U.S. Army   **Twentieth General Hospital**

The Twentieth was formed in 1942 by staff from the University of Pennsylvania, Elsie's alma mater.

We arrived in Bombay, India, in March 1943 and had quite a trip getting there. Our orders were for "Destination Unknown," and from the time we left training camp we were told to keep quiet as to how many of us were in the unit. In Long Beach, California, we waited a week at a nice, big hotel to board the ship, under strict orders to be unobtrusive. When the ship was ready to sail, we were driven through town in buses with police escorts and sirens blaring. Anyone with half an eye could see us. When our ship, the USS *Monticello*, stopped in New Zealand, again we were told not to divulge how many of us were there, but they had us parade through the streets. The next day they tried to parade us around again, but I wouldn't go.

Our hospital was in Margarita, near Ledo, India, along the Burma border. It was a big place, with 1,500 beds for Americans and 1,500 beds for Chinese patients. We lived in bamboo huts, called "bashas." The floor was brick with bamboo matting covering it and burlap lining the walls. The windows were screens with a wooden flap that closed. During the thirty months I was there, the bashas became old and had to be rebuilt.

There was a separate room for showers and a cement trough in which we washed clothes. When we first arrived, we had to give laundry to local women who took it to the river and hit it on the stones. The bathroom was separate, but we had no privacy. There was a lineup of toilet boxes, six in a row, and no partitions. It was quite an experience.

At first we wore blue seersucker uniforms, then they changed to brown-and-white seersucker, wraparound dresses. There was a cap that matched, and one of our chief nurses made us wear it, which was sense-less in that climate. Monsoon rains brought mud up to our ankles, so we bought leather boots at the local bazaar to work in. Nothing ever dried. Then, in the dry summer, we had dust and dirt up to our knees.

Some people came down with malaria, though everyone was supposed to take Atabrine. We used to wonder why one girl didn't turn yellow like the rest of us, because the Atabrine made our skin yellow. When she became sick, we found out she wasn't taking it. We used it to dye curtains and anything else. Everything was shades of yellow.

At the end of the longest supply route in the world, way up in India, by the time we received anything we were usually shortchanged. When we left the States we were told to bring as much Kotex as we could get in our bags, but eventually ran out. The bazaar in town had some British supplies, and we could buy pads there. They were small and compact, and we used to say they were dehydrated. One day I was talking to the boys about supplies and found they were using Kotex to clean their guns. I said, "Damn you, anyhow! I wish you were a woman for a month!"

A real treat was when we were invited to the British tea plantations. The British had been in India for years and had shipped in supplies we could get at the bazaar, like canned butter. One of the little things that made us happy was having Lipton Chicken Noodle Soup and cooking a pot of it when we went off duty.

I was the last of the original group to leave and felt they forgot me after thirty-and-a-half months. We left behind furnishings in the bashas for the girls who came in after us, and they didn't think it was much. They didn't know how rough it had been.

Florence Edginton U.S. Army   *Seventy-third Evacuation Hospital*

Working in Los Angeles with the physician who was forming the Seventy-third, Florence was quick to join up.

We trained at various places up and down the California coast and joked about joining the army to defend California. We were in San Luis Obispo, Sawtelle Hospital in Los Angles, and Fort Ord. In January 1943 we sailed from Compton and didn't know where we were going until we arrived in Bombay, India, in March. Blackout conditions were in effect all the way on the trip across the Pacific, and we were supposed to have everything in place so we could find it in the dark. Two girls joked about their toothbrushes being wet all the time and then realized

Florence Edginton (73EH-CBI) and her sister Esther (187GH-England) meet in California after the war.

they were using the same one. The ship stopped in Fremantle, Australia, and I can still see the silhouettes of all the ocean liners in the harbor, like the *Ile de France* and the *Queen Mary*. They had been converted to troop ships.

From Bombay the nurses were sent by train, then took a ferry boat on the Ganges River. GIs who were musicians and had brought instruments played some great music on the boat. When we arrived in Ledo, we stayed with the Twentieth General Hospital, then moved into our own bamboo bashas.

Many of our patients in Ledo were Chinese, and we learned to converse with them. One of the doctors was good at picking up the language and taught us some phrases. I still can ask in Chinese, "How many bowel movements did you have today?" They would hold up their fingers to answer. I would ask about today, how many they had yesterday, and then, to see if they really understood, how many they would have tomorrow. If they laughed, I knew I was getting through. Not the thing you would use later in life in America, but I still remember the words.

One time I was at a loss for words in any language. The Chinese patients were clustered together at one of the beds and making a lot of commotion. I went to see what was going on. They had the patient's penis wrapped in gauze and tied, with a long strip of gauze, to the bed, and they were pulling on it. I had one of the interpreters come and check this out. The patient had edema, and his legs and groin were swelling. His friends thought the "spirits" were putting his penis back into his body because of his sickness, and they were attempting to pull it out again. The interpreter told me this with a straight face, because he also believed in the "spirits."

Penicillin was new and we only gave it to American patients. The first patient I ever gave it to had been attacked by a tiger. He'd been on guard duty, and the tiger really dug into his head. I can still hear the soft, southern dialect of that patient saying, "That tiger sho' thought he was gettin' some good meat."

Tigers weren't the only things to be afraid of. We moved to Shimbuyung, Burma, after about a year, but didn't have night duty because it wasn't safe for the women. One night I was sleeping alone in my tent and felt something brushing my feet and hands. I opened my eyes to see a man run out of the tent.

I remember silly things like a ceramic ashtray I brought with me that looked like a coiled-up snake. One of the doctors borrowed it to play a trick on another doctor who was afraid of snakes. It was hidden in the footlocker of the scared young doctor, and he found it when he was unpacking. He found a gun and shot it. Of course, I never got it back.

A doctor told me, when we were back in the States, that we learned some things while taking care of the Chinese. For instance, when they had an operation, the Chinese got up right away. We had a hard time getting them to stay in bed but found that they didn't clot like the American patients, who were kept in bed for recuperation. Now the practice is to get patients up as soon as possible to keep their blood from clotting.

Elsie Ott Mandot U.S. Army Air Force
First Troop Carrier Command,
803rd Medical Air Evacuation Squadron

Elsie was credited as the first flight nurse and the first to receive the Air Medal for her conduct and achievement.

There were five very ill men who needed immediate care, and I was chosen to accompany them on an "experimental" flight, which took seven days and covered ten thousand miles. I had only a few hours' notice to prepare for this flight from Karachi, India, to the United States in January 1943. I'd had no flight training and didn't even know about the school that was just starting to train nurses for air evacuation.

The plane wasn't equipped to carry patients, and every night we stopped at airfields in different countries where the patients could be checked at medical facilities. The contagious ones were placed in the bomb bay because there were other passengers on board. There were limited medical supplies and water on the plane. This was my first flight and I was a little airsick the first day out, but the patients were all right.

When we landed in Washington, D.C., the patients were taken to Walter Reed Army Hospital, and I was given two weeks' leave, surprising my family by going home to New York. They thought I was still half-way around the world. That's when I found out about flight nurse training at Bowman Field, Kentucky, and joined the next class, instead of going back to India.

After graduation, the 803rd was assigned to Chabua, Assam, India, and from then I was officially a flight nurse.

Audrey Rodgers McDonald U.S. Army Air Force
                    803rd Medical Air Evacuation Squadron

Chief nurse of the 803rd, Audrey was decorated with the Purple Heart for wounds and the Air Medal for conduct.

The airfield at Myitkyina [pronounced Mitch-i-naw] in Burma was strafed while I was picking up patients, and my leg was hit with shrapnel. The Japanese planes first dropped "daisy cutters," bombs that burst just off the ground, and then strafed us. I was loading a patient who was on a litter, and he died instantly after being hit in the head with shrapnel. The rest of us took cover in weeds off to the side, and one of the pilots gave me his shirt to tear up for bandages. I remember he said, "Be sure to save my wings."

Essie Baer was the other nurse and fortunately wasn't hurt, so she took over helping everyone. The plane was full of holes but the pilot decided it could fly, and we put the patients back on and took off. The doctor, who was also wounded, decided that we had to stop at Ledo, India, to let the patients off, including the one who died on the runway, but the crew stayed on the plane in order to get back to Chabua, our home base. I was in the hospital for a few weeks but went back on duty.

Our squadron was a lot like a family, and every time I sent people out on missions, it was like a brother or sister going, and we thought about each other until all returned.

We carried Chinese patients from Burma to the hospitals in India, and they were the source of many strange and interesting incidents. The litters were in tiers on the planes, and the top litter was about shoulder high. I remember one Chinese patient on the top layer vomited down my neck when I was working near him. Another time we were waiting in Burma for a plane to land and pick up some Chinese patients, when one of them was brought in with a five-inch gash in his scalp, split wide open. The other soldiers explained that he'd gone berserk, so they beat the "devil" out of him, and I heard he passed away after he was at the hospital. Pilots told us that sometimes the Chinese laborers would run across the runway in front of a plane when it was landing, and if they made it, then the dragon behind them would be killed. Sometimes they didn't make it.

Their culture and ways were so strange to most of us, and we never had an explanation of how to deal with these people.

A group of black nurses and doctors stayed with us in Chabua, on their way to Ledo. A friend of mine who worked with them in Ledo told me the Chinese patients didn't know what to make of these darker nurses, and to avoid problems, they were told these were American Indians. The patients could understand that, somehow.

Betty Berry Godin U.S. Army Air Force
803rd Medical Air, Evacuation Squadron

A redhead, "Redberry" was her wartime nickname and still is favored by friends.

Our duty station was in Chabua, Assam, India, and when we first arrived in August 1943, we pitched our own tents. The place was very primitive, but conditions improved as time went by, and we moved into bashas, which we could decorate and make more comfortable. It was awfully hot, so the engineers built a big swimming pool, and we had some relief.

We flew the "Hump" [Himalaya Mountains] to different air bases, bringing back injured and sick soldiers to the Twentieth General Hospital. Our patients were many nationalities and particularly a lot of Chinese. One flight I remember well was when I had a planeload of Chinese soldiers who were considered psychos, and we ran into a monsoon and had to land to wait for the weather to clear. The patients were sedated, but we waited so long they began to wake up. I was getting pretty nervous, but the weather suddenly cleared enough to take off, and they dozed off again.

There were air raid shelters in the tea patches, and we had to get into them quickly when the Japanese planes came over. Once during a raid, there was a twenty-foot python in there with us, and an MP shot it. I asked for the skin and had it treated when I went to Calcutta, then brought it back to the States in my footlocker. Years later, my husband was stationed in Spain with the Air Force. I had moved many times with this python skin, so I had a handbag and a pair of shoes made from it. I still have the shoes.

Jean Yunker Johnson U.S. Army Air Force
821st Medical Air Evacuation Squadron

Flight training followed immediately upon Jean's graduation from nursing school in Oregon. She received the Distinguished Flying Cross for heroism.

We sailed from Virginia on the USS *Randall*, thinking we were going to be stationed in China. The captain of our ship had been a German submariner in World War I and seemed to be a little spooked. He didn't let us on the deck for air very much, which made the troops seasick. When we got off the ship, the men who'd been riding below looked like they were coming out of a prison camp.

We wound up where the Ledo Road started in India, and went up into China. Our patients were British, Indian, Chinese, and American. We also had Japanese prisoners, and many of them had been educated in the United States.

There weren't hospital planes in those days. A plane with nurses and techs (enlisted men) flew out to various places, along with cargo and supplies, and we were let off one or two at a time, often right after the fighting stopped. We stayed with patients at the field until a plane came in, and flew back with them. We'd signal the planes down, and they had to come in for patients. Everything from food to mules was parachuted into the jungle. There were no doors or windows because they would just kick or push things out. Depending on what the cargo was that day would determine the condition of the plane when we put patients in it. Sometimes what was left on the floor of the plane got pretty thick, especially if the cargo was livestock. Most of the time we just put patients right on the floor because there were no seats.

The Chinese could be quite a problem. I saw them jump out of a plane in the air, and another time they pushed another guy out. They thought it was fun and just pushed each other out! We carried 45s even though it was against the rules of the Geneva Convention. We weren't taking any chances.

There were some very long flights, and these could get a little spooky. Something would touch the patients off on these flights, and they would get agitated and sometimes violent. Mostly they were shell-shocked, and we would have to give a shot of morphine to calm them down. The pilots and engineers helped us handle them.

We flew almost every day but could leave anytime because we were volunteers. A couple of girls who did were married to men who had been in the Bataan Death March and left when their husbands were released from the Japanese prison camps.

There was a Chinese-language teacher on the ship, and it came in handy with the Chinese patients. When I first came back to the States, a group of us nurses who'd been in the CBI thought we were awfully clever and went to a Chinese restaurant in New York and ordered in Chinese. We don't know if what we ate was what we ordered to this day.

Roberta Ross U.S. Army Air Force
821st Medical Air Evacuation Squadron

*A graduate of the nursing school at Mayo Clinic and former flight atten-
dant with American Airlines, "Bobsie" received the Distinguished Flying
Cross for her achievements in the CBI.*

My husband was sent to Europe with Patton's Third Army, so I tried to join
him by signing up for flight nurse training. When we began studying tropical medicine, I knew I wasn't going to England.

I like to remember the lighter times we had together, instead of talking
about the war. Several of us received the Distinguished Flying Cross, but
my memories are of the friendships we formed.

The food was the hardest thing to live with. Cans of tuna came with our
rations, and after a while I wrote home asking for a jar of Hellman's
mayonnaise so we could make tuna salad. I never thought it would make
it, but it did, and I was offered up to $200 for that jar of mayonnaise.

I was impressed being able to meet Dr. Gordon Seagraves, who was
known as the "Burma Surgeon." His hospital was a bombed-out church at
the edge of our airfield. Dr. Seagraves was a missionary doctor who had
trained Burmese nurses to go bravely through the jungle with the famed
Merrill's Marauders in Burma, saving many lives.

Frances Thorp U.S. Army Air Force
821st Medical Air Evacuation Squadron

*The daughter of a career officer, Frances followed her father into the army
before the war.*

Stationed in Puerto Rico when the war started, I was in the dining room
when the announcement came over the radio that Pearl Harbor was
bombed by the Japanese. Everyone just stopped, and for a moment you
could have heard a pin drop. We all wondered what and where Pearl
Harbor was, and why was it so important that anyone would fight over it?

In May 1944 I sailed for India as a flight nurse. This was an interesting
experience, especially when the ship stopped in the middle of the Pacific
Ocean for about forty-eight hours while the engine was repaired. A GI had
put sugar in it, and when he was caught, all anyone could figure out was
that he didn't want to go to war.

The harbor in Calcutta, our destination, had been bombed by the Japanese so we sailed around the southern tip of India to dock in Bombay. From there we took a train back across India to Calcutta. That country was really a different world. When we were being unloaded from the ship, I saw a man carrying a foot locker on his head, and a B-4 bag (goverment-issue garment bag, with zippered pockets on each side) in each hand. The workers had a little trot, instead of walking, which seemed to help keep these things balanced.

We spent a month in Calcutta working in a station hospital, and our quarters were in a fancy, marble building, guarded by Gurkhas. We didn't dare try to enter without all sorts of identification. The guards wore huge Kuhkri knives, which were shaped like a very long butter knife. If ever drawn, they had to draw blood with it, even if it was their own.

I have laughed so many times in my life about that train trip. This troop train was both narrow gauge and standard gauge, changing to different tracks. We stopped to eat twice a day, lining up along the tracks with our mess kits. The food was prepared in a kitchen car then unloaded when we formed our line. A big vat of hot water was at the beginning of the line, and everyone dunked their mess kits in that. Then we loaded up with whatever food there was, made up from C rations, ate, then went back and dunked the mess kit again in the hot water.

It was summer and really, really hot and humid. To keep us cool, in the middle of each compartment was a big galvanized tub holding a block of ice, with a burlap sack on top. A fan blew across it. The train ran on coal and had to stop to be refueled often. Two planks led up to the coal tender, and about fifty or more girls and women, each with a basket of coal, walked up one plank, dumped in the coal, and walked down the other. They picked up more and continued this procession until we had enough to go ahead.

The scenery, and manner of dress of the farmers plowing with water buffalo and wooden plows, was like a trip across the ancient Bible. However, we always knew the GIs had been through the area before us, because urchins would stand outside the train, singing a constant chorus of the song, "Oh Johnny, Oh Johnny." Of course we all gave them our chewing gum and candy.

Our final destination was at the beginning of the Ledo road, where we replaced the 803rd. Our living quarters in Ledo were bashas. There was a community shower, and we brushed our teeth over a trough. The trough was built on an angle so the water ran out, and there was a spigot on one end. The dining and kitchen bashas were separate, and they were cooled by using a fan called a ponkah. Two pieces of canvas, about three feet wide, were connected by rope to the outside. A "bearer" sat outside and pulled on the rope to keep the fan going.

We flew from Ledo into Burma with the Third Combat Cargo, flying as close to the fighting as we could get, and brought out wounded. When flying into Burma we were ordered to wear sidearms, to protect the patients and ourselves. I remember once when it could have been dangerous, because the pilot got the wrong heading and asked if anyone knew what the airstrip looked like. Luckily, I'd been there before and helped to find it from landmarks I remembered. Once I had some Japanese prisoners on the plane as patients, and there were no extra guards. They were a little surly but more frightened than anything else.

On another trip, we went to a brand new strip where there were supposed to be snipers around. After the plane landed it pulled back into a parking area, ready to move out quickly if we had to. The engines were left running, and we saw a cloud of dust approaching. The pilot told us all to put a clip in our guns, so I did. The truck came close and had the raunchiest collection of military men I ever saw. The crew went to talk to them but told me to stay inside, out of sight. Staying inside as long as I could stand it, I walked to the doorway of the plane. I wore the usual, glamorous outfit, which was coveralls with a baseball cap, and two skinny braids sticking out underneath. Then somebody looked up and the conversation ceased. They all stared as I walked over to the sergeant, who broke the silence saying, "Lieutenant, can I touch you?"

Sometimes we took patients into Karachi and stayed overnight, which was a fun break. Children who were trained to beg were everywhere. I'll never forget one little guy, about six years old. He came up close to me, tugged my sleeve, and with big tears said, "Memsab, no mommy, no poppy, no per diem, and no flight pay." I had to give him something for that act.

My father died in December 1944, and I went home. I expected to go back to India but stayed in the States until the war ended. A funny incident happened in my hometown when I was waiting on a street corner. Someone came up to me, looked at the uniform they had us wearing then, and asked, "What are you, an air raid warden?"

Aloha Drennan Sanchez U.S. Army Air Force
821st Medical Air Evacuation Squadron

Always wanting to accomplish "the ultimate," Aloha became a flight nurse and was awarded the Bronze Star and the Air Medal for her achievements.

When our ship arrived in Bombay, India, volunteers were requested to go to China. Those of us who volunteered were taken off the ship before the rest of the squadron and flown to Ledo. In a few weeks we were transferred to Kunming, China, where General Clair Chennault and the Fourteenth Air Force were headquartered. Split up again, two of us were sent to Chengtu to work in the university hospital. Every day we were promised that we would get to the base soon to do our flight nursing, but there wasn't much of that. We had actually been requested up there to be sure there were some white females around. The nurses who were there before filled us in on what was really going on.

I remember an American soldier who was in the university hospital with Chinese encephalitis and our doctors wouldn't ask the Chinese for help because they felt the Chinese doctors didn't know very much. I told the doctors we were running out of oxygen three days ahead of time, and didn't get it, and the boy died. Whether he would have made it or not, we don't know, but my partner and I had had it, and we complained at the top. General Wedemeyer got us a transfer to the base, where I had to live in a storeroom but did get to do some flying.

But then I was transferred to Chungking, where there was no flight nursing, and it made me furious. The colonel in charge of the Chinese-American Combat Wing assigned me to a room near his, and when I wouldn't have anything to do with him, he closed off a private bathroom to keep me out. I had to have men hold up a blanket for privacy when I went to another bathroom.

I complained to the head doctor, and he talked to that colonel, who apparently agreed to leave me alone. He came to my room one night again, so I showed him my husband's picture on the dresser and told him that my husband, who was a navy lieutenant commander, had a full head of hair. This colonel was a bald-headed old guy. Our chief doctor asked the next day what happened, and when I answered, "I just said that my husband had hair," he said, "That does it, I'm transferring you."

Finally I was transferred back to B-29s and General Curtis Le May's command. I brought my accordion overseas, and when General Le May asked me to play it for cocktail hour, I had a funny look on my face. He named the colonel who'd given me a tough time and asked me if that was the problem, and I said, "Yes." He told me that this colonel was a helluva strategic officer, but that he was a problem for the Chinese officers' wives also.

The most horrible and unforgettable experience I ever went through was when a cargo plane crashed in the Yangtze River, which ran by the base. The whole river was on fire. Three of the five crewmen on board got out by swimming under the flames but were badly burned. We'd just cleaned them up when a B-29 came in and blew up, and there were three survivors from that. Later that night another B-29 cracked up on takeoff, and there were three more survivors. Anne Baroniak and I were swamped and exhausted from surgery. Then one of the doctors couldn't get an IV started, and I realized he was drunk, so I pushed him aside and started it myself. We were so tired and short of help, we had to set our alarms to get up and give medications, then try to go back to sleep.

Later, when they could be moved, I transported these patients in the bay of a B-29, on a two-day trip, to a Calcutta hospital. Many weeks later, General Le May called me to the tower to say he had a letter from one of the patients stating that doctors told him he would not have survived without the care I gave him.

Living conditions were not the best, especially because of the rats that seemed to be everywhere. I believe that's how I contracted hepatitis, which caused me to have to return to the States when I did. As I was getting on the plane to go home, General Chennault was standing by the steps to the plane in a pouring rain. My foot was on the first step, and he said, "Lieutenant, you are a helluva nurse, but you bitch a lot." I just turned and looked at him and said, "General, I haven't left yet, and I'm still bitching."

Since I was married, I realized that I didn't have to take a lot of crap, unlike some of the young nurses. I did have a fantastic career over there, however. I wouldn't play the accordion for the officers, but I wore it out playing for the enlisted men and had to get a new one when I was back home.

Wilma Shackelford Ford U.S. Army Air Force
825th Medical Air Evacuation Squadron

Coming full circle, today "Shack" is a volunteer guide at the Air Force Museum, Wright Patterson Air Force Base, Ohio.

Casablanca, French Morocco, was the headquarters for our squadron in July 1944. Except for the nurse and technician, we flew with civilian crews in contract C-54s from Pan American, United, and American Air lines. We lived at Cazes Air Base in crude, small, wooden houses, with showers in the living room. Italian prisoners were house boys and chopped wood for our hot water and heat.

At first I flew to the Azores Islands, about six hours from Casablanca. If there was no nurse to relieve me, I went on to Newfoundland or Bermuda, about sixteen to eighteen hours of flying. Then I could spend a couple of days in Uncle Sugar Able [U.S.A.] before returning.

My unit moved to Karachi in January 1945, to an air base fifteen miles out in the boondocks. Our house was at the end of the base with a Gurkha camp in back of us, and we had local help to manage it. Baldie was an "untouchable" and was our sweeper. Mohammed, the master bearer, lived in a small house in the back. They heated water in the kitchen over charcoal stones: two buckets for a shower and three buckets for shower and shampoo.

We flew in the C-46, also known as the Curtis Time Bomb. The planes had gasoline heaters and since a few had blown up, the pilots didn't like to turn them on, even though it was cold at high altitudes. Flights left Karachi between midnight and 2:00 A.M. so we could reach Abadan, Iran, before the heat melted the asphalt runways. The flight could take seven to nine hours, depending on wind and weather, and we'd have a short break there while the Red Cross gals fed the patients. The crew changed, but the nurse and sergeant would go on to Cairo, another seven or more hours' flight. Due to the time change, we were always eating breakfast.

I think I remained overnight at every airfield from Casablanca to Karachi because of weather or mechanical problems. We put patients up in tents, a school house in Algiers, a British hospital in Iraq, or in Sharja, Trucial Oman. My roommates and I returned so many times to Cairo with engine trouble that the sergeant would tell the passengers, if we were on board, we'd probably be back. One night we returned to Cairo three times.

The summer of 1945 we were stationed at Payne Field, about ten miles from Cairo. Trips these days were more normal, daytime flights: Cairo to Tripoli, Libya, which took six or more hours, refuel and crew change, then from Tripoli to Casablanca for another six to eight hour trip.

Those long flights would have been more difficult except for the medical technicians who did a wonderful job of supporting us. The patients made it all worthwhile. I can never forget the freed American POWs from Japan and the Bataan death march, and Merrill's Marauders [heroes of the

Burma campaign]. This was a time you felt you earned your pay by just being an American female.

In fifteen months, the 825th squadron flew twelve million miles, and we were awarded the Presidential Unit Citation.

Evelyn Hill Page U.S. Army Air Force
803rd, 821st Medical Air Evacuation Squadrons

"Rebel" was from Tennessee; at age twenty-two she volunteered for flight nurse training because flying seemed so romantic, and she circled the globe during her tour.

December 7, 1941, will always remain fresh in my memories. I was in the student nurse's quarters at Baptist Memorial Hospital in Memphis, Tennessee, when a girl came running into the hall screaming, "The Japs have bombed Pearl Harbor. We are at war!" None of us knew where Pearl Harbor was, and we were crying and hovering around the radio, hanging onto the announcer's every word. Five classmates joined the Army Air Force with me, and when we took the physical, most of us didn't weigh the minimum 105 pounds. We drove downtown together in a taxi eating bananas and drinking milk to make us heavier. It worked.

I volunteered for the school of air evacuation, which turned into a difficult, demanding, and exhausting two months, because much emphasis was placed on making us Amazons. We worked hard, ate heartily, had fun, and upon graduation, proudly wore our gold Flight Nurse's wings.

During flight nurse training, I got married when my fiancé received orders to go overseas. We wore our uniforms for the ceremony in the base chapel, and the other nurses gave us a lovely reception in Louisville. On our wedding night, they took turns calling us every half hour—all night long!

In January 1945 I received orders for overseas. When we were out over the Atlantic Ocean we opened our orders, and I was dejected to learn we were headed to the CBI theater. I was especially hoping to go to Europe with a possibility of seeing my hubby.

We stopped in Casablanca for a week, then Cairo for three weeks and did all the tourist things; visited the Pyramid and the Sphinx, sailed on the Nile, and toured the mosques. One morning at 3:00 A.M. we were rudely awakened and told we were pulling out. The outfit in Chabua, India, had contacted Washington wanting to know where those twenty-five replacements were, because their nurses had gone home. It turned out that one of our group was dating a fellow in operations, and every time our priority came up, he stuck the card in the back again.

February 1945 found us at our final destination, Chabua, India. By the time we arrived the Japanese were out of India and most of Burma. Our flights took casualties to Karachi and Calcutta for transport back to the States, or Chinese and Indian patients to get treatment.

Those C-47s were rough, drafty, and noisy, and we usually sat on the cold metal floor without a safety belt. In the back was a portable "john" with a blanket around it for privacy. We didn't have parachutes, nor did the patients. On our return flights with an empty aircraft, we usually crawled onto a litter and went to sleep. One of the worst flights was when we were given meatloaf that caused every person on board, including crew and patients, to get sick. What a mess that aircraft was.

One memorable patient was a young fellow who'd been swimming in the ocean and was attacked by a barracuda. His body was encased in a cast from the neck to his feet. The plane we were in developed engine trouble, and we almost crash-landed. He decided the evacuation was almost as hair-raising as the attack.

Our biggest concern was developing malaria. There was a regulation that everyone must take an Atabrine tablet daily as preventive medicine, and a nurse was designated each day to pass them out. It made the skin turn yellow, and many people tried to palm them or hide them. The weather, temperature, monsoons, humidity, and boredom all took their toll on our dispositions.

Natives beat the brush daily to frighten snakes away, but the GIs enjoyed killing long snakes and placing them near the mess hall so we had to see them. One girl had cooked a steak on a hot plate, and later that night awoke to find a cougar sitting on her footlocker. She outwaited it. Deciding there weren't any more steaks, the cougar left at sunup. We were out in the boondocks, and some of the dangers were human. The girl in the next tent awoke to find a psychotic patient from the hospital sitting beside her bed. He told her all he wanted to do was talk, which he did all night.

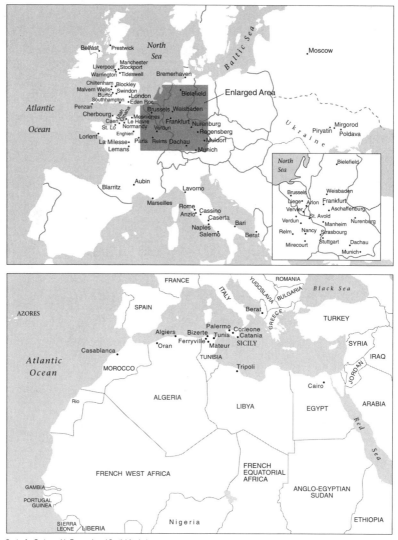

Map of North African, Mediterranean, and European Theaters of War

NORTH AFRICA, SICILY, AND ITALY

"90 mm shells would zoom right over the hospital"

Americans earned a campaign ribbon for the European theater by serving in North Africa, Sicily, Italy, France, Belgium, Holland, Luxembourg, Germany, Russia, Romania, Yugoslavia, Czechoslovakia, Norway, Denmark, or Great Britain.

From a small detachment of Rangers that went ashore alongside Canadian and British teams at Dieppe in 1942, Americans in vast numbers soon made their own attack on German-occupied North Africa. Sweeping across the Mediterranean to Sicily and a fateful airborne campaign, GIs landed next on Italian soil: Cassino and Anzio and the slog up the leg of the boot to Rome. Battles had not ceased there when Allied forces stormed onto French soil in Normandy on 6 June 1944.

Next was the rush to Paris and across the Continent, where the Germans meant to take a stand at the Battle of the Bulge. Heroic weeks and months followed, and finally, Victory in Europe. Two male voices (Medical Corps) are heard in this section.

Virginia Grabowski Shannon U.S. Army   114th Station Hospital
Twenty-first General Hospital

Of Polish ancestry, Ginny vowed to get into the war; she began nurse's training in 1939 on the same day Germany invaded Poland.

In March 1942 I joined the U.S. Army and about five weeks later went overseas. We sailed from Norfolk, Virginia, and found out at sea we were going to North Africa. Submarines were chasing us, so instead of stopping in Casablanca, Morocco, as planned, we went on to Oran, Algeria. A slow train took

123

us to our destination, Mateur, Tunisia. The two-day trip turned into five days, because we would go so many miles, then stand still because of a single track, then go on a little way, then we'd back up. I remember stopping next to another train that had soldiers on it, and they passed coffee over to us.

Six of us were in a little compartment, and when we wanted to sleep, two slept on the floor, two on the seats, and two in the overhead racks. One night a gal in the rack turned over and fell out, down on top of the gals on the floor. Everyone woke up screaming and hollering, then laughing and giggling.

In Mateur we slept in tents, but the hospital was in an unfinished building. I worked on the ward with battle fatigue patients, the psych ward. Sometimes the ninety millimeter shells would *zoom* right over the hospital. On the night of July 4, 1943, I heard a lot of noise and went outside. Our antiaircraft guns were shooting at five German reconnaissance planes. I saw three planes come down. The sky was completely lit up, and it was the most beautiful Fourth of July display I have ever seen. Then I realized I should go inside and see how the patients were doing. I'll tell you how smart they were. They had been in battle already and were under the beds with the mattresses pulled over them, while I was outside watching the gorgeous display. I got them all back into bed and had to give them something to sleep. Some of the soldiers were so young and just became battle-fatigued. Some could handle it, and some couldn't. The next day I went to see the planes that had been shot down.

When we were off-duty, we went to the Casbah, which was always crowded with people. There weren't really streets, but very narrow, brick-lined passageways, so narrow that two people couldn't pass each other. Not long after that it was declared off-limits for the military, as people were disappearing or getting killed. It was notorious for hiding criminals. The Bey was like the mayor of the Casbah, and three of us walked through his palace once, completely unnoticed. Most places had guards, but no one was in his palace so we walked all through it. Upstairs was an interesting bathroom. The bathtub was lined with fur, and there was fur on the toilet seat. It was really a beautiful place, but strange.

Often we swam and picnicked at the beautiful Mediterranean Sea beaches near Bizerte, Tunisia. Big German pillboxes built into the beaches were used to change clothes. Navy ships came in to the port of Ferryville nearby, and I ran into a navy doctor from my New Jersey hospital. That was a big break for me, because he was able to get a lot of things, like fresh food, which the navy had and we didn't.

The children ran alongside our trucks and would call out, "Bon bon, chocolate, cigarettes," and we tossed things to them all the time. The men wore coats like capes, not putting their arms in the sleeves. The women wore something as big as a bedsheet and just wrapped it all around to cover themselves. The kids never wore underpants and only wore tops. One of my impressions of Africa was that the Arabs we saw were so filthy and lived in straw and mud huts. They just used the street or anyplace as a bathroom.

In Mateur when we hung our clothes out on a line to dry, they often would disappear. No one ever saw who took them, and it didn't matter what was on the line, it was stripped. We lived up on a hill, far from the Arabs down below. We decided this went on too much, so our MPs and the French gendarmes went into the village down below and found all our clothes. They didn't wear them they just had them.

Once I was walking along a street in Tunis and along came General Dwight Eisenhower, Winston Churchill, and General Charles DeGaulle. They were in open cars, just riding down the street without any protection or fanfare. We could have touched them.

After almost a year in Africa, I was transferred to Naples, Italy. We went on a hospital ship, but all of our equipment and personal belongings were put on another ship. That ship was bombed in the Bay of Naples, and everything was lost. I'd bought souvenirs, including rugs in Kairouan, and they were gone too.

In Naples we were asked to volunteer to become nurse anesthetists. When I was a student nurse, I thought that was what I wanted, and this was a wonderful opportunity. I transferred to the Twenty-first General Hospital, which was a very experienced unit. At that time, Barnes Hospital was one of the most outstanding places to learn anesthesiology, and the Twenty-first was made up of a lot of people from Barnes and St. Louis University Hospital, so I had excellent training. Working in the neurosurgery room meant long hours. When I had a day off, I just went to bed and slept the whole time.

One of my very first patients there was a young man who had both his arms and legs missing, what they call a basket case. I had to give him a shot of sodium pentothal in a vein in his neck. To this day, I still remember his face, looking up at me, and he said, "Hey nurse, how about going out with me when I get outta here." He didn't realize what had happened to him. They brought him right from the fighting.

Our hospital in Naples was in the Mussolini Fairgrounds, a huge complex of buildings, and we walked blocks to get places. They had all kinds of hospitals: VD hospital, Orthopedic hospital, Neurological hospital, you name it. In the center of all this was a huge, olympic-size swimming pool, which we all enjoyed.

There was a ward made up completely of foreign-speaking patients, no Americans. There were Polish, Italian, and German patients. There were also big, black Senegalese soldiers, and little, short Moroccan Goumiers, with long pigtails, who fought with stilettos. One Senegalese made me a model wooden boat with little people in it, rowing. I still have it. A Polish patient wanted my address so he could write my mother and tell her that I didn't speak Polish very well.

We had to be transported in trucks back and forth from the hotel where we lived to the hospital. On the way, it was sad to see all the rubble and damage that had been done.

I went to Rome once to meet a friend from my old unit, the 114th, and, like everyone else, we went to the Vatican to see the pope. During the audience he held for the public, we were the only women, so the guards took us up on the altar where we sat along the side. The rest were sailors and soldiers who had to stand. Pope Pius XII blessed everyone in five different languages, and when it was over, we stood up and had to go past him, so we kissed his ring. He said to me, "Where are you from?" I told him I was from New Jersey. He said, "I was in New Jersey in 1939. Do you know so and so?" I said I knew of this person but didn't know him personally. I was so stunned, having a conversation like this with him. It was a wonderful experience.

I worked in Italy until it was time for the invasion of Southern France in 1944.

Marion Hein Burrell U.S. Army   Eighty-first Station Hospital

Before joining the army, "Heinie" worked in Milwaukee for the American Red Cross Blood Bank, collecting blood donations from various institutions, including prisons, factories, and colleges.

Everything was so secret when we left Camp McCoy, Wisconsin, to go overseas. We boarded the ship at Camp Shanks. I never knew what state it was in. Each group was isolated from others so we couldn't talk about where we were going. The *Cristobal* was a converted luxury liner and was filled to the rafters. Bunks were in the ballroom and even in the swimming pool. The rules were: "No nurses or smoking on deck after sundown."

There were constant drills, and we heard depth charges often. During one alarm, a girl returned to the cabin to get her money belt, and we really teased her about that. We were issued all-weather gear, including mosquito nets. That told us where we were going, along with the Atabrine that was on the table for prevention of malaria.

Wearing our Class A uniforms, we landed at Oran, Algeria, late at night, climbed into trucks, and were driven to "Goat Hill." We had to sleep in tents on the bare ground in our Class A uniforms. Our thin bedrolls were stuffed with civilian clothes as a ground cloth, of sorts. The next day we were up at dawn, looked out, and saw thousands of people all over.

In May 1943, we set up our first tent hospital at Bizerte, Tunisia. Our patients were from everywhere, British, French, Arab, German, Polish, Australian, and South African. We heard all languages, and a lot of mime was used to communicate. Most of the Moslem patients had the name Mohammed, and to keep things straight we fastened baggage-tag envelopes to the patient, with their records inside.

The hardships I remember were that there were no home permanents or sanitary napkins. The climate was very, very hot in summer and very, very cold in winter. When the television show "M*A*S*H" came on years later, I thought it was exaggerated truth about much of our lives then. We didn't fraternize like they did on the show, because the male officers and the nurses were separated with a huge field in between. There were broken hearts, however, when some married men dated without revealing their status.

In the spring of 1944 we transferred to Naples, Italy, working in a hospital that was run by the French. Our patients were the Free French, Arabs, Goumiers, Sudanese, Senegalese, and other people. Most of us found the Arabs fascinating. They seemed so huge, and their skin was very tough.

Temporary-duty nurses came to our hospital in Naples to fill in. I remember in particular a girl from New Orleans. When I saw her in the ward with the patients, who were all these different nationalities, a lot of them dark-skinned, she would be playing cards by herself instead of taking care of them. Once a transfusion ran too long because of her carelessness. I was asked to decide what should happen to her and suggested that she be made to "special" the patient—stay by his bedside—until he died. Which is what happened, and the next day he died.

In July 1944 we moved to Livorno, Italy, where we had a POW hospital for Germans and Poles. The replacement depot was near the historic Roman Baths. I remember being in a lobby one day, and a stunning, classy-looking woman wearing a beautiful uniform came in to talk to the clerk.

After she left I asked who she was, thinking she might be a movie star. He told me she was a U.S. Navy nurse.

A World War II Hospital Vignette

Hi Johnny, I've come to be with you
During this air raid.
Don't worry, Johnny,
I won't leave your side.
You're in traction, Johnny,
But we'll see this through together.
We'll talk and try to ignore the War
And what might have been.
I'm a Red Cross girl from Texas.
Where are you from, Johnny?
New York? Oh, I was there in '42.
I followed my husband there
Before he was sent "across."
We danced to the music of Harry James.
Oh, you were a dancer,
And won contests and loving cups?
Johnny, I know you lost a leg,
But you are alive.
And soon will leave Italy for home,
And be fitted with a new leg.
Your girl—this is her picture, isn't it?
She's so pretty, Johnny;
She will still love you
And will be waiting for you.
Let me hold *your* hand, Johnny.
Go ahead and cry, Johnny.
My tears are falling, too.
I feel for you and your loss.
You see, my husband's plane
Was shot down in flames two years ago,
And we will never dance again, either.
Hold *my* hand, Johnny.

by Mildred Vorpahl Hutchinson Baass
American Red Cross
Eighty-first Station Hospital

Rosemary O'Connell Smith U.S. Army   Eighty-first Station Hospital

As soon as she graduated from nurse's training, "Connie" joined the Army Nurse Corps which sent her to North Africa.

"Goat Hill" in Oran will forever be indelible in my mind, and anyone else who was there. Long chow lines were always present, because of the thousands of people that had to be fed. The food was piled one course on top of the other, with dessert on top. I've had apple pie, mashed potatoes with gravy, and roast beef, all in the same mouthful. To this day, I am not a fussy eater. The Hygiene and Sanitation officer made sure the drinking water was safe by putting in extra chlorine. We counteracted the terrible taste by floating lemon drops in our canteens. However, there was one place he missed for sanitation. The flies made a regular tour from the latrine to our sleeping quarters and back. As a result, most of us were hospitalized with dysentery.

In Bizerte, we were on "hospital road." There were about eight hospitals, each assigned to treat a particular wound or illness. The patients came to us right from the fighting, as Rommel's army had not left yet. Then we had patients from Sicily, and also Italian prisoners, who were happy to be captured. The Italian Air Force bombed several nights a week. One night a

Goat Hill in Oran, Algeria, the first stop for nurses in North Africa, known for its rocky, uneven ground under bedrolls. 81st SH nurses pose in Class A uniforms, which most agreed were unsuited for the terrain and climate.

Climbing in and out of trucks was a challenge Rosemary O'Connell and all nurses will never forget.

plane unloaded bombs between the hospitals. We guessed he didn't want to get shot back at. The winter months were rainy and cold, and we used newspapers as insulation in our sleeping bags. The hot summers brought ants crawling up the legs of our cots, and they bit the hell out of us.

One of the first encounters with celebrities didn't set too well with us. Bob Hope came with Jerry Colona, the comedian, and Frances Langford, the singer. They had all the supplies they wanted, while we had been going without all the time. Frances Langford walked through the wards in a beautiful, long evening gown, stroking foreheads and saying, "What a pity, they haven't seen a girl for such a long time." What did she think we were, chopped liver?

A funny episode happened when several of us were invited to a French-African family's home for dinner. There were many courses, and it's polite to at least taste some of everything. We did fine up to the fourth or fifth course when a small animal—head intact with ears—was brought in on a platter. We all looked at each other, someone asked, "Has anyone seen the cat?" Our hosts were bending over backward to serve us a proper dinner and would have killed anything to do it. Finally, one of our doctors left the room. When he came back he said, "The cats are outside." Some people tried to eat whatever it was, but I didn't. We had no ill effects the next day.

When our hospital moved to Italy, our quarters in Livorno (Leghorn) were in a monastery that overlooked Mount Vesuvius. In the other direction we could see the troop ships going to and from France, and knew when we'd be getting new wounded.

Esther Edwards U.S. Army   Tenth Field Hospital

Born and raised in Kokomo, Indiana, Esther went right back home after the war and a lifetime worth of adventure.

When war broke out, I decided that if my brothers joined the service, I would too. One went into the navy and one to the marines, and in November 1942, at age thirty-nine, I was sworn into the Army Nurse Corps. My mother saw me off at the train station, and she always said the whistle of a train brought back the painful memory of sending her children off to war.

I volunteered to go overseas, and one thing I remember is the huge amount of uniforms and supplies we were given to carry:

Lines to get on the ship, and lines to get off. Nurses carried as much gear, or more because of personal items, as the average GI.

Blue uniforms

White uniforms

Blue seersucker shirtwaist uniforms

Overcoats with zipper linings

Navy blue capes lined with red

Duty caps

Dress uniform caps

Clothing to wear in case of gas attack, including one-piece underwear,
    and coveralls with a cap that covered the head and neck

Two musette bags, [knapsacks with shoulder strap, one for clothes and
    the other to carry cosmetics, toothbrushes, etc.]

Bedroll [piece of canvas that could be used as a ground cover for sleep-
    ing, and we rolled up our civilian things in it, carrying it by straps on
    the outside.]

Two army blankets, rolled tightly

The blankets were to be carried on our shoulders, one musette bag in front
with the strap around our shoulders, and the other on our back, and we had
to wear a large woven belt with a tin mess kit and drinking cup attached.

I still laugh remembering one small nurse, less than five feet tall, who
put on all these things and promptly sank to the floor. We marched aboard
the ship loaded with all this gear and two helmets.

We were in a huge convoy when we sailed in February 1943, landing in
Oran, Algeria. It was a new experience for me seeing Arabs in white robes
everywhere, and I met French and English nurses. Our hospital, under the
command of Colonel Earl Ross, consisted of three units. I was put in
charge of the Third platoon. On Easter Sunday we left by truck convoy for
the war zone. Bivouacked in Tunisia, my platoon was sent out to care for
patients from an Air Corps unit.

One of the first patients I remember was badly burned over most of his
body, and the doctors in the field decided maggots might eat away the
burned flesh. He was in such misery and his condition was very critical.
Bertha Miller got rid of the maggots, debride the blisters, put sterile, wet
bandages on his burned body, and we sent him to a general hospital.

My platoon rejoined the hospital in May at Mateur, Tunisia, where we
lived in old French barracks. It was a pleasure to be in a building and not
have to use an open trench for a toilet. These were unusual toilets,
though. Metal holders for feet provided stability while one squatted over a
hole in the floor.

With the invasion of Sicily, we left by ship from Ferryville, Tunisia, landing just in time to see a German plane get shot down. Patients were waiting, and we went to work before the tents were put up. The next morning I noticed something in the grain field opposite the hospital tent, and found a soldier's body there. He'd died the day before, and there was no morgue to take care of bodies. He was taken away the next day, and I often wondered whose son or brother he was. We all had that thought in the months to come.

The troops moved fast, and we hardly stayed in one place more than a few days. There were so many casualties as we followed the battles, working steadily, then moving on, setting up, and working again. We traveled in trucks, and it was rough and hot. The Germans had blown up bridges, so our engineers made roads down steep banks and across streams.

Near Corleone, Sicily, we had patients who'd parachuted in before the invasion, were wounded, and hid until the hospitals were available. Near Termini we were flooded with patients. We could see the fighting on a strip of land that curved around the coast line. Those casualties came to us within an hour. We had so many patients that our one hundred officers, enlisted men, and six nurses could not care for them, working hours on end. An auxiliary surgical team came to help with surgery, which went on around the clock.

Injuries included bullet wounds, wounds from bomb fragments and artillery shells. Shrapnel from artillery shells made the worst wounds, because they often tore large areas of tissue, nerves, and blood vessels. Bullets had to be extracted and tissue cleaned and resewn. Mines caused limbs to be amputated. Lung wounds called for suction-type treatment. Abdominal wounds had to be cleaned, repaired, and suction used to keep the intestinal tract clear.

The Germans were pushed farther to the east, and we had some rest. Trips to the beautiful towns in Sicily and parties with every army unit in the area kept us busy. We had dinner with some engineers in a castle, and there were linen tablecloths, silverware, and even flowers on the table. The menu was spam and canned vegetables, and a string of ants crawled along the tablecloth.

There were changes in personnel. One major who had an affair with a nurse was transferred out, and so was the nurse. It was a warning that affairs within the unit would not be tolerated.

In October we crossed into Italy, following the troops who had landed before us in Salerno. Our convoy took a week to get to Caserta, driving past bombed-out buildings and tanks. The people cheered as we rode by, and we stopped to try to buy eggs or bread. Usually they said the Germans had taken everything, which was true. Mount Vesuvius erupted while we were in Caserta, leaving a flame burning that was visible for miles, and made a good landmark for the German bombers that flew over Naples. Most of our patients were wounded from the battle to cross the Volturno River, and we heard of some unbelievable feats. One patient had been in charge of carrier pigeons that were used to get messages back to head-quarters, and one of his pigeons took the message back when the army crossed the Volturno River. He gave me the band from the pigeon's leg, which is on a charm bracelet I still have.

In December 1943 we moved to Capua, into tents, and it rained and rained. It was so muddy, we wore galoshes to work in. Our patients suf-fered from exposure, malaria, and trench foot, in addition to the deluge of battle casualties. Other surgical teams came to help, and surgery went on all day and all night.

The corpsmen weren't adequately trained to do all that was needed, and we held classes to help them take more accurate temperatures, count pulse rates, and notice signs of distress. They were sympathetic to the injured men, but they seemed to feel it was punishment to be assigned to ward duty. We needed their help immensely and tried to instill a sense of pride. I think it worked.

As the winter of 1944 wore on, the troops were bogged down in the fight to capture the Cassino Monastery. My platoon was near the lines south of there. Another nurse and I, a doctor, and three corpsmen were sent to care for some patients who could not be evacuated. On the second day, the Germans exploded an ammunition dump along the only road between us and the platoon. We were isolated for over twenty-four hours. It was frightening to know that no one could reach us. When the road was reopened, the patients were evacuated, and we returned to our unit.

Anzio was our next stop, and we went out to different areas, keeping up with the troops as they moved toward Rome. The fighting was furious, and there were many badly wounded patients to care for. I remember giv-ing patients baths with little water available, working all day until it was difficult to stand up straight after leaning over the low cots. We were really close to the fighting, and one night German artillery landed across the road from the hospital. I heard the explosion and crawled under the cot with my helmet on my head, though a cot wouldn't have been much protection.

In June the Germans in Italy surrendered, and the Tenth went into Rome, following the victorious troops. As we passed the Vatican, the commanding officer stopped the convoy, and all the officers and nurses went inside. We were welcomed by some Italian men and taken inside to a small room where Pope Pius XII greeted us each with a handshake. Later, our major was reprimanded for stopping at the Vatican instead of proceeding directly to our bivouac area.

Dorothy Lonergan Jouvenat U.S. Army Air Force
802nd Medical Air Evacuation Squadron

Before the war, Dottie was a private duty nurse but decided the army might provide opportunities for travel; she volunteered for the flight nurse program's first class at the end of 1942.

We were all volunteers, very eager and excited to be in the program, but our training was mostly calisthenics and filling out papers for wills and allotments. We didn't get actual flight training until returning from overseas. Twenty-five of us made up the 802nd MAES, and in January 1943 were sent to North Africa, by ship. Most were seasick, but while I stood along the railing to get fresh air, I remember being fascinated by the beauty of the ocean, especially with the moon shining on the water.

At first we were told there would be a Red Cross symbol on our plane while we had patients aboard, but the Geneva Convention forbade that because we carried supplies and cargo when we went to pick up patients. We began flying out of Algiers, as close as possible to the fighting, close enough to hear the guns. Sometimes we had fighter planes as escorts. Patients were in ambulances or on the ground in litters waiting for us, and their wounds were only hours old. We evacuated all nationalities, and when we had POWs, they were accompanied by armed guards. While in Anzio, Italy, some days we evacuated one thousand patients, flying two missions a day. The 802nd had ten invasions to its credit, covering the North African, Sicilian, Italian, and Southern France campaigns, going to the German border.

We started out wearing makeshift uniforms, because we wore slacks that nothing matched. Several of us had uniforms made out of our overcoats or capes. As the members of our first group of flight nurses were transferred back to the States, other nurses arrived to take their places, and all of these new girls wore regulation uniforms and had their wings.

Air evacuation of patients took hold during WWII, when the first class of U.S. Army Air Force flight nurses and technicians graduated from training.

Ordeal in Albania

The 807th Medical Air Evacuation Squadron had been based at Catania, Sicily, for two months, and the Italian invasion was on. Flight nurses and surgical technicians, who were enlisted men, would fly into various places in Italy to care for wounded who were being brought in from battle, and then fly with the patients back to a hospital.

This story begins when bad weather grounded the C-47s, and each day more people were added to the group waiting to take off in Catania. On 8 November 1943, a C-54 was brought in to take the medical crews to their stations in Italy. Three flight nurses and a surgical technician relate their experiences.

Agnes Jensen Mangerich—Trained in Detroit, Agnes was sent abroad with the 807th in August 1943. Lois Watson Mckenzie—After school in Chicago, Lois immediately joined the Army Nurse Corps. Harold Hayes—Sergeant Hayes enlisted from his hometown, Indianola, Iowa. Ava Maness—Growing up near Paris, Texas, Ava joined the army in 1942.

Agnes: It was supposed to take about ninety minutes to get from Catania, Sicily, to Bari, Italy, and after three hours I realized the pilots were lost. The radio quit, so we had no contact with anyone. Once we tried to land and it turned out to be a German airfield, and they shot at us, so we climbed again. Most of the time we couldn't see the wingtips because of the weather. The thirteen nurses were stoic, but the twelve enlisted men were young kids and pretty nervous. I thought about getting a Mae West (life jacket), but there wasn't one for everyone, nor were there enough parachutes. I tried to go to sleep, deciding it was better to not be aware if we hit the water or a mountain.

Finally, the pilot stuck his head out the cockpit door and said we were landing, though no one knew where we were. He said we should buckle up tight in case we had to make a wheels-up landing. If we hadn't been buckled up tight by then, we would have been out in the aisle or through the roof because of the rough turbulence. After a five-hour flight through the most horrible weather that you can imagine, we were just happy to land. We came in for a very rough landing on a muddy, former lake bed. The wheels really made big ruts, and the plane stopped down on its nose. I was so relieved to be on the ground that I didn't think about our predicament. You feel someone will find you.

Some men appeared and told us in very limited English that they were Albanian partisans. They said the Germans might have heard or seen us, and to pick up our things and come with them. We grabbed everything we could, our musette bags, some parachutes, the rations. Some of us had rubbers and wore them over our oxford shoes. We wore wool slacks, and the nurses had storm coats with zip liners and hoods. The enlisted men were just in their field jackets, so we divided up our liners and outer things with the men.

We expected help, and our optimism was high. The first days however, we hardly had anything to eat. We were taken to a village and put up in a house, but the people there didn't have much to share. They finally killed an ox to give us something to eat. The partisans worked hard to get us to help their political cause and were always badgering us. One of them, who'd been in the States, kept after me to tell the others what it was like to live in the United States, but I avoided it because he was always trying to talk politics. Then he finally said, "Tell them how you open the door and milk is waiting there in bottles. You don't have to milk the cow!"

After a couple of days we started for the town of Berat, and I thought we were being led to safety. I also expected the pilots knew what to do in enemy territory, and I kept waiting for them to solve our problems, but they didn't know any more than I did because they just flew routine, short trips.

One Albanian, who spoke good English, stayed with us and almost casually mentioned that some British were in the country. We quickly wrote a note and he sent someone to find the British, but it was two weeks before the runner came back.

Italy had surrendered by this time, and some Italian soldiers stranded in Albania heard that Americans were around and thought we might be able to help them. One morning about one hundred of them followed us along the road. While we were walking, we came up over a hill and gunfire broke out, so we ducked for cover. The band of Italians that joined us made us look like a big army, but they took off in one direction, and we ran to some houses. A couple of patients were even brought to us. The skirmish was between opposing Albanian groups, who quit firing toward evening, and they all seemed to decide to go home for supper!

The Italian army had invaded Albania earlier, and when they gave up, there was no way for the soldiers to return home. They were just wandering around looking for food, and the Albanian who stayed with us said there was no animosity toward them, but they had nothing to help them with either. We saw the Italians in the towns once in a while, like they were waiting around for something to happen. Once an Italian officer came over and in his broken English wanted to know what the heck we were doing there, since he hadn't heard of an American invasion of Albania. When I told him, he said they didn't know how to get rescued either. We never knew what happened to them.

When we left Berat three nurses were left behind, but we didn't know where they were. We'd all been staying in various houses, and their hosts kept them hidden too long, thinking they were protecting them.

We walked to the British camp, which was at the very east side of Albania. They had a radio and contacted their headquarters in Cairo, which notified our Air Corps to let them know we were alive. We stayed with them a few days and tried to get some supplies, but they didn't have much as they were only occasionally supplied at night by parachute when their big planes were able to fly in between the mountains to a small drop zone. A lieutenant and a sergeant were assigned to us. They strapped wireless equipment to donkeys, and we started across the country on our long trek to the coast.

We were all young and healthy to start, which was a really big help getting us through this ordeal. Everyone had lice, fleas, and constant dysentery from drinking water from streams. We didn't touch things that weren't well-cooked or milk when it was offered. In the villages sometimes we were given cooked beans, but I couldn't stand to look at most of the food because it was soaked in grease.

We almost got out before Christmas. We heard that an American OSS man had been landed early in December to look for us, which lifted our spirits. But, to avoid the partisan fighting, the British lieutenant had us turn back to avoid getting trapped. We became very discouraged then.

When we turned back, our pilots had the British lieutenant send a message to Cairo to request air evacuation for us. We stayed in a mountain village about ten days, and finally, we received a message that an American plane would come the next day with fighter escort. The Germans were nearby, so when the planes came, the lieutenant didn't think it was safe and wouldn't signal them to land. He said we didn't need any more people on the ground.

That was really heartbreaking. We watched from our hiding place as a British Wellington bomber and two C-47s circled with their wheels down, and then eighteen P-38s arrived to protect them. No one expected that much coverage, and watching them leave was just terrible. We also were kind of proud that the Air Corps thought that much of us to send so many planes.

In early January we heard a rumor that the OSS man had been captured, but then the second day out we were walking along a trail and met him. We were elated, though we had a long way to go yet. He had guides, an interpreter, donkeys, and gold to buy things in the towns.

From then on we could only travel at night and had to cross one more mountain pass. The OSS man went ahead and made arrangements for us in a very nice village, where we stayed in a home that had light, a pot-bellied stove, and the woman of the house was dressed western style. I knew they had to be on the German side when they served tea with a big bowl of sugar. For the first time, we sat on chairs and drank that welcome tea.

He had a truck for us and told us we would be riding at night, and if car lights were seen, it would probably be Germans. We would have to hurry out and hide, and the driver was to pretend motor trouble. If the Germans were too curious, we couldn't fool around, "Understand?" The men who were armed nodded. They understood.

We took off in that truck and were so cramped, sitting on the floor, practically on top of each other, with the truck swinging and swaying on the mountain road. Pretty soon someone said, "Get out! Get out!" We ran

Agnes Jensen (middle, top) and Lois Watson McKenzie (middle, bottom) recuperate in Bari, Italy, with 807th nurses who were rescued from Albania after crash-landing in 1943.

off to the side of the road and down the hill, lying flat behind big rock formations. Pretty soon a car came up and stopped, and we could hear they were Albanian. I think they knew someone else was around, but they drove on. We climbed in again, started off, and the same thing happened. We jumped out and ducked behind bushes. Sometimes you think you've stopped breathing, you are so frightened. Again it was Albanians.

We stopped in a safe house for a while, but the OSS man wanted us to get over the mountain before daylight.

The British saw us walking down the hill and came running up with cigarettes and chocolate. They said, "Welcome to this side of the mountain, we have been waiting a long time for you." They sent up donkeys for us to ride on and gave us oranges, tea, and greasy chicken broth.

We slept in a cave that night, and everyone was so exhausted, we just crawled over someone and found a space and fell sound asleep. I remember someone waking me up saying, "The boat's here," and I grabbed my shoes and coat and went to the water's edge. There were bunk beds on the boat, and two or three of us crawled into each one and went right back to sleep.

When we arrived in Bari, Italy, our commanding officer and some photographers were there to meet, and interrogate, us.

Lois: My parents took me to the train when I joined the army and left for my first assignment at Camp McCoy, Wisconsin, on December 1, 1942. I remember Mom saying, "You might accept sending your son to war, but not your daughter." My flip answer was "Oh, Mom, I could slip on a banana peel and break my neck here." Before a year was up, I would be hiding from German soldiers, trying to find my way out of Albania.

I left Camp McCoy after five months to go to Bowman Field in Louisville, Kentucky, for flight nurse training. That grueling training probably prepared me for the two-months' ordeal in Albania, though no one had that in mind.

After the rough landing in Albania, the crew chief and I were the only ones with any visible injuries. We'd been sitting near each other, and his foot must have hit me in the face as he flew through the air. I had a split lower lip, loose upper teeth, a cut under my right eye, and, later, a black eye. The crew chief had a nasty cut on his leg.

I remember the farmhouse we spent the first few nights in, and the word "primitive" is mild. It was a stone building about fourteen-by-fourteen feet with no panes in the windows. There was a fireplace but no chimney and no furniture. We walked to Berat, which was a village of about six hundred houses, most of them similar to the one I just described. The Germans shelled the town the fourth morning we were there, so we headed out of town, with German planes strafing the small, crowded road. We scattered and when we regrouped, three nurses were missing. We had to go on without them and hoped they weren't captured.

We were filthy, having picked up body lice in the native homes. The lice were embarrassing when we sat by a fire and began to warm up, they would run foot races across our middle. We wanted to scratch but didn't want to offend the hosts. We wandered from village to village in search of food. The people were anxious for us to move on for fear that the Germans would find us, plus, we were eating all their food. They also feared the Ballista, or Ballys [opposite of the partisans], who were collaborators with the Germans.

On our way to the British camp, near the Greek border, we crossed a mountaintop and ran into a violent snowstorm with a howling wind. We were in single file on this narrow path, when suddenly the nurse in front of the sergeant in front of me slipped and started sliding down the side of the mountain. He reached down with one hand, grabbed her waist, and pulled her back up on the trail. Not a word was said, and we plodded on. When we reached the next village, the people ran out calling us heroes, and told us no one ever crossed that mountain between September and Spring. We did have a few frostbitten fingers and toes.

We came to the British camp December 1st, and I received badly needed shoes and socks, as I had practically no soles left on my shoes. The new ones were in men's sizes, and it took several pairs of socks to fill them up. They had hobnail soles and were heavy as lead.

We were near Agrisicostr when the British officer wouldn't signal the American planes to land, and it really lowered my spirits. This led to a forced, seven-day march to the sea, and believe me, going down from the mountains is as painful as going up. This was the most grueling experience I have ever had, and most of us were ill the last days. By the time we started the downhill side, my knees were locking every little while and I'd take a tumble.

A few at a time we were rowed out to a British motor launch, climbed up a landing net, and for the first time, I felt safe. With muffled motors, we left Albania, and the crew aboard the boat broke out their rum. In the morning we arrived in Bari, over two months late.

Backing up my story to Camp McCoy again, that was where I met the charming man who was to become my husband. About that time, the concept of flight nurses was evolving, and both of us were interested in flying. He applied for transfer to the Air Corps and I to Air Evacuation Training. Somewhere in here we decided to get married, and in March 1943, I married Nolan McKenzie. He left in April for primary flight training, and in May I went to Kentucky.

The army kept in touch with my parents while I was in Albania, and they in turn let my husband know what was happening. The first Westen Union telegram from Dad to Nolan read,

Heard radio report plane Africa to Italy November 8th overflew destination hoping.

On November 27 Dad's next telegram read,

Received message war department Lois missing since November 8th No other details.

On December 5 my parents were notified that I was safe. Nolan wrote to the adjutant general in Washington on January 2, 1944, requesting information about me, and asking if I was in enemy hands, or what my status was. On January 11 the general responded saying "a communication will be received from your wife in the near future."

Report now received states your daughter second lieutenant Lois E Watson returned to allied military control nine January.

My parents and Nolan received this telegram on January 20.

Front page headlines in the *Chicago Tribune* on November 30, 1943, read: 13 Nurses, 12 Soldiers Lost. Ann Markowitz and I were from the Chicago area, and were featured in several articles. Many newspapers throughout the country followed the story from when we were missing until our return to the States, and our pictures were in papers and magazines everywhere. *True* was an adventure-style comic book that told our story, titled *"Balkan Escape."*

Harold: I was a surgical technician with the 807th and on the flight that crash-landed in Albania. When the pilot finally saw an open spot where we could land safely, he thought we would be in western Italy, but we'd flown across the Adriatic Sea without knowing it.

The band of partisans, who met us at the site of the crash, were a big help, but after about the tenth day we found out we were in more danger from the civil war that was going on between the Albanians than we were from the Germans. One group was for the Germans, and the others were communists. This group did not want to turn us over to the Germans, but they could have helped us escape earlier than we did. There were British all over the Balkans, and the partisans could have put us in touch within a day.

One of the biggest problems we had was shoes. It was later estimated that we had traveled about seven hundred miles, almost all on mountain trails. Not many people were experienced hikers, and the nurses were terrific the way they kept us from getting too discouraged.

We all were greatly discouraged though, when the planes flew over to rescue us and they couldn't land. An interesting aspect of this story is that when the British contacted their headquarters in Cairo, Egypt, to request a plane, the message came back, "Men are expendable and an airplane is not." So we asked them to send a message to the American Air Corps, which radioed right back, wanting to know the particulars of the field.

After we were back in Italy, I was interrogated and told not to say anything, and several times on the trip home I was questioned and required to sign a statement of secrecy. I was back in the States about a month later, and when I told my family I couldn't tell them where I'd been, everyone said they had read about me in the newspaper already.

After sixty-two days of unbelievable living, they were safe. Three nurses were still in Albania, where they were to spend four-and-a-half months in hiding. The OSS man turned around to bring them out. The three nurses left behind in Berat found themselves in a rather primitive house, with a family that cared for them with their meager amount of food. They didn't know how or when they would ever leave or what happened to the others. Ava Maness relates what happened to them.

Ava: The third night that we were in the house in Berat, I heard some popping sounds, which sounded like gunfire up in the hills. The next day we found that the rest of our group had left town when the shooting started, and we three nurses were the only Americans still there.

We could see enemy troops were bivouacked across the street in a school yard, and a member of the family we were staying with told us the Germans knew we were there and were coming to look for us. He told us not to worry but not to try to talk to them, which we couldn't do anyway. Later I realized that our hostess knew a lot about these troops, some of whom spoke Hungarian. Her family was from Hungary, and she could hear some of what they were saying in the school yard.

Soon I heard men talking, and two nice-looking, young soldiers came in to the room where we were. They looked at us, and we looked at them. Finally one of them gestured about our insignia, and I said the Italian word for nurse. As they left, they told our hostess that we should stay there and not to let us go outside.

We stayed there, inside that house, for almost five months.

We didn't know what to expect, so there wasn't much point worrying over it. Our host's brother had been in the United States for a couple of years and spoke a little bit of English. He lived across the street and came over every morning to tell us what was happening, which wasn't much.

This family consisted of a man and his wife, his mother, and their

Ava Maness and Wilma Lytle rest with their guide on the long trek across Albania in March 1944 after surviving five months of hiding from Germans.

nephew, about seven years old. The wife was kind of smart and seemed to catch on very quickly. She didn't speak English, but we understood her, and she had no trouble understanding us. The host's mother wore black all the time, and everyone called her Mama. We slept with Mama on pallets in the living room. She put blankets and quilts on the windows until there was no light, but we supposed it was to keep people from seeing inside.

The family was Orthodox, and we were there for Advent and Lent, the only time we ate meat. They ate a lot of beans, and I'll never forget one day during Lent, Mama held out a pot of beans and said, "Beans! Beans! Beans!" That was her only attempt to speak our language.

We had to sit on the floor, as there was no furniture. The kitchen was the room next to the one we stayed in, and I think I only went in there once. I'll never forget seeing the plates on the floor with cats licking them, but we couldn't let that bother us.

The house had no plumbing or running water, but there was a well downstairs. The "toilet" was in a little room that had a barrier in front of it.

Helen Porter had a deck of cards, so we played a sort-of-bridge. Sometimes we'd argue a little about the hands, but it was just to keep our blood pressure up. Wilma Lytle was the third nurse, and we got along well. We just felt we would get out sometime. The family did the best they could for us, and we didn't wonder too much.

One night, a local man who seemed to be important took us for a ride in a car, which was the only time we were out of the house. It was nice to get out and we just rode toward the hills and back.

When we finally left, we weren't sure what was happening, but they let us know they were going to try to help us. All that time we only had our uniforms to wear, so they brought material and the hostess made native dresses and headscarves for us. No matter what happened, we were not to look men in the eye, which would be a dead give-away for blue-eyed Helen and Wilma. Dressed as native women, we were driven off in a car, with me in the front seat holding the driver's rifle.

Once our car was stopped at a guard station along the road. A man came over to my side, but I didn't look at him, and we drove on, spending the night in the mountains on our way to the coast. The last night, we met an American officer who was in the country to take us out. He brought us to the coast and the boat that took us to Italy.

Looking back, the reason we had to stay where we were was because our hosts were scared to death. The noise I thought was gunfire that first night scared everyone else to get up and get away. But our host was too scared to go out. I've always hesitated to say too much about that family because Albania has had a lot of problems, and something might cause them harm, even today.

USS *Refuge*

Five navy nurses assigned to the hospital ship, Refuge, *relate shared experiences during eighteen months' duty in the Atlantic and the Pacific. Their stories here begin early in the war during crossings of the Atlantic.*

Helen Wentz Miller   **Esther Wallenga "Wally"**
Ernestine Hess Davey "Hessie"   **Betty Torrance Staats**
Bessie Glembocki Daniels

Helen: Another nurse and I were driving down the street in Palm Beach, Florida, when on the car radio we heard President Roosevelt's speech declaring war. My friend's immediate reaction was that she should return home to Alabama and join the army. I told her I would join the navy in my native Pennsylvania, and that's what we did.

Wally: The nurses forged such close friendships during my eighteen months aboard the USS *Refuge*. How fortunate to have such a terrific group to work with.

Hessie: We served in three theaters of war: the North Atlantic, Mediterranean, and the Pacific.

Betty: Sometimes we picked up patients, treating them on the ship while we stayed in a harbor, or we serviced other ships. Eventually, we would come back to the States with a full load of patients. We could carry six hundred, but did push it up to eight hundred sometimes.

Helen Wentz, who served fourteen months on the USS *Refuge* hospital ship, is shown wearing "abandon ship" gear.

Wally: We crossed the Atlantic the first time to bring casualties back to the States from North Africa. In the Mediterranean, we looked after the men wounded in Italy, at Anzio. Other trips back to the States included casualties from the Normandy invasion.

Betty: Twice we transported German prisoners as patients from Southern France to Naples. The story was that when the Americans went into the south of France, they found a German hospital with patients left behind, but no doctors or nurses. The patients wore makeshift bandages made of newspaper. They were very hungry, and the first meal they got was lunch, but none of them finished it. When the corpsmen tried to take the trays, the patients resisted strongly, because they thought it was all they would get. That night they had another meal, and the next day they received three meals and were amazed.

Patients were always divided on board according to injury, and this resulted in Allied patients being mixed with Germans in the same ward. That proved to be a major mistake! The Allied patients would say things like, "You've got six live Germans here today, but tomorrow there will be six dead Germans." It wasn't good for recovery and caused a lot of bad feelings. Needless to say, similar arrangements were not made on the second trip.

I was assigned the job to get everyone identified, with the help of a wounded German officer. When he asked for name, rank, and serial number, the other Germans resented it, because they thought he was collaborating with us. I don't understand German, but he had to struggle to convince them that he was just trying to get them accounted for.

Bessie: The Germans thought we were going to poison them and wouldn't eat until one of our corpsmen ate something off their food tray.

Helen: Some wounded German prisoners were just young boys who were scared to death, not knowing if we would torture them or what. When they were on board I remember being told if we were bombed and had to abandon ship, they were to be left on the ship.

Betty: The *Refuge* anchored offshore in the Bay of Naples, and we took small boats in to the dock. It was sobering every time when we had to pass a capsized luxury ship, the *Rex*.

Helen: Once when we were in Naples, an army officer I knew back in Philadelphia found me and took me around. I met some army nurses then because I would stay overnight in their barracks, and I found out why they envied us. They were eating off tin plates, with rationed food, while we had nice white tablecloths and fresh food. I remember they couldn't get things like Kotex, so we would give them a supply, and they thought that was really wonderful. We thought they had it rough, and when we were in port, invited them on board for dinner. One of our trips back to the States we had some army nurses as patients, who were shell-shocked from the buzz bombs in England.

Bessie: Everyone went to Rome when they had the chance, and a highlight of my visit was being able to attend an audience with Pope Pius XII. Before the war, and before he was pope, he was a patient at Georgetown

University Hospital where I had my nurse's training. I was at the audience with several of my shipmates and many other military people, all in uniforms, and none knew that I'd ever met him. We'd been instructed not to interrupt or try to carry on a conversation with him and were lined up around the sides of a huge room as he walked past us. He looked at me and said, "It's nice to see you." My shipmates were speechless, and so was I. Then he said, "I will pray for a safe voyage for your ship." "My ship" did have a safe voyage from then on.

Betty: When I was at a papal audience, the pope asked everyone where they were from and I told him, "A town in New Jersey that you probably never heard of." When I said it was Kearny, the pope said, "That's Mayor Hague's bailiwick, Hudson County." I couldn't believe what I was hearing. Hague was the mayor of Jersey City, and Kearny was nearby in the same county. I had another "small world" experience when we were bringing patients out of Naples and two of them were from my hometown, Kearny, New Jersey.

Helen: On our last trip back to the States from Europe, we heard about the death of President Roosevelt. Everyone wondered about his successor, Harry Truman, and if we would lose the war now. We already knew that the *Refuge* was going to the Pacific soon.

ENGLAND

"Buzz bombs, blackouts, and barrage balloons"

When war was declared on Germany in 1941, American military nurses were on duty in England, supporting the Allies. Their numbers multiplied by the thousands during the next years, anticipating the invasion of the Continent in 1944.

Evangeline Bakke Fairall U.S. Army   **250th Station Hospital**

First assigned to a POW camp in Illinois where she attended to disabled and ailing German prisoners, "Bakke" was ready and eager for her overseas duty.

I didn't think I'd ever know what it was to be warm after we landed in Liverpool, England, in January 1944. It was night and pouring rain, and we marched in formation carrying our heavy packs to the train. We stood for what seemed like hours while the rain beat a tattoo on our helmets, like rain on a tin roof. The American Red Cross greeted us with doughnuts, hot coffee, and gum after we boarded the train. It was wonderful, for all we'd had to eat was breakfast that day.

Blackouts were always in effect, so we had to do a lot in complete darkness, often without the aid of even a flashlight to show the way. Utter, pitch-black darkness descended about 4:30 P.M. and lasted until 8:30 A.M. Because of air raids, the blackout system was so complete that you never saw even a crack of light when a door was opened. Almost everyone had black and blue marks on their knees from bumping into signs, posts, and fences.

We soon learned to dread air alerts but had no desire to ignore them. Many a night, and often on consecutive nights, we climbed out of bed, put our trench coats over pajamas, went to the wards to be with the patients,

151

**Nurses disembark wearing helmets and Class A uniforms. They have
musette bags slung over each shoulder, in addition to carrying various
kinds of gear grasped in their arms.**

and remained there until the "all clear" came. I remember getting patients
up and putting them under each bed. It could be an hour or two hours
later before we could return to our tents, cold and hungry. The tents were
so cold, and heavy rains kept everything damp. We kept clothes under the
pillow at night to keep them dry. The latrine and showers were up a hill,
and we had to walk there out in the open, day or night.

From January to May we moved several times, staying with other hospitals or in private homes. We worked at Cheltenham, Ullenwood, Swindon,
Burford, and just before the D day invasion, set up a hospital at Grim's
Ditch, near Salisbury. Stonehenge was across the field from our camp, and
we often walked there among the giant stones.

We knew D day was coming but weren't supposed to talk about it,
even among ourselves in our tents. I'll never forget the morning of D day.
Very early we heard thousands of planes going overhead, toward the
Continent; just thousands. As the day went on, they were coming back,
and we knew fewer were returning. Everyone was quiet.

When we heard our first convoy of battle patients was coming, we
were very excited, because we could finally get to do the work we had

come to do. We couldn't do enough for that first group of one hundred patients. Then, as more came, the number soon jumped to over a thousand. My first battle patient had a bullet wound in the spine and was paralyzed from the neck down. I'll never forget that first patient.

This went on for several weeks, and everyone was busy. Then we were told we were to be a rehabilitation hospital, caring only for convalescent patients, getting them in shape physically and mentally to return to combat. Our spirits went down with a thud, but we gradually adjusted to the change.

About three months later our status changed again, and we received new battle casualties. We worked like beavers, never enough nurses to go around. One nurse might have responsibility for nearly two hundred very sick patients, spread over an area of approximately two city blocks. With the aid of competent wardmen, we managed to get along.

We had every type of case, and sometimes those sick, sick patients kept our morale up more than we did their's. They came to us in many ways, sometimes by plane straight from the front. Just before Christmas 1944, we were busier than ever, and I remember one patient telling me, "I was crawling out of my foxhole about 3:30 this afternoon, and here I am." It was about 7:30 in the evening when we were talking, and we were a long way from the combat area.

The number of orthopedic patients was astounding, running well over four hundred. Ward after ward was filled with fractures, almost everyone up in traction, with rarely an ambulatory patient in these wards.

One nurse who was inspecting our hospital really lifted my spirits. She had seen several of these wards with nothing but patients in traction, the nurses wearing raincoats over their uniforms for warmth, and pantlegs wet well above the knees from the heavy, drenching rain. This nurse was amazed that we could care for patients in that situation. I asked, "Have you seen the General Hospital down the road?" It was made of brick, while we were a tent hospital. They had covered ramps between buildings, and we had to walk through the rain and mud to carry supplies and food to each tent. She said, "I've been there several times, but I like this place. You have to have what it takes to work here."

Though we all remember the problems, it was a very happy memory for most. Living in close conditions and sharing the most difficult of working situations brought us together in closeness not found in many other circumstances.

The "Latrinogram" told us that we could expect to be moved as the war was ending in Europe. All notices for the nurses were posted on a bulletin board in the latrine, thus the name. It also carried rumors and notices of parties. In May 1945 our unit went to the Continent.

Theresa James U.S. Army   **168th Station Hospital**

One of only two African-American nurses enrolled in the University of Minnesota School of Nursing, Theresa graduated in 1933.

We were accepted at the university on a trial basis and were treated respectfully, like everyone else. I then became a supervisor at a hospital in St. Louis, Missouri, and while there was recruited to join the Army Nurse Corps. Forty-eight of us were the first African-American nurses in the armed forces.

My first assignment was to Fort Bragg, North Carolina, and being segregated was quite an experience for me as I had never been in the South or any segregated area before in my life. I had heard about it but was insulated from it. Here I was thirty years of age, and having to experience both the South and a segregated army.

On December 7, 1941, I was in church in Fayetteville, North Carolina, when we were told about Pearl Harbor being bombed. Transfers to Fort Huachuca, Arizona, Camp Livingston, Louisiana, and Fort Clark, Texas preceded my being sent to Europe. When we arrived in England in the fall of 1943 no one knew what to do with us. Our quarters were at a boy's academy, and all we did was march and have classes, like basic training. I remember being invited to tea at a castle, which was the home of Lady Fellows.

We were moved to several different places for three months, finally arriving at Warrington, England, to replace another unit of nurses at the 168th. The doctors and corpsmen were white, and the patients were wounded German prisoners. They were sent to prison camps in the States from there. Being prisoners, they were usually cooperative and, I thought, interesting. Regardless of your race, country, or whatever, people are people. The Germans spoke broken English, and we soon picked up broken German.

I was able to take several trips during the two years we were there, including to Scotland and Wales, and it was an adventure. During my first trip to London, Harrod's Department Store was bombed. Another time the train had a bomb scare just before we reached London.

When I returned after the war, I stayed out a few months but went back in the army in 1947, staying in for twenty-six years.

Nurses of the 168 SH went through months of training after arriving in England while waiting for assignment.

Lillie Emory Skinner U.S. Army   168th Station Hospital

Lillie was from Knoxville, Tennessee; her military service began in 1941, and she went abroad two years later.

In 1941 when I joined the army with the first group of African-American nurses, I was sent to Fort Bragg, North Carolina. We were segregated wherever we were stationed, but Camp Livingston, Louisiana, was the worst place I've ever been. I never want to go through there again. The local bus driver wouldn't let us ride the bus back to the base, and in general, the people just weren't nice.

I had a lot of fun in Fort Huachuca, Arizona, where I met my future husband, who was a dentist. Transferred to Texas from there, I went back to visit him in Arizona, and we were married. He went to the Pacific, and we didn't see each other for two years, until the war was over.

When I heard I was going overseas, I cried. I didn't volunteer. It turned out to be an adventure, and in a way, I enjoyed it. I had international patients in England, where they called us "sisters." They were French, Russian, German, and everything else. Some were kids fourteen and fifteen years old. One man was quite old, and he told me that the Germans forced him into the army. There were several Nazi SS patients, and the other Germans were even afraid of them. We weren't allowed on their ward without an armed soldier with us.

I spoke some French, and once a Frenchman told me that another patient was a spy. "You watch him," he said. While I was watching, the spy went to the officers' ward when the others went to the mess hall. I told my ward officer, and he and the corpsmen kept their eye on this guy. One night, a whole bunch of the patients were taken away, and I was told they had maps of the place and were going to blow everything up.

One of the colonels in charge of the hospital did crazy things, including writing bad reports about everybody. Soon someone from Washington, D.C., came to check on him, and he wound up at a hospital in the States as a patient. After he left, things were better.

Warrington was the town near the base where we shopped. We couldn't figure out the money exchange, and I remember thinking we always paid too much. Being from Tennessee, I bought things similar to collard greens, which they fed to horses, and we took them back to the hospital and cooked them, like back home. I took trips to Ireland and Scotland with friends and especially enjoyed the many bookstores in London.

Generals Dwight Eisenhower and Benjamin Davis came to visit our base, and we had to have the hospital all cleaned up and ready for them. I have a picture of General Davis with a patient and me.

My husband and I wrote letters all the time, and mail went between England and the Pacific theater pretty well. We weren't supposed to tell our locations, so we tried to use codes. The censor, who checked his letters, wrote a note that said, "Your husband loves you, but he talks too much."

Louise Dumond Kopchak U.S. Army   327th Station Hospital
Sixty-first General Hospital

On Christmas Day 1943 Louise was on the Queen Mary in the middle of the Atlantic Ocean, after being an army nurse for only three weeks.

The 327th was near Blockley on a lovely estate owned by Winston Churchill's cousin, but we lived in huts and tents. There were some American patients, but we had mostly German prisoners who'd been injured. I met my future husband there, and we became engaged before he went to France for D day. We wrote letters to each other until he was wounded and returned to England. I was glad to be transferred to the Sixty-first after hearing my fiancé was injured. I took care of the Germans but had very mixed emotions.

My fiancé came back to England an amputee. As soon as he was well enough, we were married and wound up having three ceremonies. The first one was at the Catholic church in town, and another ceremony was in the vestibule of the church to meet civil requirements. After that we returned to the hospital where he was a patient, and they took us into the chapel and had another blessing of the marriage by the chaplain.

At the Sixty-first, near Burford, we had only American patients, including the American POWs after they were released in Germany. I remember watching the stream of ambulances going and coming from the hospital when they were brought to us from the ships. As soon as we had them settled in the wards we began to fatten them up. They were skin and bones, suffering mostly from malnutrition, but a few had wounds. They had great attitudes.

The hospital kitchen made eggnogs and sent them around to the wards. If they didn't come quickly, the doctors would tell us, "Get busy and give them eggnogs. They've got to have them!" We had powdered eggs and milk on each unit, so I'd mix them up, making them stronger than the ones from the kitchen. Then I was told to stop making them because it wasn't my job, since I wasn't a dietitian. The doctors would tell me to not pay attention to the orders and keep on making them the way I'd been doing it.

I stayed until after V-E Day. My husband was already back in the States and wrote that I could petition to leave early, so I did.

Anna Steele Fox U.S. Army　　　　　　　　**128th General Hospital**

A civilian psychiatric nurse with the Veterans Administration, Anna joined the army in 1943.

We were located near Swindon, about seventy miles from London. Our hospital was right across from a camp for German prisoners, and one night we were told not to go anywhere, even the bathroom, without a corpsman standing by. The reason we were given was that inspectors from Washington were expected to come anytime. Later my mother sent a clipping from the *Chicago Tribune* telling that prisoners at that camp had planned to make a break and take the females as hostages. We didn't know anything about that until my mother sent the clipping.

The English had been guarding the Germans, but by the time we arrived the guards were Polish soldiers. Every Sunday the Polish guards marched goose-step to our chapel, and afterward they always stood and sang their national anthem.

Everyone rode bicycles, and there was a nice family that had us to dinner often. We brought sugar and things they couldn't get and showed them how to pop corn for the first time.

Viola Molloy U.S. Army　　　　　　　　**Fifty-sixth General Hospital**

"Molly" was in the army for five months, working at a military hospital in Des Moines, before going through basic training.

When our unit arrived at Fort Devens, Massachusetts, in August 1943, things began to be a lot more serious than I'd been through until then. We went through all sorts of maneuvers: marching every day, climbing everything but trees, and that gas chamber. We were so young, nothing bothered us, and we all had a lot of self-confidence. When I look back, we were very naïve.

We sailed out of Boston Harbor in October 1943 and kept our eyes on it until we saw nothing but water. There were ten thousand people on board. Most had never been on a ship, and I believe this was when we nurses became so close.

From October until July 1944 we worked in three different hospitals in England. The first was near an English village called Malvern Wells, and it served psychiatric, or battle fatigue, patients. We didn't stay there long because most of our doctors were from Johns Hopkins, and they were not interested in psychiatry.

Buzz bombs caused terror to the patients in England. Some of the boys said they preferred the hazards of foxholes rather than being in a hospital bombing. Our hospital was damaged a little but no one was injured when a bomb hit nearby. I went to London alone once, and on my way to the hotel, the first thing I heard was a weird-sounding siren and saw people running down the street with pillows under their arms toward a shelter. I hadn't seen or heard about buzz bombs until then but went along with the crowd.

I was happy to get back to our base and leave the buzz bombs behind, but, lo and behold, when I was back, the bombs were flying around there as well. We were told to get behind a door when we heard a bomb, or if outside, fall flat on the ground. One evening another nurse and I were dressed in our Class A uniforms, walking over to the Officers Club, when we heard a buzz bomb overhead. They made a "putt-putt" noise, and when that sound stopped, it was coming down. I ran as fast as I could across the muddy yard and crouched behind a door at the Officers Club. However, my friend did as she was instructed, and what a sight she was.

Esther Edginton Kelly U.S. Army   187th General Hospital

While her sister, Florence, was stationed in India, Esther joined the army and was sent to England in March 1944.

My sister and I wrote back and forth, but since the letters were always censored, I didn't know too much about her life there until we got together after the war. The 187th was near Tidwell, south of London. In the beginning we weren't allowed to go to London because the German V-2 rockets were flying over. Later, we just stayed in our hotel rooms or went to bomb shelters.

Troops came and went through Tidwell on their way to the Continent. Some who had been in Africa had malaria, which we hadn't expected. After D day we received a lot of wounded from the battles, and I worked in a very busy colostomy ward. Patients had usually been stabilized at other hospitals by the time they came to us, and some of them were like little brothers as they became better and on their feet.

I dated a nice fellow before he was sent to France for D day. He wrote a letter and I wrote him back. My letter was returned, marked "Missing In Action." I never knew whether he was killed, or what.

The day President Roosevelt died we had a formal military retreat: marching and lowering the flag. It was a very sad ceremony because many of us had never known any other president.

Florence Viergutz U.S. Army   **216th General Hospital**

Florence was a graduate of Grace Hospital in Detroit, becoming an army officer in 1943.

When my brother was drafted in 1943, I decided to join too. I just didn't know it was going to be so rough, but there was a lot of satisfaction because I felt I was doing something. If you really had a bad day, you could go to the latrine and shout. The army was still the army, because no matter what was happening with the war, we never knew when there would be an inspection. The generals and colonels came but they never looked at the patients. They looked at the floors.

Our one-thousand-bed Quonset hut hospital was one hundred miles outside London. We knew when D day was coming because planes were constantly practicing, and we saw more and more of them. That first week of June we heard the planes day and night.

The broken and maimed bodies of American GIs came to us from the battlefields in Europe. I never want to see another war. There's nothing romantic about it, really. I remember one young man, just twenty-six years old, and blind. He was newly-married and wanted me to write his wife a letter. She didn't know he was blind, and I sat there trying to write that letter. He couldn't see that tears were streaming down my face. The patients were so messed up, and almost all had bone destruction. They were in casts and traction. It was quite an awakening.

From England, I was transferred to Verdun, France, where barbed wire still stood from World War I. We just jumped for joy when Germany surrendered, and all we could think about was going home. After Germany surrendered I went to Stuttgart, Germany, which had been heavily bombed. The hospital I worked in was inundated with underground tunnels, to show you how well-prepared the Germans were.

Mary Ferrell U.S. Army   **101st Evacuation Hospital**

Mary joined the army from her hometown, Shiloh, Ohio, and before the war ended was awarded the Bronze Star for meritorious service in Europe.

The 101st arrived in England in February 1944, where we waited until July to cross the Channel. Thousands of U.S. troops kept arriving, waiting for the invasion. With each new arrival, we joked that the barrage balloons would fail to hold the island up. Huge antiaircraft balloons were anchored over many parts of Britain to defend against low-level enemy flights.

We were billeted in Stockport, near Manchester, and the nurses stayed in private homes with British families. Many of the Yanks, as we were called, found the local girls attractive and brought brides home after the war. A saying of the English about the American service people was, "Those Yanks are overpaid, oversexed, and over here."

Betty Theobald Blagen U.S. Army Air Force
806th, 811th Medical Air Evacuation Squadrons

"Theo" graduated from Cincinnati General Hospital and was one of eight accepted directly into air evacuation training from civilian life; thereafter nurses had to join the army first, then be admitted to the school.

The first Omaha Beach Invasion casualties to arrive back in the States were on my flight in June 1944. There were eighteen litter patients, and one of them was Pfc. James A. Lester of Clio, Michigan. My father wrote to the Lester family, after he heard me tell about the boy, who was paralyzed from the neck down. We never heard back from them, but after all these years, I haven't forgotten him. On those long flights we often came to know the patients really well.

We flew relays in C-54s from Prestwick, Scotland, to Iceland, to Newfoundland, then to New York. Sometimes we stopped in the Azores, but for that flight I was on the leg from Newfoundland to the States. Whenever I got to New York, there was often enough time to go home to Ohio for a couple of days.

Ethel Carlson Cerasale U.S. Army Air Force
815th Medical Air Evacuation Squadron

After graduation in 1942 Ethel wanted to become an airline stewardess but found herself in a Medical Air Evacuation Squadron.

We sailed from New York on the *Ile de France* in March 1944, in preparation for the invasion of Normandy, then waited in England until we were needed to evacuate patients. There wasn't much to do, but we had training flights in B-17s to learn the effects of high altitudes (20,000 feet), and how to use oxygen masks. Everyone about went crazy during several alerts for the invasion but knew it was for real when we were restricted to quarters a few days before

D day, June 6, 1944. We watched from the rooftop as hundreds of C-47s flew over in formation on their way to France and eagerly awaited news of their return. Some did not come back and we all mourned their loss.

Two weeks after D day I made my first air evac flight from England to Normandy and returned with a load of litter patients, which included several German officers. At first I was angry that they should be allowed swift care, possibly before our own soldiers might have filled that space. Then I realized they were being brought back for interrogation, and to prevent their escaping.

Our patients were prepared for the short trip to England in mobile tent hospitals, so our job was to keep them comfortable. Later, when we picked up tank casualties as Patton's troops raced across northern France, this was especially difficult. Many of these men were in full body casts with only a hole for breathing and one for a straw or a cigarette, and our biggest concern with these fellows was they might become airsick. They each had a scissors hanging on a string tied around their necks, so that we could snip the wires that held their jaws together, if necessary.

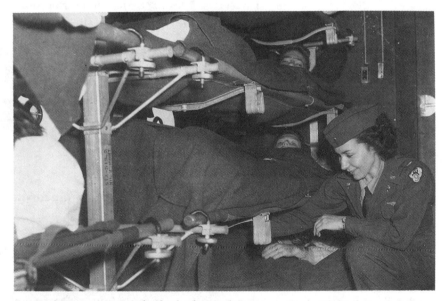

**Patients were "triple-decked" in planes carrying sick and wounded
to hospitals.**

As the war progressed we flew where the battles were, usually bringing patients back to England. Our planes carried supplies which were often grenades, tank fuel, or ammunition. It was off-loaded, and the nurse and a sergeant converted the interior of the plane to an air ambulance, putting up brackets to hold the incoming litters or raising the bucket seats if the patients were ambulatory.

Margaret Carlson Larson U.S. Army
USS *Dogwood*, 218th Hospital Ship

"Carly" made several crossings on the Atlantic before the Dogwood sailed into the war in the Pacific. The Dogwood was originally the Liberty ship George Washington Carver converted for hospital service.

I joined the Army Nurse Corps in 1943 and went through basic training at Camp Miles Standish, Massachusetts. The assignment to ship duty came as a surprise, but I enjoyed it. We went over empty and picked up about six hundred patients each time at the docks in England.

"Abandon Ship" drills were always taking place. We were assigned certain patients to assist and told how to take them with us into the lifeboats. It would have taken a long time to abandon that ship. These trips took about twelve days each way. The *Queen Mary* was a luxury liner converted to a troop ship and would be docked when we left a port. She was a lot faster, making about two trips to our one. She'd catch up on her way over, and we'd meet her again on the way back.

Our ship always traveled alone, unarmed, and completely lit up. Painted white all over, it had a big red cross for identification. Once when we were traveling empty, we became mixed up with a convoy of ships and had to shut off the engines. We sat in the lounge with our life jackets on, waiting for something to happen. It was hard to knit with the Mae Wests on.

I worked in many different wards on the ship, and it never mattered to me what I did, because the GIs were the greatest patients on earth. The psychiatric ward was usually filled with boys who had combat fatigue, mostly from seeing a buddy killed or wounded. I remember one young man who had amnesia, and nobody could get him to talk. At that time, I wore a cologne called "Woodhue." One day the psychiatrist gave him sodium pentathol, and we waited for him to respond to the drug. All of a sudden he said, "Oh, lieutenant, I love that perfume. What do you call it?"

Now this is the first time he had said anything. I told him it was "Woodhue." He said, "Would I!" His recovery went on rapidly from there.

The boys cared about each other so much and didn't want anyone to know they had problems. We had to hide injection needles when we came into the ward, because the patient who was getting medication didn't want his buddies to know and worry about him.

Ruth Lawrence Little U.S. Army   USS *Dogwood*/218th Hospital Ship

After leaving New England, Ruth enjoyed duty on a hospital ship, recalling the lighter times shared by the nurses.

Who can ever forget her most embarrassing moment on the ship? Our small cabins opened out to a narrow passageway that was usually empty. We washed out our undies in the evening and hung them on the handrail running along the passageway outside of our door to dry for the next morning's wear.

One "next morning" I stepped naked out the door to retrieve the undies, and my foot just missed landing on a mop on the floor. As I followed the mop handle up, I came to the person of an enlisted man who was about to mop the passageway floor. I'm sure both of our faces mirrored extreme shock, but I didn't stop to think of that as I catapulted back into the cabin.

That was embarrassing, but even more so was the follow-up later that day. As we were going down the stairs to supper, the enlisted men were loitering around the foot of the stairs to await their call to chow. I heard a whisper from the ranks of the men, "Here she comes!"

One of my cabinmates, Rusty, spent most of her off-duty time on our trips across the oceans face down on her bunk. She would emit a moan or groan occasionally, indicating her seasickness. The frequent and famous words in our cabin were, "I'm getting a transfer when we get back to Charleston!" When we landed somewhere the sickness would fade from memory until the next time the ship left the dock. Sure enough, Rusty was on board again to renew her misery.

We were all excited the first time the smell of fresh-baked bread wafted through the ship, so impatient as we waited to get to the evening meal. Surprised is hardly the word when we saw the long-awaited delicacy peppered with small black specks, which we recognized as bugs! But we ate it anyway, and it was good. A protein addition didn't stop us from enjoying it.

The *Dogwood* made seven trips across the Atlantic between Charleston, South Carolina, and England before being sent to the Pacific.

FRANCE

"Normandy, and the Battle of the Bulge"

A fter D Day, 6 June 1944, hospital units crossed the English Channel, landing on Utah Beach and Omaha Beach in Normandy.

Mary Ferrell U.S. Army

The 101st crossed the English Channel in LSTs, landing at Utah Beach on a pontoon dock. Allied planes patrolled constantly overhead as we went ashore. Soldiers and cargo swarmed over the beach like ants, and everywhere were shattered concrete pillboxes, shell holes, and smashed buildings. The enlisted men from our unit marched several miles, laden with their field equipment, to a transit area to pitch pup tents. The nurses and officers settled in an apple orchard. We slept on our raincoats and shared it with a buddy, using her raincoat as a cover. During the night we climbed into trucks to go by convoy to the Thirty-fifth Evacuation Hospital to await our equipment. German planes zoomed overhead as searchlights constantly probed the sky and antiaircraft fire chased the enemy planes. We waited there until Patton's Third Army became operational on August 1, 1944.

Our hospital then followed the XII Corps and the XX Corps of the Third Army throughout the war. We moved fifteen times the next ten months. An evac hospital had to pick up and move with the troops, stopping at each battle to treat the wounded. Then, we'd load up a truck with the equipment and our belongings and move to the next one.

Marlene Dietrich visited our hospital several times and sang "Lili Marlene" and "The Boys in the Backroom" for the patients in the wards. She changed clothes in my tent, arriving in army fatigues, then appearing in the wards in a very shiny, sparkling, long gown. She was beautiful and would always show the calf of her leg to the patients as she left. I remember the boys liked to sing the risqué song, "Roll Me Over."

Most of my nursing was in the shock ward of our hospital, or as the men called it, "The Chamber of Horrors." We received casualties from the admission tent who were in varying degrees of shock. If their postoperative condition was poor, the patients returned to us until they were stabilized or transferred to another hospital. We tried to evacuate all the patients to the rear as soon as they were able, so we could be ready to move on as fast as necessary. I don't like to talk about patients and cases, but there is one man I can't forget. I had to send him to surgery before he was strong enough to stand an anesthetic. He knew it was going to hurt plenty, so he said, "Let's sing." He and the doctor sang all through the operation, ending up with "Spring Will Be a Little Late This Year."

I'd like people to know how much I admired those boys. I would never have believed what they could take. It was the army nurse's privilege to give the best nursing care possible to the sick and wounded soldiers. The words of a badly-wounded man, as he looked at you giving him plasma, were thanks enough for us all. They would say, "Are you real?" or, "You are wonderful," or, "You are here in hell with us!"

In February 1945, while in Arlon, Belgium, I was awarded the Bronze Star for meritorious service. I also proudly wore five campaign stars.

On V-E Day we were operating in tents at Parkstettern, not far from the Danube River near the city of Regensburg, Germany. We moved into an old abbey and operated as an emergency hospital for awhile. By the time V-J Day came, I was in a school of tropical medicine in Paris, anticipating being sent to the Pacific.

Mary was featured in a moving article by Ernest Hauser in the Saturday Evening Post, 10 March 1945. He describes her work in the shock ward, with two patients who were in no condition to be moved:

> *"Sometimes," Mary said, "I think maybe it's a good thing their mothers can't see them when they die." Hauser writes, "I can't help feeling that she was wrong that time. If the mothers of these two boys could have seen Mary Ferrell standing by their sons, keeping them silent company through that long cruel night, and escorting them gently up to the threshold of the last, wide-open portal—if their mothers could have caught a glimpse of it, I think it might have made them feel just a little better about it all."*

Grace G. Peterson U.S. Army   **Eighth Field Hospital**

After the rigors of basic training at Camp McCoy, Wisconsin, Grace, whose hometown was Cleveland, went overseas in September 1943.

After working in England for several months, right after D day in June 1944 we were sent to France and landed on Utah Beach. When people argue about women being in combat, I think how silly they are, because we already were. In France we had 88 mm artillery shells flying right over our heads. It was unsettling to hear the 88s, but we figured this was what war was like.

When the ships unloaded, everything was piled up for each unit in an area called the "dump." Every day our officers went out to look for our equipment, going from one "dump" to another. About the fifth day they spotted a pile of boxes with an ironing board on top of it, and said, "That's ours!"

Our first destination wasn't really captured by the Americans for a month after we landed, so we moved several times. Today, we take so much for granted about running water, electricity, and bathrooms, for instance. Living and working in tents was a different story. I can remember getting up in the night during heavy rains and having a river of water running through the middle of the floor. The men who put the tents up forgot to dig a ditch around them. When it rained, the tent ropes had to be tightened up, and when they dried, we had to loosen them, or the tent would be down on top of us.

Our field hospital was designed to have three one-hundred-bed sections. Patients were brought from hospitals at the front, and we cared for them until planes came in to take them to England. There was a small landing area for C-47s. One day an evacuation plane didn't have any nurses to accompany patients, so two of us were ordered to rush and get on board. It was my first plane ride. When the plane landed in England, we were taken to quarters, but then we didn't know what to do or where to go, and the flight nurses absolutely ignored us. The only money we had was French francs. The next morning we found a plane headed back to France, and landed at a small airstrip some distance from our's. Again we were ignored. We hadn't eaten anything since the day before, but finally found a D ration chocolate bar. By afternoon we found a place to eat and then decided to hitchhike back to our camp.

The P-38s were small, fast fighters, and they were hedgehopping very low to the ground all around us. In the evening we had pilots coming over to meet the nurses, and they told us how they hunted for the tents with red crosses on top.

About five days after Paris was liberated, the Eighth Field Hospital moved to Le Bourget Airfield. Finally, we were in buildings. Our patients usually came to us three to five days after being injured, and we prepared them for air evacuation. The hospital was an old school building with litter patients on the first floor and ambulatory patients on the second. The enlisted personnel were quartered on the third floor. Officers were quartered about a block away, at an inn, and we walked back and forth.

Stationed there was a platoon of about one hundred men and officers who handled litters for us and did various other jobs. The officers were white, but the enlisted men were black. They were great, and we worked well with them. There was also an ambulance company that worked around the clock, picking up patients coming in from the front at the train station. During the Battle of the Bulge, we shipped out close to seventeen hundred patients, and received about eight hundred more in one day. Approximately seventy-five thousand patients went through our hospital during the six months we were there, so we had to work well with everyone under those circumstances.

Our medical work was interesting. We had orders to exteriorate the gut when a patient had any gut surgery. With so many patients having abdominal surgery, some of the intestinal holes might be missed, so when patients finally reached the hospitals in England, their intestines were put back in. We did a lot of cast splitting, because of the chance of swelling. It could happen in a plane because of the pressure, and the cast might need to be pried loose. One poor patient I remember had fractures on arms, shoulders, and leg. He was in plaster basically from his neck to his feet. They had not made a hole for his stomach, and he couldn't eat much because of bloating. He was so relieved when we split his casts and opened the cast over his abdomen and buttocks and taped it so it didn't rub his skin.

Paris had a lot of entertainment for us to enjoy, and we often went downtown to the opera house in our free time. It was fantastic. Before the last act though, we all tried to rush out because they played the national anthems of France, United States, and Great Britain, and we had to stand at attention through all three.

Austin R. Grant, M.D. U.S. Army   **100th Evacuation Hospital**

Orders to report for duty came one week after Dr. Grant was married in September 1942. The 100th landed in England in February 1944 and on Omaha Beach in July and followed American troops across the Continent into Germany until the war's end.

The experience I had in the war was great training as I'd just finished my internship. I did everything a surgeon could do. We followed the First Army, then switched to the Third Army, staying right behind the fighting. We were in France, Luxembourg, Belgium, Holland, and Germany. A few of us surgeons, nurses, and technicians, volunteered to assist another hospital during the Battle of the Bulge and got as far as Malmedy, Belgium. We checked in and found everyone was retreating because the Germans were coming up the hill, so we left too. I later heard the doctors who were still operating were captured, but the nurses had been evacuated. At one time, we all had to jump into ditches because of the German advance.

On V-E Day the 100th was in a meadow at the River Elbe, waiting to join up with the Russians. Some fellows made a big victory bonfire to celebrate the occasion. We treated many prisoners, including several British soldiers who'd been captured back in 1940. There were displaced persons from Russia who didn't want to return. Our commander took us to the prison camps where we saw German guards burying the dead Jews. It was a horrible sight.

I was transferred to a station hospital in Luxembourg and was there on V-J Day. Hitler's yacht was available for trips on the Rhine River, and I went once while waiting for orders to return to the States.

When the 100th returned from Europe in 1945, members of the unit put together its history in a book filled with warm-hearted anecdotes, GI humor, and cartoons. The authors are Robert Hoenig and Robert Needleman, with cartoons by Joe Kiebzak. The following cartoons exhibit incidents shared by World War II nurses everywhere.

"NURSES ARRIVE AT MANEUVER AREA"

The first group of nurses had not been told what was in store for them when we were sent on maneuvers before leaving the states, so with characteristic female tendency, they came with Class A uniforms, evening gowns, high heeled shoes, and nylon hose. They accepted their fate with a minimum of grumbling and griping and within a week were veteran field soldiers.

Mr. Mouse became the object of a council of war among the tent-mates. Each nurse armed herself with a lethal weapon such as a hatchet, slipper, or hair brush, ready to sally forth prepared for mortal combat.

Nurses try to kill a mouse.

MAYOR WATCHING POP CORN POP

One of the many friends we made in Fleetwood (England) was the Mayor, His Worship, Tom Roberts, usually bedecked and behung with his golden oversized dogtags, emblematic of his office. His Worship was introduced to and initiated into the grand American custom of popping corn, among other mysteries of American Life. After seeing the little kernels increase to an edible size he was fearful of eating them. "What happens to them in my stomach?" he asked. "Do they still continue to pop in there?]

In France the Air Corps quickly discovered that the 100th had a group of charming, pleasant and beautiful nurses. Planes would buzz the area, frequently dropping notes by parachute to the girls asking for dates that evening. On one occasion, a cub plane flew over the area slowly and dropped a bouquet of flowers. An attached note read that, if able to go on a date that evening, a nurse was to wave a pair of pink panties. In less than two minutes, ten pairs were being waved vigorously and frantically in the hot summer breeze.

- NURSES RESPOND TO AIR CORPS

Viola Molloy U.S. Army

In July the Fifty-sixth General shipped over from England to France to set up a tent hospital. One of the hard things about working in a tent hospital was that the cots were so low we had to kneel by each one to keep from bending over all the time. Liege, Belgium, was our next destination, and we were glad it was a building instead of tents.

During the Battle of the Bulge in December we were so close to the fighting the patients had to be evacuated. They were just about to evacuate us nurses when the Germans retreated, and we stayed. The casualties came in so fast, nurses had to start blood transfusions, which only doctors had done before. Whatever needed to be done was done by everyone. There was no limit. I'll never forget those young patients, hurt so badly. I felt worse when I saw they were wearing a wedding ring.

Martha Vroeman U.S. Army   168th General Hospital

Martha was graduated from a Little Rock nursing school in her home state of Arkansas.

After three days on the *Queen Mary*, Winston Churchill, prime minister of Great Britain, appeared at our roll call in the auditorium of the ship. He gave a short speech and welcomed us to England. I'd been playing cards with Churchill's aides during the trip and was surprised to find out who they were and that he was on board.

We waited in England and went across the channel to France three months after D day. I'll never forget the sight at Omaha Beach of rows and rows of white crosses that marked the thousands of graves from the invasion that took place in June.

Our hospital was in St. Lô at first, but after a few months, we moved to a location near Reims, which was General Eisenhower's headquarters. German doctors from the University of Heidelberg worked with us in our tent hospital after they were captured. One of them spoke English very well and accompanied me to Catholic Mass often.

In May 1945 the Germans signed the surrender in Reims, and that night I stood with several other military people in front of "The Little Red Schoolhouse," the name given to the former education building where this all took place. In the middle of the night the Germans drove up in cars, and about 3:00 A.M. Ike arrived.

After that I was sent to Germany to pick up the American GIs who'd been in prison camps, and brought them back in ambulances to the hospital in Reims. The first man I spoke to was from Arkansas and was so glad to hear my Arkansas accent! He'd been shot in the arm and hadn't had any care while he was captured and was just skin and bones.

The Army Nurse

What is a nurse? the little boy asked
    As he walked in the hospital ward.
A nurse is one who takes care of the sick.
    Was his mother's quick reply.
But she was anxious to get to her husband's bed
    As she passed other visitors by.
The boy's father had come from a battlefield
    Where the enemy had left him to die.
He looked at his son who kept watching the nurse
    And a vision passed before his eye.
A nurse, so bright, was there that night
    They were bringing the litters in.
She was dressing men's wounds and easing
    Their pain not once . . . but again and again.
The man looked at his son who kept watching the nurse,
    And with a tear in his eye he said:
"A Nurse, my son, is so many things,
    She really is hard to define.
She's relief from pain, She's legs for the lame,
    And often she is eyes for the blind.
She's the one who can smile when the going gets tough.
    She takes Army life with a nod.
It's easy for her to be kind to these men,
    Because her Commanding Officer is God."

by Martha Vroeman R.N.
(written in France, 1945)

Florence Heermance Wiechman U.S. Army 217th General Hospital

The 217th was billeted in a cow pasture in France, requiring some adjustment for this city girl.

Crossing the English Channel in August 1944 was an experience I'll never forget. One hundred five nurses waited and waited on the dock, finally being told that all the cabins on the British ship were given out and we would sleep in the crews' mess hall, in the very bottom of the ship. With the cheery words, "We know what jolly good sports the American nurses are," they hustled us aboard and down several wall-mounted ladders to *E* deck. We slept in three layers. "Upper" was a hammock, "Middle" was on the crude wooden mess tables, and "Lower" was on the floor. I drew a spot on the floor by an open pipe which dripped water and smelled like sewer. We ate in this dungeon also, being served the same food the crew ate. Another nurse and I made friends with some American officers on *A* deck, who snitched food for us from the officers' mess.

It took three days to cross a distance of twenty miles. The commanding officers of the various units on board were said to be squabbling over who would get to be the first to land on Utah Beach in Normandy, even though the famous invasion was long over. When we did land, it was about midnight, in a cold rain. Then we waited several hours for transportation, without either raincoats or bedrolls, resting in the wet sand.

Our next stop was a cow pasture, literally. Being a city girl, it seemed wherever I turned there were cows in my way, even in the creek where we had to bathe and wash clothes. We had nothing to do for weeks, and the boredom magnified all the primitive details of our camp.

The latrine was unforgettable. At first we had a slit trench dug in the ground, about twelve inches wide. The idea was to straddle it and squat. It was raining everyday and water filled the trench, with mud all around. Surrounded by a wall of canvas, the latrine was open to the sky, and the Army Air Corps pilots loved to fly overhead and dip their wings at us or swoop low. One memorable day, our chief nurse made a visit to the trench, assumed the position, slipped in the mud, and fell "kerplunk" right into all that excreta. I have to tell you a bit about her before I go on. Absolutely no one got along with this woman, except the commanding officer, who was equally unpopular. Everyone called her Aunt Fanny, the traditional nickname for Frances, and it was synonymous with calling her an ass.

As news spread around the camp about Aunt Fanny's predicament, there were many cheers and, in the evening, several glasses were raised in celebration. Soon after her adventure a set of wooden privy seats was delivered to us nurses. What a sight: a twelve-holer, surrounded by canvas!

Our drinking water was from a lister bag, and purification tablets were dissolved in it, which made it taste strongly of chlorine. We were allowed one canteen of water each day and added lemon crystals from our K rations to help the taste. We usually ate K rations, which were small cardboard boxes filled with hardtack crackers, a tin of either cheese spread or potted meat, a fruit

Nurses cared for GIs on hospital trains bringing patients from the front lines to treatment in hospitals throughout the Continent.

bar made usually of ground raisins (on rare occasions ground dates), an envelope of lemon crystals, and envelopes of powdered coffee and sugar. Sometimes we had the dreaded D rations, which made K rations seem like a feast. D rations were only thick, heavy, sweet and strong chocolate bars, loaded with vitamins. If you gagged just trying to eat them, you could always dissolve them in hot water and have hot chocolate.

My pal, Aggie Flynn, and I walked along a country road one day in search of some normal food, and since we both spoke French, made a deal with a farmer's wife for tomatoes, potatoes, onions, and two pork chops. We hustled them back to our tent, made a small fire on the ground between our two cots, and cooked a sort of stew. All went well until the smoke seeped out through the tent seams. Naturally, Aunt Fanny came charging across the pasture and caught us enjoying our feast. "You can't eat food from the local farms," she shrieked. "It could be contaminated." We ate it.

Besides cows, we had apple trees. The apples were sour and not good for eating, but were grown for making Calvados and cider. Calvados is a bad-tasting alcoholic beverage, but the old lemon crystals helped the flavor when, on a few occasions we sat on the grass, at eventide, trying to create an officers-club atmosphere and chatting with the medical officers.

The army way of getting somewhere just to wait created an almost unbearable boredom among our camp. Singing was one of the few diversions, and having had voice training, I was often called upon to sing requests as we sat in front of our tents at twilight. We didn't just sing songs that were popular, either. Some clever nurse or GI would use the tunes everyone knew and make up words to show our feelings about the situations we were in or to express something about our jobs. The men made up words about women, and the nurses made up songs about men. Parodies of songs I remember singing over and over were to the tunes of "Bless Them All," "Mademoiselle from Armentiers" and "Roll Me Over in the Clover." The length of the song "Alouette" became so tiresome, but there was one doctor who would start it and, naturally, we couldn't drop it until all made-up verses covering the entire human anatomy were sung.

We were waiting to move into Paris after it was liberated from the Nazis, and in early September, we received orders to proceed in a truck convoy. Our unit was the first hospital to enter Paris, and our executive officer, Colonel Wiechman, asked my friend Aggie and me to ride in the lead jeep. I rode in the passenger seat, thus was the first American nurse to enter the "City of Light." We took over the old hospital, "1 'Hopital de Pitie" from the Nazis. I was later transferred to a hospital train unit and made many trips from the front [Battle of the Bulge] to Cherbourg.

167th General Hospital

*When deployed to the European theater, these four nurses were assigned to the 167th, stationed at Cherbourg. They wound up sharing an unforgettable twelve-day ride on a troop train through France, returning together to the States after the war. **Leviatha "Vi" Nelson Jones** hailed from New Mexico. **Janet Haddon Hoffmann** was from Madison, Wisconsin. **Florence "Brandy" Brandvold** and **June Noreen Norlin** were from Minnesota.*

Vi: Before going overseas I was stationed at Fort Riley, Kansas, with German prisoners as patients in the psycho ward, and a corpsman was to be with the nurse at all times. One of the older Germans, who spoke English, told me he learned to love the Americans during World War I, but the younger ones hated our guts. I often went around by myself, and he told me to have a GI with me because the young prisoners had scissors they were going to use to kill me. So I reported this to the captain, who had an inspection, and they did find the scissors. I never knew which one hated me so much, but then I knew they just hated us on general principles, and always had my GI with me. One night a huge fire erupted in the barracks at a camp that adjoined Fort Riley, and we all watched it burning. I can remember the look on the Germans' faces while we were watching, and they said to us, "That's the Germans. They have come and are going to liberate us." They were always very arrogant.

Janet: On our way to Europe, an enemy sub was sunk while we were at sea, and everyone cheered. Nothing was scary when we were in our twenties. The GIs were down in the hold of the ship, and it was a hell hole. It stank, and once a day they could come up on deck for a little while. I felt so sorry for them because we ate nice meals in the dining room, and they had to eat K rations down below.

Brandy: Our chief nurse of the 167th was something to remember. On the ship going to Europe, she made us do calisthenics every single day, and we were the only ones on the ship doing it. When it came time to cross the English Channel in the LSTs, she directed us to wear Class A uniforms. We had to wait for the tide to go out to disembark, so we could go ashore in skirts. We were told not to wear raincoats, but it rained and rained and rained.

Still in our Class A uniforms, we slept on the ground in tents and pooled our blankets. Later when we met nurses from other units, they said, "You are the ones who came off in your Class A uniforms." The other nurses all seemed to have slacks.

Janet: After landing in England, we crossed the channel into France. Our first stop was a cow pasture, where hundreds and hundreds of nurses waited until sent on to the hospitals. I'll never forget the shower arrangement that was quickly erected for us in one huge tent where a hundred people could take a shower at once. The weather was so cold that we just went in and out as quickly as possible. The tent came to a peak, with a hole at the top, and one day I looked up and saw a GI sitting up in a tree watching us through the hole.

I don't think I've ever been so cold, even though I was from Wisconsin and had nurse's training in Minnesota. We were always cold, so five of us shared two or three blankets, sleeping together for warmth, though the ones on the ends were always shivering.

Our destination was Cherbourg, and the 167th was just a few blocks from the beach, where there were remnants of German or French guns. We could go almost anywhere, and all we had to do was walk to the road and American GIs would take us there. Local people didn't have much, but when we ate in town, they really could make marvelous things with the GI rations.

I was a nurse anesthetist, with five of us working under one doctor. The operating room was in a Nissan hut but had marvelous equipment. We lived in tents, and the patients were in tents, so we thought the huts were first class. Most of our patients were Germans, and I remember getting one of them ready for surgery one day. We were all talking to each other, thinking he couldn't understand, and then I asked him in German to count, "Ein, zwei, drei." He answered, in English, "One, two, three." We were embarrassed. I have a German dogtag that came off one of those patients.

Our chief nurse treated us like we were her "cross to bear." She was very paranoid about us doing anything illegal or immoral and couldn't have been more wrong. She hated that the doctors were in charge of anesthetists, because she wanted to rank all the nurses. It really griped her when I received a perfect rating and was promoted to first lieutenant.

Vi: Again in France, I treated mostly German patients. I didn't have any trouble there but remember some nice ones. I dated a captain, who had an older German prisoner as a "man Friday" to take care of his quarters. He made beautiful things, and I still have a wine set he made out of shells, engraved, "Cherbourg, France, 1945." He was also a tailor. I didn't have a bathing suit to take to the Riviera when I went on a pass, and he told me to bring a pair of panties, a brassiere, and some material, and he would make one for me. I gave him one of my brown-and-white seersucker dresses, and he sewed a really snazzy swimsuit.

I have pictures of the French women who had fraternized with the Germans. Their heads were shaved by the townspeople. We walked on the beach near Cherbourg, though I don't know how come we didn't get blown up. There were leftover mines all over. We weren't supposed to

Tents and Quonset huts at the 167th GH near Cherbourg.

fraternize with enlisted men, but we liked them, and one of the places we all could go was to the beach.

General Eisenhower came to inspect the hospital once, and the German prisoners shined everything spotless. Some of them admired him very much and wanted to see him, but he was late. Since they weren't allowed to work more than four hours at a time, they were disappointed when they missed him. But, Ike put his arm around my shoulder and told me what a nice ward I had. I was thrilled!

We had a ward with displaced persons from Romania, Lithuania, and many different countries. They had diphtheria, and you name it, they had it. It was hard to communicate in all these languages, but I'm from New Mexico and spoke a wee bit of Spanish. So I talked to a Spanish man, who would talk to an Italian, and he would try to talk to the Romanian, and we just hoped the message got through somehow.

The first time we went into Cherbourg to shop, one of the GI patients asked if I could speak French. When I told him I didn't, he said he would teach me some things to say. So we practiced these words, and when I went into one of the stores, I said to the man who owned it, "Voulez-vous coucher avec moi?" He said, "Oh, mademoiselle, I speak English." I later learned that I had asked him to sleep with me.

At times it was so cold there that my tentmate and I slept together on a cot, so we could share our blankets. There was a little potbellied stove that we had to scrounge around to find wood for. Every month we received a ration of two fifths of liquor, and I traded mine with the GIs, a jigger at a time, to chop my wood.

We were issued two blankets apiece, and it wasn't enough. One of my GI patients ran a very high temperature, and they couldn't find out what was wrong. They ran every test in the world, and every day it stayed high. So they decided to send him to England, and then probably back to the States. Just before he was to leave he gave me his two blankets and I was thrilled to get them. When the doctor was checking him out of the ward, he asked me, "Lieutenant, have you ever taken his temperature rectally?" I told him that I hadn't but would do it right away, and the patient sat up and said, "It's over!" He had another thermometer, and whenever we tested him, he would heat up the other one with a cigarette or something so his temp was always high. Since there wasn't anything wrong with him, he was sent back to the front lines, and I had to give him the two blankets back.

After all these years, certain patients still come to mind, and I often wonder what happened to this one baby. He was such a young, little kid, and his poor, little face was so drawn. He had been in the front lines for a long time. He was autistic and wouldn't say a thing. I've often wondered what became of him.

June: Our patients were German prisoners, and I remember the young Hitler Youth were pretty defiant. They told us Chicago had been bombed and refused to believe us when we told them otherwise. We were told not to fraternize with the enemy at all as our GIs would be demoralized, after seeing their buddies killed.

I was fortunate to get to Paris for R&R, where the opera and theaters continued performing throughout the war. I saw *Faust, Sleeping Beauty,* and *Afternoon of a Fawn.*

One tentmate was in love with an officer whose parents sent a lovely diamond ring through the mail. We packed her flannel nightgown for a trousseau and sent her off on a honeymoon to Cherbourg after the wedding. She left a few months later when morning sickness began.

Janet: After V-E Day our unit was put on a train to Marseilles so we could be shipped out to the Pacific. It took twelve days by train for us to go about six hundred miles. We were always side-lined because we didn't have priority, and our train was stopped all the time to let other trains through. I had more fun on that train. Coming through Paris, we were stopped on a siding next to a fruit train, which the boys raided, and we all just filled ourselves with the most wonderful fruit. The Commanding Officer had to pay someone on the other train for everything we took. At lunch they set up mess tents, and we ate along the side of the tracks, always making it a lot of fun. Whenever we stopped along the way, which seemed to be always, we took cups from our mess kits and ran into whatever town it was and bought a cupful of wine. If we had to move, the engine would toot, and everyone would come running. It was a ball. In the morning, we woke up and ran with our helmets to get hot water from the engine to wash our faces and clothes.

June: That train ride from Cherbourg to Marseilles was one of my most awesome experiences. I can never forget it. The worst part of it for me was that I was menstruating, and being on the crowded train made everything messy and exasperating. Before we left the States we were told to bring diapers with us, in case disposable sanitary pads were not available. These took up a lot of the space in my musette bag, which I carried over my shoulder along with the canteen, purse, and everything else. When we got to France there were Kotex pads available in little packages, and they were very compact so that we had to fluff them out.

Twelve days on a train from Cherbourg to Marseilles were memorable for the 167th GH nurses after V-E Day. Long chow lines along the track and local vineyards broke up some of the boredom.

The bathroom on the train was just a hole in the floor, not to be used while the train was standing still, which seemed to be most of the time. There was no privacy in our little compartment, where we were squeezed in with all of our equipment. We stretched out on the floor, or anywhere available when we couldn't sit up. We often sat on the little boarding steps while the train was moving because it went so slowly, but we'd be covered with soot, and our faces were black. The enlisted men rode in "40 and 8s," which were train cars that could hold forty men and eight horses.

Janet: When we finally arrived in Marseilles, there were thousands of people there waiting to go to the Pacific. Lines for food were extremely long. We were housed at an old riding academy until we got our shots, then were sent to a small town called Eden Roc. All we did was sightsee, swim, and sun in the Riviera, went to a bullfight, and saw a show with Bob Hope and Jerry Colona. As always, there were lists in the latrines to sign up for parties. Different groups, like engineers, would send a notice that read, "Need 30 girls for party on this date." Thirty would sign up, a truck came to take us to the party, and the truck brought us back by curfew. It was fun, and it was safe.

Bastille Day, on July 14, was one of the most fun times I ever had. Coming home from a party in a jeep, we had to drive through several towns. Everyone was celebrating, and the towns were close together so it was like one big celebration. The local people were in the streets, dancing and drinking, so we would stop, get out and dance and then go on to the next town and do the same thing. It was so much fun. By this time, the curfew wasn't held too strictly.

Everyone griped about going to CBI (China, Burma, India theater). It was part of life to gripe. It was healthy to gripe, and if you didn't gripe, it meant you weren't healthy. We were still in France for V-J Day, so then we didn't have to go to the CBI.

Vi: Marseilles was a wild place to be on V-J Day. That whole town went wild, with dancing on the streets, and everyone drinking their hearts out. It was the wildest bunch of people on earth. Everyone was hugging, and there were fights. It was wild, wild, wild!

Janet: The return to the States was faster because we didn't have to worry about subs, but the chief nurse never let up her suspicions. Friends tell me that she came to my bed, thinking I was up on deck doing something wrong, and pulled the cover back. I slept through it. We landed in the

States the same day my mother was buried. I just couldn't get home any faster, though I knew about her death.

Looking back it was a wonderful time. Never had so many boyfriends and so much fun, despite the seriousness of why we were there.

Allied troops invaded Southern France in August 1944, and medical groups that had been through the battles of North Africa, Sicily, and Italy followed northward into France.

Virginia Grabowski Shannon U.S. Army

In October 1944 we were ready for the invasion of Southern France. A transport ship took us from Naples to Marseilles, then we went by train all the way through to Mirecourt, about twenty-five miles south of Nancy. There was no resistance because the Allies were attacking from the north. We expected to be based at Lyon but just kept going until we were only ten miles behind the lines. Again, we were in a hospital that had not been finished, but it had a big red cross on it. On Christmas Eve 1944 I was in my bunk when we were bombed. One girl went crazy, screaming through the building. My heart was pounding, and of course I had no idea what was hit or how much damage was done. We were near a railroad depot, which was what they were aiming at.

There were so many casualties from the battles. Wounded and injured were brought in from the Rhine, and as fast as we could evacuate them, more were brought in. It was nothing for us to evacuate two hundred to three hundred patients, and get three hundred to four hundred right on top of that during the Battle of the Bulge. Being young and having a purpose, we could work twenty-four hours a day. We had to learn a lot of things right on the spot. When there wasn't a doctor there to do it, the nurses did it. I did blood transfusions, intravenous medications, and even sewed up secondary closure wounds.

German prisoners worked in the hospital, and they acted like they didn't understand us. Outside the operating rooms were bulletins posted telling the progress of the war. One day I saw them clustered around the bulletin, reading it and talking to each other. So, in English, I told them I was glad to know they understood, and they couldn't get out of anything after that. I remember some were only seventeen years old, and very handsome. Among the German prisoners were doctors and nurses from the University of Strasbourg Hospital.

Everyone in the town skied because a snowy hill was right there. I managed to find a pair and left them outside the back door of the operating room. During free time we would just change our clothes and go to the snow.

Nuns did our laundry, as they needed the money. I'll always have the picture of a nun riding a bicycle down a road with her habit flying behind her, and this big, white, starched head cover on, flapping in the breeze. The people stuffed old worn out bicycle tires with paper, or whatever they could find, because they couldn't replace the tires.

The man I had become engaged to was killed in the Battle of the Bulge. He was an engineer who'd been putting up temporary bridges for the troops to move across. On New Years Eve he and a driver were coming back from the front and were strafed by a plane. A few months later, just before the war ended, I came home because my father was quite ill, and the war was winding down.

Esther Edwards U.S. Army

The invasion of Southern France began, and the Tenth landed right behind the troops, who were moving very fast. The rains really came down in October 1944, and the whole countryside was a sea of mud. We sank to our ankles every time we stepped outside, but the engineers made wooden floors for our tents. We had many patients, including French soldiers and civilians. We traveled by convoy, and once our truck picked up a hitchhiker carrying a gunny sack over his shoulder. We asked what was in the sack, and he explained that he was part of the French underground and was taking the remains of his buddy back home. He departed near Lyon with his burden.

In Strasbourg we were housed in university buildings. The Germans left behind patients who could not be moved, so we had to care for them. A few German doctors and nurses were taken captive, and I was startled once to hear a nurse reporting, "Heil Hitler," before she left the building.

The local people in Strasbourg were French citizens but spoke German, and there were many German sympathizers who were barely civil to us Americans. The Americans took over the home of a German couple who had refused to return to Germany, and one night I went there with some other officers before the couple moved out. They served us in their living room, and we listened to their radio. A few days later, when they moved out, the local people threatened them, and they hanged themselves. Refugees were everywhere in France, as in Italy and Sicily. They walked for miles, taking whatever they could carry or load on a cart. Food and medicine were scarce.

We eventually were able to rest, and I went to Paris on a three-day pass with another nurse. We were stopped several times by the MPs and asked to give the password of the day. If we didn't know it, we were asked about baseball teams until we could come up with some answers. A Jewish doctor with our unit had relatives in Paris and asked us to deliver food to them while we were there. They hid out during the war, and we had to be very "hush hush." We found the address he gave us, a man opened the door, and we gave him the food. He was reluctant to talk, but we felt we had accomplished something important.

In France the Tenth Field Hospital moved constantly, following the troops fighting the Battle of the Bulge. We moved from buildings to tents, and back to buildings, depending on where we were. Sometimes the patients had to be moved from one floor to another for surgery, which was a hard job for the corpsmen. A few French nurses were attached to our unit for a while. Near Saint Avold, the Allies fired artillery shells over our building, then the German artillery answered back, over the hospital again. Some shells fell short and landed close to us, but luckily we were never hit. One nurse was using her helmet to bathe when the firing came too close, so she dumped out the water, put the helmet on her head, and sat there naked until the firing stopped.

Patients came by ambulance and helicopter all day and night. It was overwhelming. When I tried to rest, I couldn't sleep, thinking of all those wounded patients and all that needed to be done for them. There were some I cannot forget to this day, like one whose leg was amputated, and when he was told, he was so furious he wanted to die. There was little we could do to comfort him. Another man's jaw was nearly blown off and he needed more care than was available in our field hospital, so we hurriedly evacuated him to a larger one. Some developed kidney failure from shock and injuries, and died because there was nothing we could do for them there.

GERMANY

"V-E Day"

Esther Edwards U.S. Army

The Tenth moved from France into Germany, following the fierce battles of the Seventh Army. They were moving fast, and the patients were coming in even faster. We lost the most patients then, and were getting the men right off the battlefield. In Aschaffenburg our hospital was located on a hill, and we could see the fighting below. Very badly wounded patients were being brought in, including German children. Some German soldiers who were patients refused intravenous treatment because they didn't trust us. During April 1945 my platoon moved five times. We had a hard time keeping up with the troops. On April 28 we crossed the Danube River and arrived in the town of Dachau. That's where we were when we heard the war was over. Right after that, an American soldier was brought in with a bullet wound and died. He'd been shot by his own gun when a German soldier who was taken prisoner took it away from him. It was so tragic.

We were all so relieved that the war was over, after what we'd been through the last three years. I couldn't find enough words to express how I felt. I had said many times that when the war ended, I would cry for all the soldiers who had such terrible wounds, and who had died. One night a friend came from another unit. We drank some wine, and that night I cried for the men. It was a long night. Some of us went to the nearby concentration camp at Dachau, which had been taken by the Forty-fifth Division only a few days before. We saw the horrible barracks and the crematorium, where there was a room filled almost to the ceiling with bodies, waiting to be burned. Bodies were everywhere, hundreds of them. It was unbelievable.

There were some freed prisoners still there, waiting to be processed, and hundreds were dying every day from starvation, cholera, and typhus.

German guards had put on prisoner clothing when they were taken over, and they were captured and being held. It was so awful that I had nightmares later. Three American hospital units were there, trying to bring order. After a couple of weeks' rest in Munich, we moved into Camp Dachau. We lived in rooms in barracks where the prison guards had lived, and were quite comfortable. The whole camp was extremely depressing. We were there a month.

Most of the patients had been prisoners in the camp and were not able to move, and many had no place to go. They died every day from malnutrition, dysentery, and tuberculosis. Mostly German and Polish, the patients were difficult to communicate with. They hid what they could not eat for fear they would get no more. They were just skin over bones.

From the time the war ended, a lot of people from our hospital were getting orders to return to the States, and what was left of our platoon went home by ship in October. I was discharged in New Jersey, and just before boarding the train for Kokomo, Indiana, one of the nurses patted me on the back. She said, "My heart is as heavy as that pat on the back." We both realized we would not be seeing one another again, and it was sad to leave people who had become as close as members of my family.

The Tenth Field Hospital was awarded seven battle stars. No other hospital received as many in World War II.

Grace G. Peterson U.S. Army

In March 1945 we went by ambulances from France into Germany, crossing the Rhine on a pontoon bridge. White material to indicate surrender floated from the windows on the other side. We went to Bielefeld, near the British sector. There we received one thousand ex-POWs as patients. They were mostly Russian, and about one hundred Poles. We put them in tents but couldn't really do much for them. They had been prisoners for years and were literally skin and bones. We couldn't give them hypodermic without hitting a bone. It was something. We took chest X-rays, and at least half of them had tuberculosis. They were absolutely starved, and hoarded the food we gave them, so their cots had to be searched about twice a week. We gave them fresh oranges, and they didn't know what they were.

After V-E Day we were moved by 40-and-8 train cars to Southern France. I was sent to Biarritz, where we set up a hospital in a hotel. Troops were sent to Biarritz to attend classes taught by college professors. This was apparently meant to keep people busy while they awaited being shipped off to the Pacific theater. When we could be shipped back to the States, we left from Marseilles.

RUSSIA

"The Eastern Command"

Lucile Rosedale Tubbs U.S. Army

Ninetieth General Hospital

"Rosie" joined up in 1942 in Atlantic City and by 1944 was working with the Ninetieth General in England.

I wanted to get into some kind of duty other than a general hospital and requested a transfer. It was all top secret when twelve of us were sent to the Ukraine, attached to the Air Corps. We knew we were going to what was then Russia, and I was really excited. I wanted adventure.

There were three bases in the Eastern Command, with four nurses at each one. I was at Piryatin, a fighter base. Missions came in from England and Italy, and we waited with ambulances at the field for the planes. The planes were usually running low on fuel after bombing places in Germany or Poland, and the pilots had to find our little base in this flat, flat country.

The first mission was the most exciting. The planes came zooming in, over the hospital area and the field, circling around before landing. The pilots stepped out of the plane, then stepped out of their flight suits, and were in Class A, dress uniforms. The Russians were there in fancy uniforms, and everyone had cameras. There were ceremonies, parties, and almost more than we could handle. It was really something.

The same thing was happening at the other bases, because this great plan had been in the works for I don't know how long, and everyone was excited that it had been accomplished. The first mission went smoothly and there were no casualties. The second mission brought wounded men on a B-17 that had been shot up. Our base was the first one they came to as they flew in from Germany.

That second night, we had air raid warnings, and here came the Germans. They flew over our base and went to Poltava and bombed and

193

strafed. The B-17s were there, all lined up, and the Germans shot them up. There were casualties all over.

The next day, I flew up to Poltava to help out. It was so sad to see the damaged airplanes and buildings. That was the first time we used the cemetery, and I have always wondered if the Americans' bodies are still buried there.

During one bombing raid, the Germans dropped a lot of little parachutes with mines on them. Our GIs ran out of the air raid trenches to pick them up for souvenirs, in the dark. Surprisingly, none of them were hurt.

There was a little village near our base, and each morning the women came out with rakes over their shoulders, singing together, and went off to the fields to work. In the evening, they came back, still singing, with their hoes and rakes over their shoulders. On the base, Russians worked in the kitchen, the laundry, and did guard duty.

If we went off base, we were told not to go far, because local Russians wouldn't know we are Americans, and might think we are Germans. One day an American fellow walked into our base, and we were just flabbergasted. He'd been shot down somewhere and burned badly. The Russians didn't treat him well, because they thought he was a German. We don't know how he found us.

The GIs went to the village to meet girls. They must have had some experiences because they came into the hospital with venereal disease. Penicillin was new then and saved a lot of lives. Sometimes we had wounded Russian soldiers as patients, and their doctors didn't believe they would live. But we gave them penicillin, and they kept on living.

Our water came from a lister bag and tasted awful. The only good thing we had from the Russians was their bread. Most of us wrote home to have our mothers send Lipton's Chicken Noodle Soup. It smelled wonderful when it was cooking, and we'd give it to the really ill patients. Everyone else was jealous.

We all had swimsuits, and one afternoon I was swimming in the river with the other girls when two truckloads of Russian soldiers came and started stripping down to nothing. They saw us but didn't care. You never saw three women get out of the water so fast, back into the jeep, and back to the base.

Our outdoor shower was just shower heads with canvas around the outside for a wall. We went together to the shower at 4:00 in the afternoon, and almost every day a little plane circled overhead. We knew why he was there.

Florence Jacobs U.S. Army   **Third Station Hospital**

While stationed with the Third in England, "Jake" asked for a transfer and quickly found herself on the way to Russia.

Just before the D day invasion, in June 1944, I received orders to report to Air Force Headquarters in London, as soon as possible. The assignment was "Top Secret," signed by General Eisenhower. I left the Third Station Hospital in Tidwell, England, not knowing where I was going. The whole thing was so secret, when I went to the office of the head surgeon, instead of telling me where I was going he pulled out a map and silently pointed to it.

I had to get shots quickly, and when the nurse asked where I was going, I said I didn't know. She said, "I've had a lot like that," and gave me every shot she could. From London I took a train to Penzance, staying in a hotel where most of the people were civilians. They were intelligence people, and no one was talking to anyone else.

My first plane ride was in a converted B-24. As we flew out over the Bay of Biscayne, radios silent, they taught me to use a Gibson-Girl radio*, in case we crashed and I wound up in the water. An intelligence officer traveled with me. We stopped in Casablanca, where the French were celebrating the Normandy invasion, and then to Cairo. A C-46 took us to Iraq, then to Teheran, Iran. We couldn't go on without a Russian pilot, so we waited about two weeks. Finally, the Russian pilot was ready, and we flew across the Caspian Sea into the Ukraine.

We were there to set up bases and hospitals at Poltava, Mirgorod, and Piryatin, in the Ukraine. Apparently, President Roosevelt and Stalin cooked up this project so the American planes could bomb Germany and go straight east to land in Russia. They wouldn't have to turn around and meet the German fighters. It didn't really work, because the second night I was there, the Germans bombed our bases, and for several nights after that.

I was stationed at Mirgorod, where the hospital was just a few tents at the edge of the airfield. When they bombed us, we moved the hospital hurriedly into the protection of the woods. Other nurses were there already, and I was a replacement for one who'd left after becoming ill.

---

* The Gibson-Girl radio was indented in the middle and wide on the top and bottom. It was named after the women with cinched-in waists made famous in drawings by Gibson.

This area in the Ukraine had been occupied by the Germans, and most of the buildings were destroyed. The Americans put down a runway using steel mats. The main street of the village was intact, the church was open, and there was a Russian military hospital. Russian soldiers came to Mirgorod for recuperation because it was an area with mineral spas.

Our doctors helped the Russians, but they wouldn't let any of us nurses go. The Russian nurses came to the river near us and washed the linens on rocks in the river. Russians did most of our housekeeping and guarding. To their amazement, we had a washing machine. The laundress was Russian, and she was the talk of the village. She would fill up the washing machine, then sit on a couple of bags of dirty laundry, and read *Pravda*. We called her "Queen of the Laundry."

Once I missed some of my slips, and when I asked the interpreter about them, she told me the laundress took them to the village to show the other women. She told them we weren't really workers, but aristocrats, because we wore satin underwear under our dresses.

They had a hard time understanding who we were. Because they thought we were aristocrats, they treated us with greater respect than was necessary. Our men had fun with this, and when the Russians were around, they treated us with great deference. It was a big joke. If we drove up in a jeep, a couple of the men would rush over to lift us out. Otherwise, we jumped out the best we could.

Averill Harriman was ambassador to Moscow then, and his daughter, Kathleen, came to visit, inviting the nurses to Moscow. We went two at a time, staying in the ambassador's residence, and they took us places, like the theater. We rode the subway and walked around the Kremlin. The people seemed to be cut off from the rest of the world and just stared and followed us. They were almost childlike, touching our uniforms and admiring our shoes. The ambassador invited us to a luncheon where there were several news correspondents, and they seated us in between aides so we couldn't be questioned. We were carefully briefed and warned not to talk about our assignment.

Germans had been out of Mirgorod long enough for the Russians to plant crops. We arrived in summer, and there were fields of wheat and sunflowers. The weather was very hot then, but by the time I left in October, it was very cold, especially at night. The Chief Surgeon in London knew we only had trench coats to wear, and not knowing how long we would be there, he had a London tailor make up heavy coats for us. We were back in London before they were finished and received them there. They were beautiful, melton wool, dress overcoats, and the pockets were lined with white velvet.

My grandmother was from Russia, and when I was a kid I picked up a few words from her. Once I overheard a Russian officer talking about something, which I passed on to our intelligence people, who passed it on to England. The Russians knew everything before we did, and a lot of our people were really intelligence officers, there to find out where the Russians got their information.

I have since found out that the Russians had dossiers on each one of us. A few years ago, I met a woman whose husband was with our group. She applied to go on a trip to Russia with the League of Women Voters and was refused a visa, supposedly because of her husband's experience. I believe the real reason we were there was because President Roosevelt was trying to get information on what the Russians had done about moving their industry east of the Ural Mountains.

When we left in October 1944, we were told this was a personal project of the president and these were our allies. By this time we were pretty sour on the Russians but were told to keep our mouths shut. On the way back to London we stayed overnight in Naples, and the hotel had a room for everyone but me. While I waited for them to get a room ready, an American officer said, "Too bad. Come in the bar and have a drink with me." I did, and he began to ask a lot of prying questions, which I didn't answer. Finally, he said, "You passed," and showed me his identification card. He was with Intelligence, and it was all staged.

Back in London I was assigned to the Air Corps, staying in England until the war was over. We were awarded the Bronze Star for our service in Russia.

166TH GENERAL HOSPITAL

"Raining again"

While stationed at Camp Ellis, Illinois, in 1944, Captain Shirley Payne Sweet was asked to form the 166th General Hospital, enlisting nurses from army camps in Illinois and Wisconsin and preparing them for deployment overseas. Several nurses in the 166th relate here what they experienced together, from basic training, to the trip on the Queen Elizabeth across the Atlantic, to the actual work they joined the army for, treating wounded soldiers. After being together for a year under the most demanding and, yet, satisfying circumstances, mixed emotions are explored as these gentle women were separated from each other because of the war's end. Tying these memories together are excerpts of original letters of one nurse, Lorraine Krause Taylor. Her letters exemplify what army life was like, what she didn't want family at home to worry about, and the comradeship, humor, sisterhood, spirit, language, and attitude of the young women of this era.*

Lorraine Krause Taylor U.S. Army

During basic training, this redhead was nicknamed "Torchy" by her new friends. In the next year-and-a-half of army service, she traveled around the world and every week faithfully wrote letters to her family in Chicago. Excerpts follow:

> *May 1944, Camp McCoy, Wisconsin.*
> *Dear Family, Was met at the train station by a soldier with an army truck that had seats, but no springs. We have double deck bunks—think I will sleep upstairs. I need a formal gown for the dances on Saturday nights.*

They gave us shots for tetanus, typhoid & smallpox all in one arm. Went swimming Sunday and am real sunburned. Monday we started training - classes, drill, calisthenics. Glad I brought my Ouija board.* It's getting a real workout. Received the white dress. Send white slippers and beaded bag. They taught us how to salute today! Love, Lorraine

*Ouija: Lighthearted board game popular during WWII that gives telepathic messages. Vibrations from fingers cause planchette to move around board and answer questions.

June 1944: Our schedule is class, calisthenics, class, drill, lunch, class, more drill, class. I look like an Indian from being outside so much. Look in the department stores for summer beige suits for army nurses. And hat. And if they will send it C.O.D. Also olive drab dresses. The army is going to issue them, but don't know when. All the girls are crazy about the Ouija Board.

I signed up to have a War Bond taken out of my check each month, and an allotment for the family. They give us $21 a month for expenses, and then charge $1.25 a day for meals. Also have to pay for laundry.
Love, Lorraine

July 1944: [After a weekend at home] *When I went back on the ward, a yell went out, "Red is back from Chicago!" Everyone either calls me "Torchy" or "Red." Guess why? Col. Blanchfield, head of the ANC, is arriving today from Washington, so we are getting all cleaned up. Had a letter from a nurse in France—says that the boys need all the prayers that can be offered for them.*

Have been going to dances every Saturday night. Sunday we go swimming and have a weinie roast afterward. The hospital personnel go on a road march every Thurs. nite now—it is quite a mob! About 300 nurses, besides the M.D.s, dentists, administration people, wardboys, etc., and you should see our dust! Whew! Have beer and sandwiches after.

There are Japanese prisoners here in a separate compound that is guarded by dogs. Their hospital ward is locked and the nurses can't go in without armed guards.

Forty girls were alerted to leave, but have been put back to work. They sat around ten days waiting orders. One of the men I know stopped to see me just before he shipped out. He had been very anxious to go but when it came right down to leaving, I could see he was sorta' "pale around the gills." He's with the infantry, and those fellows know what their chances are of coming back alive, let alone in one whole piece. Love, Lorraine

August 1944: A lot of excitement around here. Nurses are leaving for various assignments, but we are definitely going to the 166th. Some girls left Tues. nite by plane. They said they were going east, but their luggage went west, so maybe they will get it some day. Don't think we'll be here next Sunday.

Went through the gas chamber again yesterday, and was exposed to chlorine gas. You should see the clothes. Shoe laces faded white, brown slacks spotted and bleached and some girls' undies faded. It sure penetrates. All leaves have been canceled for now. We were told to be sure to make out a will and power of attorney. Don't know what I need one for, but orders are orders. Will write more when I can. Love, Lorraine

Shirley Payne Sweet U.S. Army   Chief Nurse

Called to active duty from Marlette, Michigan, in 1941, marrying in 1942, Shirley volunteered to go overseas when her husband left for duty in Europe in June 1944. She was asked to take over the position of chief nurse for the 166th General Hospital.

Uniforms were hard to come by, and getting them for my nurses was a great challenge. Before the war we wore blue suits and hats and our own white uniforms and school caps to work in. A wrap-around dress was issued later, which was tan-and-white striped seersucker. Early in the war, nurses weren't issued a complete uniform. The new color was called olive drab, then an off-white summer dress uniform came out. There was also a one-piece dress, one was navy and the other was off-white. We didn't take these light-colored items overseas. Most of us were able to write home and have things sent to us, like stockings and even uniform items.

Once when I was still in the States, I was asked to be military escort for Marlene Dietrich, and I didn't have the complete uniform set. Jackets and skirts didn't always come at the same time, so I borrowed pieces from other nurses to make up an "official" uniform. We picked Miss Dietrich up at the train station and drove back to camp. The only words I remember her saying to me were, "That's not a very attractive uniform, is it?" I think it was a sympathetic statement, but I was already feeling pretty dowdy sitting beside the very fashionable Marlene. At the end of the day she and I were standing together, and I overheard a soldier say, "I'll take the nurse anytime." I felt vindicated.

I'll always be thankful we had time to visit New York City from Camp Kilmer in New Jersey, because we were able to purchase wool slacks for our trip. By the time we were ready to ship out, things were happening fast in Europe, faster than the army's quartermaster could keep up with. I expected to be issued field clothing before we left the States, but when it was apparent we wouldn't get anything, I advised the nurses to buy slacks to wear as uniforms. We all paid for them ourselves.

Helen Wenning U.S. Army

Helen graduated from University of Michigan nursing school, worked in California and Alaska a few years, then returned to Detroit in 1943 to become an army nurse.

When I left Camp Ellis to join the 166th and go overseas, we had German prisoners as patients. There were two German doctors to care for these patients and one American doctor to oversee them. One of the German doctors was every bit as fine to work with as our own, but the second was a dyed-in-the-wool Nazi. He had an intense dislike to having a woman give him any orders, which I had to do.

Lorraine Krause Taylor U.S. Army

September 1944, Camp Kilmer, New Jersey:
Dear Family, We are on the East Coast at a busy camp. It is quite different here. It is REAL ARMY compared to the last camp. Met a 1st Lt. the second night here, and have gone out with him every night. Everyone is out for a good time before they go overseas.

Went to New York City and saw the sights. One of our girls fell when we were leaving to get into the trucks, and broke her leg. The worst part is that my Ouija board predicted it the second day we were at Camp McCoy. We all laughed, but it worried her, and that was the first thing everyone thought of when she fell.

Mailed a package to myself yesterday. In case I don't get back, you are to take it to a commissioned officer to be opened. We don't know where we are going, but they say it won't be too bad. Hope they know what they are talking about! Went on a road march the other day that turned out to be a dilly. We waded through water up to our knees and in real deep mud, over tree trunks and finally scrambled up a hill. We were a mess, but it was fun. Will write more soon. Love, Lorraine

Fannie Kasmer Bruner U.S. Army

While working in Michigan, a bill to draft nurses was before the Congress, and Fannie joined up to beat the draft. The bill failed, but she and classmate Violet Raiche were already in the army.

Basic training included long hikes, where the tallest women were in the lead to set the stride. Being only five-feet tall, I always had to double-time to keep up. I remember having a drill on the side of a mock-up ship, where we had to climb down rope netting, wearing helmets and fatigues. The woman under me froze from fear and refused to move. I couldn't go around her or anything and stepped on her helmeted head several times, and finally, she went down.

When we left Southampton to cross the English Channel, we left the dock in tugboats and had to jump from a tugboat onto another boat. They tossed our bedrolls into the bottom of the boat, then we jumped on top of the bedrolls. When the water made the boats come together, we jumped, then waited, and more would jump when the boats came together again. Short legs didn't make it too easy, and we lost a couple of bedrolls, but didn't lose a nurse.

Jean Kolczak Sciora U.S. Army

Jean joined the army in 1943 after receiving a degree in Physical Therapy from Northwestern University.

Basic training was the worst time for me because I was not athletic at all. My future husband was one of the sergeants who drilled us, and we really didn't like each other yet. He thought I was pretty clumsy.

The hardest thing for me was climbing down the rope ladder, called "Jacob's ladder," when we had to practice abandoning ship. I didn't like heights to start with and went down with my eyes closed. There was a moat around the mock-up ship, and our chief nurse was in a boat with some GIs to help us get into the boat. People stepped on my fingers, head, and shoulders as they passed me. I didn't know I was at the bottom until I heard Captain Sweet say, "Lieutenant Kolczak, open your eyes and put your foot in the boat!"

On the *Queen Elizabeth,* I asked for the bottom bunk, and was that a big mistake. All the others were seasick, except me. What a mess! The toilet, sink, and bathtub were used as receptacles, and some didn't quite make it in time.

Another test of my agility was when we crossed the English Channel to France. We had to jump from a big boat into small ones that were very greasy and dirty. Waves made the boats bounce against each other, and I waited a long time to jump. There were a lot of catcalls and jeers, but I laughed last because some who'd been teasing me jumped too quickly into the small boat and slid on their butts from one end of the boat to the other, through the grease.

Myrtle Brethouwer Hoftiezer U.S. Army

Mert took the army physical in Wisconsin with a classmate, hoping to go together, but the other nurse failed, and Mert joined up alone.

After training at Camp McCoy, we had more to go through at Camp Kilmer where we learned to use the gas masks, were put through an obstacle course, and more marching. I remember the GIs yelling and whistling from every barracks window as we went through the mud and did pushups.

One of my first memories of Europe was the public toilet we had to use in England. We were at the dock, waiting to cross the English Channel, and while I was seated in the "privy," a young man came in and sat next to me. When I told the other nurses about it, they asked what I did. "I passed him the paper," I told them.

Lorraine Krause Taylor U.S. Army

October 1944, Somewhere in France.
Dear Family, Arrived safely, and had a very nice trip. We crossed the ocean on one of the largest & fastest ships afloat. I didn't get seasick! We had a lot of fun on the ship. Never played so much poker in all my life. We had to carry a life preserver with us at all times. I left my stateroom without it once. A guard stopped me, made me give him one of my shoes, and

Private Breger Abroad   **By Dave Breger**

"Oops! Sorry! I thought it was some Germans surrendering!"

Cartoons like "Private Breger" were popular throughout the war years, running regularly in *Stars and Stripes* and syndicated in most hometown papers.

I had to go back to get the preserver. Then I had to report to him to get my shoe back.

One rough day I was trying to take a tub bath and the ship would sway to one side and the water would all be on one side of me. Then she'd roll back and it would all run to the other side. It is impossible to get a lather in salt water. You just get gummy. The night we climbed across the gangplank, the Red Cross was there with hot coffee and doughnuts, and the army sent out a hot band. They played, "Pistol Packin' Momma" and "A Pretty Girl Is Like A Melody." Some combination!

We are anxious to get to work, but our permanent tents aren't set up yet. Don't worry about me as the Nazi troops are a long distance from here. They tell us the "jerries" never fly over here anymore. Raining again today. All it seems to do on this side of the world is rain. We hang our boots on the corners of the cots to keep them dry overnight. All we do is make bandages and drapes for surgery. Then they make us drill and do calisthenics. Tenting with Eleanor Behnke from Wisconsin. Wish you could see our tent. We each have a cot. A rope is stretched across the middle and is filled with p.j.s, undies, etc., drying. We have a box for a dresser. Have an olive drab towel over it and it is loaded down with cologne bottles and a bouquet of dahlias. It looks sorta homey!

Last night the engineers who are building our hospital had a party for 40 of us. During the day they sent word that if we wanted to take showers, they would provide hot water. A gang of us went over and believe me it is the first real bath I have had since I left the States. These "bird baths" out of a helmet are not very satisfactory.

When it isn't raining, the countryside here is really pretty, with rolling hills, and the leaves beginning to turn colors. The natives are very friendly. Yesterday they came out in droves and walked all over the place. They stood around and watched us line up for chow. The French women do our washing, and we pay them with soap and cigarettes.

You should see some of the towns around here, or rather what is left of them. Just a few walls standing, here and there. Went through an old chateau the other day. It was beautiful, but everyone is taking things like the pretty doorknobs, etc. We went to a dance the other night in another chateau, built around 1640. The Gestapo had been living there so they just stripped the place. We had a five-piece orchestra, and everyone had their liquor rations, so we had a great time.

Although we are allowed a pint of gin and a fifth of scotch each month for $2.50, today they withdrew liquor privileges. Seems things were getting out of hand, or perhaps the black market, but we now have curfew at ten P.M.

What style hats are you wearing this fall? The ones we see on the French women are real tall crowns, and they wear their hair real high in tall, fuzzy pompadours, which is not very becoming. They are pretty until they open their mouths, and they all have very discolored teeth. Must be the water.

We have a darling little puppy, called "Jeep." He owns the place, and we take him all around with us. We aren't working yet, so go to a lot of parties at various outfits in the area. They pick us up in trucks, and we wear our four-buckle arctic boots to and from the dance. The boyfriends give us cosmetics and soap. At home, if any fellow gave you a bar of Lifebouy soap for a present, you would never speak to him again. Here you are tickled to get it. Will write again when I can. Love, Lorraine

Shirley Payne Sweet U.S. Army   **Chief Nurse**

Once we were off the ship in Scotland, we traveled straight through that beautiful country and England in a crowded train, not getting to see London because of blackout conditions. Local people met our train with pastries and tea at different stops. Trucks were waiting at the train station for us, and we were driven to the docks in Southampton. There we took a ferry boat for an overnight trip to France, some of us getting seasick.

We landed at Omaha Beach. I can still see us trudging through the sand, in single file, to the top of a cliff, wandering around until I found a reception area. They didn't know we were coming, were overwhelmed to see us, and didn't know what to do with us. While we waited around in the dark, they eventually pitched some tents in a cow pasture so we could get some sleep. We slept on litters (stretchers) right on the ground. It was cold, rainy, and very muddy. That pristine little cow pasture soon became a mud hole.

I heard about a quartermaster "dump" (depot) near Caen, and soon everyone was able to buy long underwear, fatigue pants, jackets, and, the love of our days in France, paratrooper jump boots. I still have mine. Most of this clothing was made for men. Our footlockers didn't show up until December, three months after we shipped them.

We went by train to our hospital area at the village of La Milesse, near Le Mans. The most frustrating time for the nurses was waiting for the hospital to be ready. But when we got to our hospital area, everyone enthusiastically pitched in to help set up things, making bandages, preparing the operating rooms, and whatever else needed to be done. Finally, in early November, our first patients arrived and we were ready. This was what we had come for.

Gladys Weltzien Hesson U.S. Army

Several classmates from Milwaukee were going into the services after graduation, and "Red" chose the army because she liked the uniform best.

Landing at Omaha Beach, we hiked up the bluff. To the left was a cemetery that was a sea of white crosses, and a sad reminder of those who had gone before us. Before our hospital in Le Mans was set up, several of us were assigned to work on a hospital train based in Paris. We lived on the train, in the railroad station, and transported patients to Cherbourg where they were put on ships going to England. Our patients came from Belgium and had mostly amputations and abdominal wounds. The train car had litters in three tiers, and the top tier was high enough that we often stood on a pail to reach that patient. After several weeks we returned to our unit near Le Mans.

Helen Wenning U.S. Army

After landing at Omaha Beach, our first stop was a cow pasture between the "Red Ball Highway" and the town of Saint Mere-Egliese, the first town in France to be liberated. I was in a command post tent, presumably better than others, but in the rain it was worse. The flat top held the rain until it was too heavy, then came down on us. We slept in our clothes to keep warm and awoke in the morning with wet clothes and wet cots. All we had to do in the morning was to put on our boots and neckties. I remember shining my boots at bedtime, religiously, only to tramp through mud every morning.

The first patients came by train to our ambulances, which transported them to the hospital. Most stayed a short time, either going back to duty or sent to hospitals in England. I remember one of our biggest difficulties when we received our first trainload of about three hundred fifty patients was food. We couldn't fill them up. Second and third servings disappeared like magic. The poor guys had been on C rations for so long, they seemed unable to get enough of our hot food. Our cooks were very good at making things like powdered eggs taste like the real thing, at least to the patients.

Life in a tent hospital . . . or, Here is Your War

> Writing letters makes me ga-ga
> So guess in verse I'll tell my saga.
> We're set up in a pasture "somewhere in France"
> "How thrilling" you are thinking—"How full of romance!"
> That's one way of putting it—but let me go on.
> A portable latrine is our only john.
> My tent has a stove, but what good does it do us,
> If we're caught lighting fires, our CO will sue us.
> We were issued a candle to light our way to bed.
> QM's now out of candles and our flashlights are dead.

We bathe in a helmet to keep clean and nice,
But to get at the water, we must first break the ice.
Meals are like a garden party, as on the grass we stand
And try in vain to balance all our mess gear in one hand.
Our favorite topic of conversation
Is ways of disguising our daily C ration.
The vegetable hash ties my stomach in knots
And half of our outfit now has the GI trots.
We are mighty impressed by the Army cuisine.
(Let me never see Boston, the home of the bean.)
We dream of Paris, that makes us merrier
For the moment however, it is not a leave area.
We're just ten miles from mild civilization,
But woe is me, there's no transportation.
Then darn it, we'll work and make that our salvation.
Yes, but first some patients must hit our station.
My tale is now told, so I'll cut out the bitching.
I'll even grant that this life is enriching.
If I weren't so afraid of losing face
I'd confess I love the darn place.
And it would take a helluva lot
To make me swap the deal I've got!

by Janet Macleod Gordon, October 1944
American Red Cross, 166th General Hospital

Irina Stahovich U.S. Army

*Assignment to the 166th was a relief for Irina because she had been wait-
ing months at Camp Kilmer to go overseas. She replaced a nurse who
broke her leg leaving Camp McCoy.*

After leaving Russia when I was a child, my family had lived in France
before we moved to the States, but this was a different experience altogether. The staging area at La Milesse was the first time I was ever in a tent.
We were in a cow pasture, and one dark night I left the tent to brush my
teeth with water out of my helmet and came nose to nose with a horse.

I was assigned to the operating room and thought it was fantastic to see
how they worked under such difficult conditions. I had "on-the-job training" in anesthesia, under the supervision of the nurse anesthetist.

Lighthearted memories include the time I bought a chicken from a local farmer and cooked it in the operating room autoclave. My tentmates and I adopted a puppy, naming him Centime [1/100 of a French franc], and a corpsman built a tiny dog house near our tent. He was great company and made us very popular.

Frances Tremper Howard U.S. Army

From Chicago, Frances became an army nurse in 1944.

From the time we started to set up the hospital at Le Mans until the first patients arrived, the nurses made bandages and lined the operating room with sheets and did things like that. The sheets were put all around the inside of the tents, as well as across the top, to keep dust and dirt from coming down on the operating tables.

One of my tentmates was Irina Stahovich, who had lived in France after her family left Russia. It was wonderful to go places with her because she was so at home in Paris and took us with her to a French home on Christmas Eve.

The patient I'll never forget was Corporal Samuelson. He was teased mercilessly about his wound. It seems "Sammy" was on his way to the latrine and was shot in his butt. For three weeks I dressed his wound, and then it came time for the Purple Heart to be awarded. I was given the job of questioning several eligible patients about their injuries. One question was, "Where was the geographical location of your wound?" Sammy got very red in the face and was embarrassed and said to me, "Lieutenant, you have been dressing my wound for three weeks, and you ought to know where I got hurt." The answer should have been "Holland." The boys in the ward never let him forget it.

He wrote me later, saying he was back on duty, and "Yes, I did get the Purple Heart."

Myrtle Brethouwer Hoftiezer U.S. Army

It rained and rained at the beginning of our stay in France, and we often had to move the cots we slept in to higher ground to stay dry. We ate outside from our mess kits, often in the rain. Our first hot meal was Cream-of-Wheat, which tastes wonderful in a muddy field in France. We wore the

**The rainy weather and muddy hospital grounds were topics that every-
one at the 166th GH could agree to gripe about. Walking between tents in
the mud, eating outside in the rain, and never having dry clothes to wear
during rainy seasons, were complaints heard throughout all theaters of war.**

ugly, olive drab underwear for a month without being able to wash it. Our
bathtub was a helmet, and the latrine was a dug-out trench with a canvas
screen around it, open to the sky and the pilots who flew overhead.

Everyone was excited when we were finally told to make beds and get
ready for a trainload of patients. After all, we hadn't come to France to
enjoy the winter climate. My strongest memory is how many times a
patient would say, "Get to me when you can. He needs you more than I
do." I've never taken care of patients like that since.

My brother worked in General Eisenhower's office and surprised me on
Thanksgiving Day with a visit. We shared a mess-kit dinner. It was a very
special time for us.

Lorraine Krause Taylor U.S. Army

November 1944, Somewhere in France:
Dear Family, Having a $100 allotment sent home each month. Buy a
$37.50 Savings Bond for me out of it. Send clear nail polish and some

Lorraine Krause, 166th GH relaxes in front of a German pillbox on a French beach

hose, as our footlockers are still in England. Can't buy much in the French stores either because we don't have ration points for them, or it is junk. Sending two hankies to show you what the junk is like around here.

We are really busy and I honestly feel like an army nurse now. Yesterday we received a train load of patients from the front, and I wish you could have been there when they came in and saw the brand new beds with those beautiful white wool blankets. They simply could not believe their eyes. They are the nicest fellows, and you feel like you can't do enough for them. Just coming from the front, their morale is a lot higher than ours. When I went off-duty later, I didn't want to because they are so grateful for everything.

On my birthday three other girls and I had a champagne party. It's going to be expensive to take me out when I get back to the States, the way we guzzle champagne. Tomorrow we move into new tents that will have cement floors instead of dirt, and stoves for heat. Every night we take a canteen of water to bed so it won't be so cold in the morning to wash our faces.

The GIs climb over fences to get apples for us from the groves around here. The other day the owner presented a bill to the commanding officer. Love, Lorraine

December 1944. *Dear Family, Appreciate the package of things you sent, all except the cans of Vienna sausage. We get that with our rations, and use the cans under our suitcases to keep them off the ground. Bet*

Armour never thought they would be put to that use.

Interested in the newspaper used for packing more than the contents. How they skim over the bombings. Maybe if the people back home knew a bit more, there wouldn't be so much black market stuff. We are issued two packs of cigarettes a week and the men up front get five packs a week. You know how some men smoke, especially when under nervous tension, so you know how far only five packs go.

Whatever you do, don't forget to offer a few prayers everyday for the fellows up front. We may be winning all right, but even so it is costing a price. So don't forget them. Remember that when the news sounds good, we are the busiest. Someday we'll be able to tell some stories, but at present there is so much I can't tell.

Laura Borup, one of my tentmates, and I picked holly and mistletoe along the roadside to use for Christmas trimmings. The other day we went to town, which has narrow, little, alley-like streets with cobblestone paving. You hear the youngsters clomping along in wooden shoes, which they wear as protection from the mud and rain. Sending a money order home to buy each of the kids [a nephew and two nieces] an $18.75 bond. Will write again soon. Love, Lorraine

Helen Wenning U.S. Army

On Christmas, we wore our Class A uniforms, instead of the fatigues, and put holly in our hair to show the patients how glamorous we could be. Some girls were good at giving home permanents, which they brought from the States or had sent from home.

Janet MacLeod, the Red Cross worker assigned to our hospital, gave French lessons. I was her poorest student. A French woman who did my laundry was always talking to me, and me to her, though neither of us ever understood. After a while, Janet found out that this woman invited me several times to her home for dinner, and thought I'd accepted. Well, I never showed up because I didn't know what she was saying, and soon Janet was able to clear things up, and we went to the woman's home together.

Mary Budway Atkinson U.S. Army

Six months after her husband was killed in the Pacific, Mary joined the Army Nurse Corps, going to France with the 166th.

One memory that is with me still is a young man, about eighteen years old, who was one of our first patients. He'd been in a hospital in England with a very bad cold when his unit left for the Continent, and he insisted on crossing the English Channel with them. He wound up in our hospital, where we did special duty for him. My last evening with him, he was seeing angels. The next day, when I came to work, he had gone with the angels. It really hit me hard because he was so young and eager to please.

Lorraine Krause Taylor U.S. Army

January 1945.
(Printed stationery): Lt. Lorraine M. Krause
Somewhere in France

Dear Family, Johnnie had this printed in Germany for me. Had a very nice Christmas with a lot of parties, so I think everyone felt pretty good for being so far from home. Went to Midnight Mass.

I didn't mention anything earlier about the bad times we were having at Christmas as we all felt too badly about it. The Allies are certainly going to town now, and look what the Russians are doing! I could tell you stories of the atrocities of the Germans that would stand your hair on end. We have quite a few patients that were captured by the Germans and in turn were captured by us. All nationalities, Czech, Polish, Russian, etc. They are the saddest sacks you ever laid eyes upon. They can't get over how well the Americans treat them. You should see the marks left on them from being ill-treated. We certainly should thank God we are Americans.

One of my patients told my fortune today and said my family was worrying a lot about me. There isn't anything to worry about. He also told me there was illness at home - are you holding out on me? Who is it? He told me I was very aggressive and ambitious and that I was in line for a promotion, which is the bunk. He also said I'm going to marry a lawyer soon. He has been telling everyone's fortune around here, and seems to be good.

I put in an order for a dressy uniform coat instead of the trench coat. If I ever get to Paris, I'll have to dress up a bit.

Had my first taste of Coca Cola since leaving the ship. We are allowed one bottle a week! Once I dreamed I was squeezing oranges and was about to drink it and someone woke me up. I could have killed her! She was so sorry when I told her about it.

We do the most exciting things on dates! One night on a date, Behnke and I mentioned how much we miss a bathtub, and our dates said to use the one at their 'chateau.' They were living in a big French house with several other officers. So we lost no time getting in that tub, believe me! Another time we fried fresh eggs there, and even had fresh celery to eat. What I wouldn't give for a big wedge of lettuce and a fresh tomato!

I'm working in Supply at nights now, and the sergeant working with me is a hairdresser from Antoine's in New York. He does my hair when he can, and is really good! Received a box that you sent last September, while we were still in the states. Thanks anyway! Will write again when I can. Love, Lorraine

Jean Kolczak Sciora U.S. Army Physical Therapist

Physical therapy treatment over there was mostly hands-on exercise. If the boys were better in thirty days, they were sent back to the war. Otherwise, they went home. Most wanted to go back to their buddies, but one case I can't forget was a man who attempted suicide by shooting himself in the chest. We treated him for limited-arm motion, but he was very depressed and wouldn't talk to anyone. He was sent back to the States, and I often wonder what happened to him.

Fannie Kasmer Bruner U.S. Army

A patient once held a gun to my head when I tried to awaken him for breakfast. The food got cold fast, and he had the sheet over his head, so I tried once, then twice to get him to eat. He threw back the sheet and pointed the gun at my head, threatening to kill me. A doctor disarmed him and sent him to the psychiatric ward. This GI was there in the first place because he'd shot himself in the foot, to get off the front line, but we didn't know he still had a gun.

We had nothing but POW patients eventually, and though I understood German, I never let anyone know. The young Germans were quite militaristic and would shout "Achtung" when I came in the ward. They referred to me in German as "Holy Sister of the Sick."

There were other nationalities also, who'd been captured by the Germans. Many of them had been locked up, tied up, and found in boxcars.

The first time I was asked to find out how many hadn't had a bowel movement, I couldn't think of the right words. I had a German orderly helping me and tried a couple of words that probably weren't nice. He just stared at me, so I took him to the latrine and showed him the enema can. He caught on and went around the ward asking about bowel movements. We understood that some of them had dug it out of themselves with their fingers because they were so dehydrated and constipated. Sometimes it took an hour to get an answer, by the time my question was translated into German, then Polish, then Russian, and all the misunderstandings.

When the ward was called to attention, the patients were supposed to sit up or stand, or just be still when "Attention!" was called out. We had a black patient who seemed to ignore the order. Turns out he was French-speaking, from Africa, and no one knew it. We didn't have many black GIs as patients, but when we did, I can remember some of the GI wardboys had bad attitudes toward them and told me I was too nice to them. I straightened them out.

Eva Yungblut Lapham U.S. Army

When Eva transferred to Paris, she met, and soon married, her husband there.

I worked in the psychiatric ward at the 166th, and the patient who held a gun to Fannie Kasmer's head was sent to my ward after that incident. We got along well, and when he went home, he sent me a beautiful compact made of mother-of-pearl. His note said, "I'm sending this to you because you remind me of General Patton, who carried a pearl-handled pistol." I still have the compact. He was from my hometown, and when I returned, I realized his family had a very prominent business there.

Everyone tried to use their high-school French with the local people, but the GIs had no trouble at all. They learned the language in about two days, especially the sentence, "Voulez-vous coucher avec moi?" (Will you sleep with me?)

My husband and I married in Paris, and as soon as I found out I was pregnant, I was able to come home.

Shirley Payne Sweet U.S. Army **Chief Nurse**

One of our patients informed me that my husband was wounded and was to be sent back to the States. He was in a hospital in Paris, so I hitched a ride in an ambulance to see him, and we spent three days together in a tiny French hotel. I remember the room had steam heat, which I would like to have taken back to my tent. I was surprised several weeks later, when I thought he was in England waiting to go back home, that he showed up in Le Mans. He stayed in an army hotel, and I "commuted" back and forth to work for a few days, until he did return to the U.S.A.

Lorraine Krause Taylor U.S. Army

February 1945.

Dear Family, We are getting passes to Paris, but the girls who have relatives to meet there get preference, which is fair. When someone returns from three days in Paris they seem so clean, because they don't have to stay in tents. Got a new permanent wave, from the French. I let them set it the way they wear it and I was about six feet tall when I left the shop. Real fancy!

Just finished censoring a whole big stack of mail written by the fellows who work in surgery. I simply detest doing it. They write their wives and sweethearts and it seems so much like eavesdropping, but it has to be done.

Have been seeing a lot of a really nice guy named Pat, and he surprised me with a proposal this week. He called while I was on duty, with a wardman standing right next to me, and he asked if I would "put the double harness on with him." I didn't know what to say, so he told me to think it over. Then last night he called again and said, "Are you shining up the double harness for the big event?"

I like him a lot, but Johnnie still keeps coming around, and I don't know what to do. We wouldn't get married over here anyway, because of all the paperwork. He's stationed in a nearby town in one of those beautiful French homes. Thinks that I have it so rough, living in a tent. Will write again soon. Love, Lorraine

Eunice Phelps Carr U.S. Army

From Indiana, when Eunice became a young widow in 1944 she joined the army.

To make the ground drier and warmer inside our tents, we got some straw from a Frenchman and improvised a straw mattress. Soon we needed insecticide because of the fleas in the straw. Our mode of living compared to that of a semi-modern farmer's. It's the little things in life; so long as we had heat in our tents as well as the hospital, we gained a measure of contentment. To get coal we walked a half-block with our pail, and between the four tentmates, we kept the stove going.

A two-day pass in Paris was too short, but I saw some wonderful programs. *Faust* was at the Opera House. There were at least 250 in the cast, plus a sixty-five-piece orchestra. The next day I was lucky to get tickets to a performance by Lily Pons and Andre Kastelanetz. The military audience of about 2200 people was thrilled. The Kastelanetz orchestra was composed of 110 performers from five different professional GI bands. Traveling through France, we were always shocked to see the bomb damage to the cities. It was a surprise that the French didn't try to clear up rubble from the streets and make travel easier for themselves at least.

Another shock was the type of diseases we were finding with prisoners. When medications became scarce for the Germans, diseases popped up which were already rare, such as virulent diphtheria and typhoid. Our Russian patients had been prisoners of the Germans, and forced to work in underground factories. Most of them had tuberculosis.

Lorraine Krause Taylor U.S. Army

March 1945 France.

Dear Family, It's quite cool, but haven't had any rain for a couple of days. Violets are blooming and the trees are starting to blossom. Mert (Myrtle Brethouwer), one of my tentmates, and I went out Sunday and picked violets. They have the sweetest smell. Went into Le Mans and took pictures of the pretty cathedral. Saving most of my film for Paris.

The Chicago Tribune comes in batches. Won't get any for a while, then seven at a time. Noticed they are making all kinds of slurring remarks about the Russians not doing their part. Believe me, the soldiers over here don't feel that way about them. Isn't it wonderful that the Americans were the first to cross the Rhine River? The Germans kept saying it would never happen, that we could never do it. Be sure you say some prayers for all the fellows over here. Also for the boys in the Pacific. Love, Lorraine

March 16: *Got back from Paris last night! The four of us were allowed to go together and had a wonderful time. Mert's brother is stationed in Paris and got dates for us, and they showed us a grand time. The first night we went to Montmartre to a night club. It is in the slum section, and you should see all the streetwalkers. They sure do a big business there.*

Took a tour the next day and saw all the famous sights. Sending souvenirs home, and bought rosaries for you at Notre Dame. That night we went to the Follies. A lot of naked women, but they are beautiful. The dancing was good, but they don't have good singing voices. Then we went to the Lido and saw a good show, but not as good as the Follies. Mert's brother dates a girl in the chorus. She had a featured part that night because Mert was in the audience.

Shopping the next day. Went to Guerlain to get perfume but couldn't buy it because we didn't have an empty bottle. You have heard so much about how beautiful Parisian women are and what beautiful clothes they wear. I wish you could see them. The most artificial things and not at all beautiful. Their clothes were awful. The only thing new was the color of their hair: purple!! And Pink!! It was a shock. The young girls are pretty, but they don't age well. But, we certainly had a good time.

We only have a few patients now, and they are PWs. It is so pretty around here now, with beautiful flowers. We think we may be moving soon. Love, Lorraine

April 1945. *Dear Family, We just received some really bad casualties and are rushed to death. I'll write while I have a little time.*

On Easter Sunday, three of us kids went for a long walk and visited the prettiest little church in the village. Behnke and Laura started to cry when we were in there. We are more homesick today than at Christmas, because we were trying our darndest to cheer up the patients then, and now we have time to think about ourselves.

Received the box with egg dyes about five days after Easter. Will try to find some fresh eggs and dye them. The box with flannel pajamas and bottles of cokes came. Boy, did those cokes taste good! We've been told we can now wear our beige uniforms. Please send them to me as quickly as possi-

ble. *That includes the suit, dress, hat, maroon neckties, white shirts and that white dickie if you can find it. Also, will you go to Marshall Fields and buy me a beige overseas cap and an olive drab WAC officer's cap.*

Wasn't it a shame about President Roosevelt dying? And right now, too. Hope Truman can carry on. We had a nice memorial service on Sunday. The chaplain said that even tho our president had died, the government would continue, as our real ruler is God and all of America was founded for God. As the Declaration of Independence proves, and our coins state, "In God We Trust."

We have company right now, a mouse, and I hear him crunching on something. Love, Lorraine

May 1945. Dear Family, Here we are in Paris! Several of us were transferred up here, but not all to the same hospital. The four of us (Eleanor Behnke, Laura Borup, Myrtle Brethouwer) are still together, and we are right in town. It is really nice being in buildings, with hot and cold running water, and real beds with springs.

We wear brown-and-white seersucker uniform on duty, instead of fatigues, and I bought a new khaki uniform with a short jacket. It reminds me of a bellhop's uniform.

What do you think about Hitler being dead? I wonder if it is true. Mussolini got his too. Hope this business over here ends soon. It is supposed to. Love, Lorraine (Germany surrendered May 7, 1945.)

May 18: Now that the censorship has been lifted, I can tell a few things. Before we sailed we were in New Jersey, but don't know why we had to keep it such a big secret. We took buses back and forth to New York City, and the name of the camp was in huge letters on the bus.

I crossed on the Queen Elizabeth which is the largest and fastest ship afloat. They are getting her ready again as a luxury liner, but was never used except as a troop transport. We were on the main deck, and I loved looking out the porthole and watching the ocean fly past. We were told before we got off the Elizabeth that we had to dodge German subs a couple of times in the Atlantic.

Crossing the English Channel was the only time I felt uneasy. The danger was from mines, but nothing happened. We landed on Omaha Beach, and I'll never forget the scene at the top of the hill. There were acres of white crosses on graves. We first stopped near Cherbourg, where the hedges were still full of German mines. That territory had gone through a lot of very bitter fighting. The natives were on the side of the Germans.

Went through St. Lo. It is a complete ruin. They wouldn't let us go out without male escorts, and there were guards around our area always.

The Battle of the Bulge was going on around Christmas and we couldn't go to town. One night we could hear planes flying over constantly for almost an hour. Had a lot of casualties then. Toward the last all we had as patients were German PWs.

I was just shifted to another ward and have night duty. It's hard work, but more than that, the poor fellows are in such terrible condition. Most of them hopeless with brain and spine injuries. I could put my fist in a hole in one poor fellow's skull. God certainly should punish those who started the war.

Most of the patients are "RUSPS" (recovered U.S. prisoners) or "RAMPS" (recovered allied military personnel). They are very malnourished and just need food mostly.

V-E Day was really celebrated here. All lights were turned on and bells rang. Three of us found a GI to drive us to the Place de la Concorde. It was so crowded. People were climbing over the jeep, and we couldn't move. On the subway I saw a woman carrying two baby goats in a bag. It was like a gunnysack. Just their heads were sticking out and they kept baa-ing all the time. At first I thought a baby was crying behind me. Imagine doing that on the Chicago subway? Will write again when I can. Love, Lorraine

Myrtle Brethouwer Hoftiezer U.S. Army

German prisoners were our patients eventually. Some of them were pretty cocky and let us know what they thought of the Americans. Our doctors sent them right back to their prison camps when they heard a German being disrespectful to us. The four of us who'd been tentmates were happy to stay together when we transferred to Paris. There was plenty of time off to see the sights, and I remember thinking that traveling the Paris subway must have been heaven to a garlic lover.

Lorraine Krause Taylor U.S. Army

June 1945 Paris.

Dear Family, Just came back from a nice trip to Brussels, Belgium, with Laura. I don't expect to be here long, and the sad part is that none of the other girls are going with me. I have to get the shots for the Pacific Theater, or CBI. Turned down a chance to go to Germany with the Army of Occupation. Love, Lorraine

June 15: Arrived in Marseilles, and what a set up! I keep pinching myself. They are just grand to us. You ought to see how blue the Mediterranean is, and the weather is grand. We don't even have to make our beds, because the PWs do it. Have a week's leave to go to the Riviera. This life here is too good to be true. Have gone out with a navy officer. The navy really has it great. Fresh meat and vegetables, and Budweiser beer!

Ran into Mert's brother here. He's on his way to the Pacific too. I have to go to some training classes, with the gas chamber again. Will write again soon. Love, Lorraine

Gladys Weltzien Hesson U.S. Army

Our tent hospital in Le Mans was divided into blocks, with five wards, a kitchen, doctors office, and a nurses office. The nurse in charge of each block was known as a "Blockhead."

When I heard we were going to be treating German prisoners, I thought to myself, "This is not what I'm living in a tent for." I didn't mind at all doing it for our GIs, but not the Germans. I never mentioned it to the others and followed orders.

I was sent to Le Havre for reassignment, but after V-E Day transferred to Marseilles for assignment to Okinawa. The day we sailed from Marseilles the atom bomb was dropped. We sailed anyway, but at sea our orders were changed to return to the States.

Eleanor Behnke Williams U.S. Army

During basic training at Camp McCoy "Behnke" gave the nickname "Torchy" to Lorraine Krause. Tentmates until June 1945, they were separated in Paris.

From Paris, I was sent to Muldorf, Germany, assigned to the Sixtieth Field Hospital. There were no patients, so I traveled around the area, sightseeing. I visited Bertchesgaden, Hitler's retreat, and saw what had been the "baby farms." *[Hundreds of young German women were recruited to bear children fathered by Nazi SS officers. The women were honored to be selected.]* We were also shown bones of babies that supposedly were killed because they weren't perfect German specimens.

Because the war ended and there was nothing to do, I was transferred to the 132nd Evacuation Hospital in Munich, where we were located in an insurance building. I soon had enough points to return, and spent twenty-one days on the ship, with 108 nurses in one huge room.

Laura Borup Wild U.S. Army

Laura, "Mert," "Behnke" and "Torchy" shared a tent when the permanent hospital was completed at Le Mans. Hardships molded close friendships and the four nurses were like family during the months they cared for the wounded. Transferred to Paris together, they eventually split up, with Laura and Mert staying in the same unit.

The war in Europe ended while I was waiting in Marseilles for orders to the CBI, along with thousands of other military people. I didn't have enough points to go home, so Mert and I were sent to Weisbaden, Germany. The first night there I met my husband-to-be at a party.

When we decided to marry, I was told nurses would have to stay six months longer, so George signed up to stay that long too. A German seamstress made my wedding dress out of parachute silk, and the Red Cross girls found some pretty material for Mert's bridesmaid dress. The first ceremony was by the Burgermeister in City Hall on December 15, with an interpreter standing by to tell us when to say, "Yah."

The next day we had a service with the army chaplain. All these years George celebrates December 15th and I celebrate December 16th. The commanding officer walked me down the aisle, with the head nurse sitting in the "mother's place." The cooks put on a beautiful wedding dinner that night, and afterward we all danced.

Our honeymoon was a trip to the French Riviera, where we stayed in a bridal suite at an elite hotel the officers used. Coincidentally, one of the band members at the hotel had grown up with George in a little Oklahoma town. The first night we walked into the dining room, the band played "Here Comes The Bride." Of course, I blushed. The next night we waited until intermission to go in, but they burst out with "Here Comes The Bride" again. When we returned to Weisbaden, my hospital was closed, and everyone had orders to go home. So I went back to the States immediately, and George had to wait six months.

Right after we were married, I was sitting at George's desk, playing solitaire, when a new private stood in front of me, saluting. He looked at me strangely as he said his name, and that he was "reporting for duty." I returned the salute and welcomed him to the outfit, knowing all the time that the hall outside was full of sergeants, listening and laughing.

Myrtle Brethouwer Hoftiezer U.S. Army

After V-E Day I was in Marseilles waiting to get on the ship to go to the war in the Pacific, when President Truman ordered the atom bomb dropped. Bless him! I was also promoted to first lieutenant. Laura and I were then sent to Germany, to the Eighty-fifth Evacuation Hospital.

My husband had been a P-47 pilot, and forty years later the French government invited a group of them to France to honor them for their part in the liberation of France. We were in Paris, being lavishly entertained, when I fell and broke my hip. I ended up at the American Hospital and asked the doctor where the American Military Hospital would have been in World War II. He smiled, saluted, and said, "Madame, you are in it."

Shirley Payne Sweet U.S. Army   Chief Nurse

I was promoted to major in France, when there weren't many nurses with that rank. In Paris two soldiers passed me, saluted, and I can still hear the voice of one saying, "Jesus Christ, a major!"

As the war front moved further into Germany, the 166th took care of German prisoner patients and then turned the hospital over to the Germans after V-E Day. The 166th moved to a Quonset hospital at Le Havre, where we tended the wounded waiting to board ships for their return to the States.

The whole five years of my time in the Army Nurse Corps was a wonderful experience. I would have been the last to know about things like dating between nurses and enlisted men. That was good because I would have had to "do something" about it. One woman with our hospital knew an air transport pilot who let her fly with him to New York for a long weekend. The ensuing Court Martial resulted in nothing more than a slap on the wrist. I never felt I had any problems with the nurses, as they were grown women.

**Nurses of the 166th and 170th GHs march proudly in the V-E Day
Parade in Le Mans, France.**

Helen Wenning U.S. Army

One hot, dusty day in June 1945, we climbed aboard trucks for the all-day trip to our new hospital site near Le Havre. The new location was Camp Philip Morris, one of the many camps code-named for cigarettes and occupied with deployment troops. Instead of battle casualties, we had patients injured in accidents such as land mine explosions, shootings, and vehicles. This was a time of rapid turnover of personnel, as people were being sent home or reassigned to other areas. I took a concentrated workshop on tropical diseases, presumably in preparation for assignment to the CBI. V-J Day was the cause of a lot of celebrating, and many people headed back to the States as soon as possible.

In March 1946, four of us were the last of our unit's original nurses, and we boarded the *Sea Perch* for the voyage home. It was a far cry from the luxury liner we went overseas on, but I didn't know the difference. When the *Queen Elizabeth* sailed for Europe, I ate one meal and spent the rest of the trip in the infirmary, seasick. My first experience with seasickness was a ten-day trip across the north Pacific when I went to work in Nome, Alaska, before the war. The third, and I assure you, last, was sailing home from Europe, again in the infirmary for the entire trip in 1946.

Fannie Kasmer Bruner U.S. Army

I was transferred from the 166th to the 62nd General Hospital at Enghien and Aubin for a while, then to Paris. After the war ended, I went to Belgium, where eventually I worked in Liege, in an ancient fortress turned into a hospital.

I am Jewish, but we never knew about the atrocities against Jews until the war was over. A family who'd been released from a concentration camp were put in my care, because they had a premature baby who was near death, and I'd been a pediatric nurse before the army. I was able to find bottles and nipples and gave him canned milk and Karo syrup. We used pillow cases for diapers. It was a joy to watch that family get better.

My husband and I were married overseas. He was a sergeant who worked in the post office. By this time I was with the 196th, and when I became pregnant, they flew me home. When I came off the plane in New York, I knelt down and kissed the ground.

My daughter, Regina, tells everyone she was "Made in France." Her most distinct memory of our home as she grew up is the scent of perfume. What happened is my husband had to stay in Paris awhile after I left, and won $500 in a craps game. GIs were only allowed to bring home one month's pay, so he had to spend the $500, and the only thing he could think of was perfume. He went to the Rue de la Paix, to the perfume houses, and spent it all. In the following years, everyone received perfume from us as a present; for showers, birthdays, graduations, or anything. We still have some!

Eunice Phelps Carr U.S. Army

We sat up most of the night on V-E Day, listening to the radio. The Officers Club served free champagne for three days. Parades went on all day, with our nurses marching in Le Mans from 9:00 A.M. to 11:00 A.M. All the Allied participants together made a parade more than a mile long. At night, there were street dances on several corners, plus a circus was in town. You haven't seen a circus until you've seen one in France. They have everything except popcorn and peanuts. The French drank and danced all night for two days. The next day was for religious services.

I volunteered for the Pacific in June, but the age limit was thirty-five, and I was a month over that.

Jean Kolczak Sciora U.S. Army

Stan and I didn't date until we'd been in France several months, then did it on the sly because I was an officer and he was enlisted. There was a major who was always trying to catch the nurses who dated enlisted men. The Protestant chaplain let us meet at his tent, or took us with him on trips so we could be together.

I was sent to Liege, Belgium, after V-E Day, and Stan was transferred to a unit where he played football, on the Normandy All Stars. We often went to Paris and visited the Shrine of the Miraculous Medal, 140 Rue de Bac. Two nuns became close friends of ours, and we asked them if we could be married in the chapel. The Archbishop of Paris had to approve it, and since there had never been a wedding there, we were asked to be discrete about it. Schiaparelli was a famous fashion house in Paris, and they were loaning wedding gowns to GI brides. However, I was asked not to wear a gown. I found out many years later there was never another wedding in the shrine again.

Our wedding was set for November 27. First we had to go through a lot of processing, both by the army and the church. The army made us sign an agreement that we wouldn't embarrass the army, because an officer was marrying an enlisted man. We had a civil ceremony in the local courthouse performed by the mayor of the area. Besides the legal fee, Stan gave him some bars of soap and cigars.

When we arrived at the chapel, we were surprised to find it packed with people, and we were trying to be unobtrusive. It turned out to be the anniversary of the vision of St. Catherine Laboure when she received the miraculous medal at the chapel. The army chaplain in that part of Paris performed the ceremony, with all the people watching. One nun told us she heard people say, "Too bad it isn't a French girl having the first wedding in here." The nice chaplain found a hotel for our week's honeymoon.

Irina Stahovich U.S. Army

My assignment with the 166th ended in March when I was sent to the Forty-ninth Field Hospital located near Lorient on the Atlantic Coast. That operating room was busy for thirty-six hours straight sometimes, mostly because of accidents in the area.

Shortly after V-E Day, I was sent to Southern France to await orders to the CBI. It was a staging area between Aix and Marseilles, called "Tent

City," where about seventy-five thousand other military personnel were also waiting for orders. There was nothing to do, but the USO put on shows all the time. One night there was an outdoor concert, however the GIs were expecting a movie. Yasha Heifetz, the world-renowned violinist, tried several times to appease the audience, but they booed him rather loudly. He finally left the stage, for which I was sorry. I could see both sides, though.

Twenty-three years later, I retired from the ANC and am so proud to have served.

Margaret Bell Rasmussen U.S. Army

When the war in Europe was winding down, people were sent all over. Marian Gerlach and I wound up being lost for a month. We were sent from the 166th to the 286th in Cherbourg for a short time, then received orders to report to the Twenty-sixth Station Hospital in Mannheim, Germany. It took a month to get there, and most of that time we spent in Belgium, waiting and enjoying ourselves.

In May 1945 we boarded a train in Cherbourg, and two days later were pretty surprised when we got to Vervier, Belgium, near the German border, and were told it was the end of the line. There were no trains going into Germany. The Red Cross at the train station directed us to a cafe with rooms overhead, where we stayed several days. We finally found army headquarters in Vervier and had them notify our hospital. Then we discovered a nice hotel and the officer's club and waited. We made many friends, mostly men, did a lot of sightseeing, and waited. After about a month, an ambulance showed up with a doctor and a driver and took us to Mannheim. There weren't many patients, and they were mostly accident victims. Soon we were sent to Weisbaden, then Bad Manheim. Marian and I wound up assigned to a hospital in Frankfurt, before being sent back to the States.

With the GI Bill, I went to Marquette University and eventually became director of a Visiting Nurse Association in Wisconsin.

Monica Godfrey Carollo U.S. Army

I stayed with the 166th, and we waited in Le Havre to go home because there was a dock strike in New York City, and no ships could leave for almost two months. Thousands of military people kept piling up, and to keep everyone busy, all kinds of classes were organized. That's when I took French lessons, when I was leaving France!

Lorraine Krause Taylor U.S. Army

July 1945 At sea.

Dear Family, Started on my trip on the 26th, but don't expect to hear from me much. There won't be a lot to write about, and we are under censorship again. Love, Lorraine

August 1945. Dear Family, Picked up your letters in Panama. We weren't supposed to be there long, but had a little trouble going through the canal, so had a grand stay. The local women came to the ship, offered to do our laundry, and invited us to their homes. The first thing we had was fresh milk, banana split, and fresh tomatoes. Thought I was in heaven. Bought a pair of silk stockings for $2.95. They are so sheer.

This is a lazy life. We eat, sleep, and take sunbaths. We are blacked out at night, even though the Japs are supposed to stop fighting, and there are subs around. Love, Lorraine (Japan surrendered August 15, 1945.)

September 1945. Dear Family, We were at sea on V-J Day. Had a 21-gun salute and the GIs got together and scratched up a band.

Now I can tell you what happened in Panama. The ship tried to steer a new course, and wound up on a sand bar. Had to wait for repairs, but had a grand time eating and shopping on shore.

We are still at sea. This is one of the longest voyages of the war. If we go to Japan, it will be the longest probably. Thought we were smart in getting out of the Army of Occupation in Germany and now look what we probably will be in. We don't know yet where we are going, but are on our way to a port near Manila.

Stopped in New Guinea for a day, and swam at the beach. Everybody was getting disgruntled and the troops were causing a lot of trouble. After leaving Panama, the atom bomb was dropped and some of the soldiers on the ship tried to mutiny. Some had been in World War I, and thought we should turn around. The captain announced he was in command and they would obey him. After the stop in New Guinea, the change of scenery had everyone smiling and the troops were singing. Had root beer there for the first time since leaving the States, and it was so good. One day we had a "Man Overboard!" A GI was trying to look in the porthole of the nurses' quarters, and when he was seen, his buddy, who was holding him from the deck above, let go, and the guy fell in the ocean. We didn't find him. We are on the USS Gen. Aultman, manned by the Coast Guard. My heart sank to my shoes when I got to the dock at Marseilles and saw this little ship, after being on the Queen Elizabeth. Funny thing is that the more traveling I do, the more I want to do. You would think that after all I've done, I'd want to settle down a bit. Guess I'll be a globe-trotter, and not doing so badly at present! Love, Lorraine

Manila Bay, September 12: *We've been waiting to disembark for two days, but weren't expected, as usual, and they don't know what to do with us. There are over 300 ships anchored here. This harbor is tremendous in size.*

They made announcements concerning conditions in the city. Water and food are polluted with disease. Liquor is mostly wood alcohol, and has caused 500 cases of blindness, five deaths in the last ten days. Prostitutes are all diseased and many have leprosy. There are a lot of Japs left, and sympathizers, who are sniping and killing right and left. Curfew is 5:00 P.M.. Nice place!! Love, Lorraine

October 1945. *Dear Family, Finally at the staging area which is about sixty miles from Manila. Expect to go to Japan, but awaiting orders. The girls with high points, married, or over 35 years have been leaving, so only half of us are left. The mail finally caught up with us. There hadn't been any since Panama. We are just sightseeing and getting suntans. Haven't worked since early June, and are so anxious to get going. Guess what? I saw Mert's brother again. Love, Lorraine*

October 31: *Finally on a ship but sat in Manila Bay for three days waiting to leave. They kept changing orders, then said they were waiting to clear the harbor in Japan of mines. Now we are bobbing around in the harbor at Nagoya, Japan, waiting to get off. It was a really rough trip, like a jeep going fast over a rough road. Love, Lorraine*

November 1945. *Dear Family, When we landed in Nagoya, we were the first American women in this area, and everyone ran over to look at us. They thought we were "comfort girls."*

I met a navy officer who is a Japanese interpreter and he took another nurse and me to meet the Jap Vice Admiral! We had tea and then hot tangerine-ade. He spoke English fairly well. We had a special ceremony for the tea, and it was explained the why and how of each movement. The woman who is performing the ceremony is very polite and graceful, and bows every time you look at her. We had to take our shoes off when we entered the room. Glad I didn't have holes in my socks. We really were thrilled about it all. There aren't many Americans here yet, and they are very nice to us.

Our hospital is in a nice big six-story building. No heat though, even in the wards. We had to set up the hospital ourselves. There are about 1,000 patients. The biggest ward is for VD patients. We work hard because nurses keep getting sent home, and no replacements arrive. Finally working though, after doing nothing for five months. I have two Japanese women working for me.

I must tell you about the toilets! Just a hole in the floor that we stand over. They are the darndest things.

The town is pretty badly demolished. Besides the bombs that were dropped here, there was an earthquake last winter. The people are certainly different from the French. Here they have cleared away the rubble and salvaged everything they could and stacked it in neat piles. In between these stacks they immediately planted vegetable gardens. Love, Lorraine

***December 1945.** Dear Family, The points have been lowered for returning, so now I am doubly eligible. I'll be on my way as soon as we get replacements. Some arrived yesterday, but not enough to send me home. Boy, you can certainly tell the difference between the girls who have been overseas and those who just came from the states. The new girls look so young and fresh and giddy, and we look so old and serious. Am warning you, I have changed a lot.*

I've been sightseeing on days off, and went to Tokyo. Took a lot of pictures and saw General MacArthur. Everyday he comes out of his headquarters building at 4:00 P.M. and stands at the top of the stairs, just looking out over the city. Then he goes back inside. There is always a big crowd waiting to see him.

Two different girls told my fortune with cards and they both said I would not marry the man I expect to, but that I am supposed to meet someone else, who is lousy with dough!

After I get home, I'll go shopping and play Santa Claus, and catch up on the last two years. I'll have to look for a job, and frankly, don't know what I want to do. Love, Lorraine

Lorraine arrived home in Chicago in January 1946. After being discharged, her old job was waiting at the doctor's office.

SNAP SHOTS

"You never know what will happen when you join the service."

Ellen Robinson Page U.S. Army   **Twenty-fifth Station Hospital, Liberia**

During the early part of the war, planes flew from the United States to Natal, Brazil, then across the Atlantic to Liberia, and from there to North Africa or England. The Twenty-fifth was in Liberia at Roberts Field.

I entered the army in 1942, and my first assignment was to Fort Huachuca, Arizona, where everything was segregated. The original hospital took only white patients, with white nurses and doctors. The African-American nurses and doctors were assigned to a new section, caring for black patients only. We nurses set up training for the corpsmen.

Orders for overseas came early in 1943, and along with African-American nurses from Fort Bragg, North Carolina, and Tuskegee Air Base, Alabama, we sailed in a convoy of ships from Hoboken, New Jersey. My home was near there, but I couldn't contact anyone because of secrecy.

The convoy took thirty days to get to Liberia. The most hair-raising experience I had was when every ship in the convoy stopped dead in the water because enemy submarines were detected in the area. When we reached the coast of North Africa, our ship sat off the coast of Casablanca for almost a week, waiting for an escort to go on to Liberia.

Our assignment was mainly caring for the soldiers stationed at the airfield who developed malaria. Troops were in Liberia also to protect the American rubber plantations. Living was very crude. The barracks building was infested with rats and all sorts of lizards. The rafters overhead had colorful lizards crawling on them, and frequently, a monkey. During the rainy season we had to put our raincoats over the bed nets to keep dry. The community latrine was in a separate area, and to go there at night we always had to have someone with us for safety. The toilet was just a bench with five holes in it.

233

Ellen Robinson (4th from left) with other nurses at Ft. Huachuca, Arizona, before assignment to the Twenty-fifth SH in Liberia in 1943. Courtesy of *The Crisis* magazine.

The hospital was made up of six or eight barracks buildings. One was surgical, one psychiatric, and the others were medical, and we took care of both black and white patients. The main illness was malaria, and many of the patients were very, very ill. The food was pretty horrible, which I wrote home about often.

Monrovia was the nearest city, where we shopped once in a while. The ambassador invited us for American food a couple of times. To get to Monrovia, we went about twenty or thirty miles through the Firestone Rubber Plantation.

We had movies and played cards in our free time, but there wasn't much to do. A few nurses were able to work at a clinic in a nearby native village. At first, most of us were disappointed that we didn't get front-line duty, but later realized how important it was for us to be where we were.

After about ten months we returned to the States because several nurses were getting sick despite taking Atabrine. Also, the direction of the war was changing and planes were able to fly from the States direct to Europe.

Dymphna Van Gorp U.S. Navy   Brazil

A graduate of Marquette University, Dymphna set up the first navy corpsman school after joining in January 1943.

Another navy nurse and I were sent to the Army Air Forces School of Air Evacuation at Bowman Field, Kentucky, in December 1943. We are the only two navy nurses wearing army wings. Brazil wanted to form a nurse corps for their new air force, and we were sent to help start it after completing the course. The program didn't develop very much because nurses in Brazil with any education were scarce then. We learned Portuguese on the job and joked about being "Copacabana Commandos." There was never much flying for us, and we set up a clinic to take care of American patients at the Brazilian Air Force Hospital. Our patients were army and navy servicemen who came off ships or civilians who were in the country during the war. I returned to the States in 1947 and stayed in the navy for twenty-three years.

Maude Smith U.S. Army   Forty-third and 114th Station Hospitals

"Smitty" retired from the Army Nurse Corps with the rank of colonel.

Officers tents were adjacent to our hospital area in Algiers. We took turns walking to the shower, about one hundred yards from our quarters. It was about noon, on a very hot, dusty day when I walked past a tent that suddenly burst into flames. It burned quickly, and there was nothing left but a burned mound of ashes.

This example of solar power was caused by a shaving mirror left on a cot. The sun shining through the open flap of the tent was reflected onto the very dry canvas of the tent. Luckily, it was a windless day, and nothing else burned. The two dentists who lived there were walking back from the shower and wound up with nothing but the khaki shorts they were wearing and the towels they carried.

Pearl Will Haugland Bach U.S. Army

Before going to the Philippines, Skagway, Alaska, was my first overseas assignment, in April 1943. Six of us nurses worked in a small clinic, which supported the GIs transporting supplies for construction of the Alcan Highway and the oil fields in the Yukon Territory. We lived in a small house, and there were some interesting experiences. One afternoon, after working a morning shift, a nurse gave birth to a six-pound baby girl. She claimed not to know she was pregnant, and we didn't suspect it either.

Both mother and baby were in good condition, and were shipped back to the States.

Another time we were all called in and questioned about the chief nurse. She was suspected of being a drug addict by some of the doctors, because no matter how much morphine the patients seemed to be given, they were always in pain. I'd wondered about it myself, but didn't know what to do about it. They found she took morphine for herself, then diluted the rest. She was convicted and shipped out right away.

I was transferred to Fort Nelson, British Columbia, before Christmas, to a hospital we took over from the Canadians. We lived in little log houses, and it was extremely cold. My boyfriend from home had been in Panama with the army for five years, and when he was reassigned to California, we married at my parents' home in Tacoma, Washington, in April 1944. I was able to work at army hospitals in Washington for a few months, but just before Christmas 1944, I sailed under the Golden Gate Bridge, destination unknown.

Ruby Lamson Gibeau U.S. Army

"Lammy" joined the army in 1943 after her husband was sent to Europe, and her first assignment was to Iceland.

After 101 days in Iceland, I received membership in the FBI: "Forgotten Bastards of Iceland." Iceland is a beautiful country, but the wind is so strong, we had to hang on to something all the time.

When we were on a ship going from Iceland to England, I remember a funny incident with two British officers. Our life jackets had lights that only stayed lit for three minutes. One Brit told the other it was because that's how long you can survive in this cold water. I don't know when I was ever that cold again.

We went to England and France, setting up hospitals for someone else to take over. We called ourselves the "Medical Engineer Work Battalion." We set up the American Hospital in Paris, which was a plush place, with private rooms. It was already there for American civilians before the war, and we turned it into an army hospital.

My husband and I were very fortunate to be able to see each other a couple of times in Europe. He was enlisted, so we had to stay off post when we met, and I ended up as a captain when I got out in 1946.

Margaret Carlson Larson U.S. Army

Whenever my ship, the *Dogwood,* was in port, I never seemed to have time to replace my duty shoes with a new pair. Each sole had a hole in it, and I was putting cardboard in my shoes. When we went to the Philippines our ship always anchored in the China Sea, and we had to take a small boat into the dock at Manila. One day I finally got a new pair, tied them together, slung them over my shoulder, bought bananas and a coconut from a vendor, and headed for the dock to get a ride back to the *Dogwood.* I was in fatigues, it was raining, very hot, and I couldn't find any boats going back to my ship. After almost an hour, the Shore Patrol sent me to the Port Command Dock for help. As I got there, I saw a small craft making ready to pull out. I ran and called, "Wait for me!" and they did.

Hopping aboard, I pleaded to be taken to my ship, and at the same time, thrust my shoes, bananas and coconuts into the arms of the first man I saw. I was complaining and talking, but not getting conversation out of the other passenger. We pulled alongside a flagship, and as he climbed up the rope ladder, the crew saluted. I thanked him for holding my shoes, bananas, and coconuts, then had a good look, and recognized the commanding general of the Pacific Theater, General Douglas MacArthur. He smiled and gave me a wave, while I stood there with my mouth open.

I asked the crew members why they hadn't told me who the other passenger was, and they laughed, and said I never stopped talking long enough. The general didn't have insignia on, and with his trademark dark glasses, I never gave him a close look. Everyone had a good time with me after that, saying I "ordered" General MacArthur to transport me to my ship in the South China Sea.

An interesting note about him is that in 1960, I read that he was a patient in a New York hospital. I mailed him a card, apologizing for my behavior that day in 1944. I received an answer from him with the words, "Indeed, I do remember you."

Prudence Burns Burrell U.S. Army

Lieutenant Lowell Burrell, adjutant of our hospital, and I had become engaged in Milne Bay. When we first left the States and were on our way from California to Australia, everyone had to "stand to" on the ship twice a day, at 6:00 A.M. and 6:00 P.M., practicing to abandon ship should the

Japanese attack. I didn't know how to swim, and Lieutenant Burrell offered to help. He's been helping me ever since. We were married on October 17, 1945, in a formal ceremony at the Navy Chapel in Manila. My dress was handmade by a Filipina from a nylon parachute. We'd become friends with the Navata family, who held the wedding reception in their home. Mr. Navata had been a secretary to President Osmena. Mrs. Navata let me borrow the wedding veil that had been used by brides in her family for three generations. These days I give talks to school children, and to get their attention, I pull out of my bag the parachute wedding dress.

Ellen Green Dellane U.S. Army

On V-J Day we all thought we could go home right away. The army didn't do it that way. I should have been used to waiting, because when I joined the ANC in 1942, I did a lot of waiting and little working for a long, long time. I was first assigned to Camp Kilmer, New Jersey, to serve on hospital ships, but the nurses who came in with patients from Europe turned around and went back overseas. I never went anywhere, nor did I do any nursing there. For a year we became good at twiddling our thumbs until finally sent to the Pacific.

Hazel Johnson Barton U.S. Army

In 1943 I was stationed at Camp Kilmer, New Jersey, awaiting orders to go overseas, when the chief nurse decided we should convert a barracks into a nurse's club. I was selected to work at the club, and what duty. I served coffee and doughnuts in the morning, sold beer and played the piano in the evening. At least it gave us a place to go and some socialization, as everybody was on edge because of where we would go next.

Althea Williams U.S. Army

I used to umpire softball games when we were in Australia. In 1984 I was on a trip to New Zealand and met some men who said they were with the Forty-first Infantry. Two of them looked at me and said, "You were the umpire for the softball team, weren't you?"

When the war ended, I went back to school, then rejoined the army to serve in Korea and Vietnam.

Elizabeth Whitlow Reith Price U.S. Army   Eighty-first Station Hospital

A month after arriving at the Eighty-first in Italy, Beth's sister was released from a Japanese prison camp in the Philippines.

My family and I didn't know what had happened to Evelyn. Our mother sent me a letter, telling of her release, and I remember feeling surprised and grateful. We were a big family of twelve children, and four of our brothers were also in the service during the war. The only word we had was a picture of some women prisoners washing in a creek in the Philippines that appeared in *Life* magazine. We wondered if she was in the picture and found out later she was. I didn't see her for a few years after she returned, and by then she'd recovered fully.

I was a replacement nurse in the Eighty-first, joining them in Livorno, and was there for six months. Just before we received orders to go to the CBI, I married a lieutenant in the Eighty-second Airborne. My ship was in the Mediterranean when the Japanese surrendered, so we were rerouted back to the States, and I rejoined my husband.

Ethel Carlson Cerasale U.S. Army Air Force

I can't forget how naive I was when I first joined the army in 1942. Arriving at St. Louis, Missouri, early in the morning after an all-night train ride from Chicago, a taxi took me to Jefferson Barracks. I met the chief nurse, Miss Bridget Mullancy, who'd been in the army for twenty-six years but refused to be addressed by her rank of captain. One of the other nurses gave me a "caduceus" pin (symbol of the medical profession), which I'd never heard of, and a gold bar to wear on the shoulder of my white nurse's uniform. On the way to the ward, a soldier approached from the other direction and gave me a big salute. I fumbled awhile...I'd been a Girl Scout. . . so I formed the three-finger salute. The other nurses hadn't told me about saluting.

Later on we were given military training from a drill sergeant, but a major was in charge. The major was a big guy with rows of ribbons on his massive chest, and he bellowed out profanities at our clumsiness. This made one of the nurses break into tears, and she told the chief nurse, and the next day the major apologized, saying he wasn't used to ladies in the service.

I volunteered for flight nurse training at Bowman Field, Kentucky, and we learned military discipline stuff, like drilling to perfection, obstacle course, infiltration course where we crawled on our bellies to avoid being hit by overhead bullets. We went on one bivouac and one ten-mile hike and had to study logistics, map reading, and use of a compass. There was some training in caring for patients in the air, also.

I met Reba Whittle in Florida in May 1945. She was a flight nurse who was taken prisoner by the Germans when her plane was shot down near Nancy, France, and was the only woman in the prison camp for five months until she was repatriated. When she arrived for R & R in Miami she looked awful, having suffered a head wound in the crash, and her head had been shaved in the prison camp. She was hollow-eyed and very thin, with little hair. Years later I met her again, and she had recovered beautifully.

Mildred Irene Clark Woodman U.S. Army

In February 1941 I sailed from New York, stopped off at the Panama Canal, and on to Honolulu. I lost twenty-two pounds on that twenty-one-day voyage because of seasickness, making three trips to each meal. I volunteered for duty in the ship's hospital to keep my mind off the nausea, but only cheese and crackers stayed down the entire trip.

In those days, arriving on a ship at Honolulu Harbor was an unforgettable experience. It was almost sunset when we approached the shore, and there was a rainbow in the sky. As the ship neared the dock, we heard the strains of the Royal Hawaiian Band in the distance. Small boats came out to meet the ship with flower leis and messages from those ashore. My life in Hawaii was idyllic, with hula lessons, formal dinners and dances with army and navy officers, singing with the chapel choir, and horseback riding in my time off. Assigned to the hospital at Schofield Army Barracks, I was on call every other night and thought I could not be doing more satisfying and important work. This was before the war, remember.

Helen Entrekin U.S. Navy

I left Hawaii in 1942 for an assignment in Florida, then volunteered for the Aleutian Islands. There were dead Japanese soldiers still in caves when I arrived. They'd invaded the Aleutians in 1942, and their bodies were preserved by the cold. We worked in a regular hospital, but there was an underground hospital all set up because they planned to attack Japan from there. We were to go out by submarine if things became rough and were packed and ready to go at all times. A lot of dermatology patients were sent to us, because someone had the idea that the men who had caught tropical skin diseases in the jungles could be cured if they went to the cold arctic air. It didn't work, of course.

My twin sister and I both stayed in the military until retirement but were never stationed in the same area after our tours in Hawaii.

To the Army Nurse

All honor to the soldier, the sailor, and the marine.
Ours are the finest fighting men the world has ever seen.
They're deserving of their medals and plaudits of the nations
For the gallant service rendered at their various battle stations.
But Congress could not do better, and I'm sure they could do worse
Than to strike a special medal for the noble army nurse.
From the jungles of Bataan and ill-fated Corregidor,
To Tunisia, to Sicily, and to Italy's hostile shore,
Wherever duty called her, she has answered to that call,
Has left her home and loved ones to give her very all.
I asked a lad with the Purple Heart, just back from the sea
To tell me frankly what he thought of the work of the A.N.C.
He said, "I'll tell you, sir, had it not been for their care,
I feel quite sure that today I'd be permanently over there."
That this boy should know, undoubtedly, with me you will agree.
So, I offer a toast to the personnel of the loyal A.N.C.
And I offer a prayer to the Commander-in-Chief of the entire universe . . .
May thy blessing abide forever with each faithful army nurse.

Author anonymous
(from Ellen Green Dellane)

THE WAR ENDS

"I can't express how I felt when I heard it was over."

Mary Jevaraus Gallagher U.S. Army

A student in Lithuania when war broke out in 1939, Mary returned to the States to attend nursing school.

I was a young, American girl attending art school in my parents' native country when Germany invaded Poland in 1939. I remember hearing announcers on the radio asking men to bring bicycles and food and go off to the war. The American ambassador told me to leave Lithuania in April 1940, and I went by train through Germany and Italy to return to the States. I was trying to change trains in Danzig the day the Germans were invading Norway and Denmark, and the trains were all heading in that direction. Guards were constantly checking my papers, but I was able to continue. I boarded a ship in Italy, and when we passed by Gibraltar, the ship was detained three days because they thought a German Field Marshall was on board.

Back in the States, I was determined to get back to Europe to help and decided nursing was the best way for me to get there. After graduating from nurses training, I joined the army and arrived in Scotland the day the war ended in Europe, May 8, 1945.

Military hospitals were closing all over England, and my unit was the one who did it. Sometimes there were patients in the hospital, and sometimes there weren't. Things were moving so fast. I had a three-day pass to London once, and when I returned to the hospital, it was already disbanded, the nurses were gone, and I had to find my way to the next place. We transferred patients to other hospitals and then turned in everything, like fountain pens, watches, bedpans, you name it. They would dig a big hole and put everything into it. There was more than the English could use, and there was no way to take it back to the States because the ships were needed for troops going to the war in the Pacific.

We moved from place to place, and each place we went, everyone was happy to see us. The nurses who'd been there during the war were glad to be leaving, and the men all thought we were fresh young faces, which made us very popular. In England I was assigned to the 112th, 52nd, and the 178th General Hospitals in a very short time.

The same thing happened in France. As we took over a hospital that was closing, we'd care for patients until they were gone and then cleaned out the place. I worked with the 195th General Hospital there. The patients weren't war casualties by then, but accident victims, or were just ill.

One of the hardest things I had to do was to "special" a soldier who we knew was dying. He'd been wounded in the war, but now the war was over, and he was too ill to send home, and he was going to die in a foreign country. I don't know what all I said to him, but just kept telling him how brave he'd been, and how proud of him everyone was.

Venereal disease was a big problem. I remember being in Paris in Notre Dame Cathedral with a doctor, and GIs came up to him, right in church, and asked him for condoms. We usually had male escorts, and I'll never forget how the prostitutes in Pigalle came up to us and tried to pull the men away. We sent patients out on passes and gave them condoms.

My next assignment was the Eighty-first Hospital Train, based in Frankfurt, Germany. We took German soldiers and Nazi SS troops to one place and returned with our sick American soldiers, some had been prisoners, to Bremerhaven or Paris to go home. There were four medical officers and four nurses on the train. It was a very interesting time, because we went all over Europe seeing the sights, both good and bad.

The last car was our nurses' quarters. There were two rooms, with two of us in each. One day the train left the station, and our car was left behind. We waited outside, afraid another train would take us. After a couple of hours, the right train came back and hitched us up, and away we went. We went everywhere, even Czechoslovakia, and it was wonderful. I had breakfast in one country and dinner in another. If the train stopped for church on Sunday, or something like that, we'd go see the whole town.

The most horrible part was the awful odor that was everywhere. Bodies were buried under the rubble, and the stench was ghastly. The sights were unbelievable in the cities. Part of a building would be hanging from another part, radiators and bathtubs hung by pipes or wires. As we went by on the train, we could see every major city had been bombed, like Frankfurt and Munich. Heidelberg was saved and was still beautiful. It was terrible to see Frankfurt. The railroad stations were horribly damaged. Beautiful once, their stained glass windows and skylights were broken, and the roof was open to the weather. Tracks were repaired right away so soldiers and equipment could get back.

Often when we were eating and the train would stop, children and local people stood outside, staring at us. We pulled down the shades but usually gave some of our food to them. GIs threw out cigarettes and gum all the time. In no time it seemed, they really began to clean it up. The buildings came down, rubbish was piled up and cleared away, and the decaying bodies were dug out and removed.

One of the most humorous people I met was a GI who came on the train, assigned to us as a mechanic. He was very entertaining, and everyone enjoyed his stories. He seemed to have a girl in every station, and we learned he was married to a German girl. Our money was changed often, and to get it our name had to be on a list, and his wasn't. This made someone suspicious, and they found out he was AWOL, his orders were fake, and by the time they looked for him, he'd disappeared. I often wonder what came of him and how long he was able to wander around in Germany.

Although I wasn't in Europe during the war, I knew there was a difference between wartime, when there was a purpose to be there, and right after, when people were at loose ends. The years 1945 and 1946 were difficult for the Americans who were still overseas. Morals seemed to decline. Some married men were trying to get any girl they could, almost in desperation. A nurse who seemed so sophisticated would have to go home pregnant. General Eisenhower's headquarters was near us in Frankfurt, and we were very popular with his aides. We had to be pretty careful, because there were a lot of married men trying to date us.

One strange memory I have after all this time was when I took care of GIs who were black, and they would be unfriendly. When we gave them medicine, they'd turn their back on us, or I'd give a back rub, and they wouldn't respond. One black soldier I remember was so very sick, and I could never figure out how to reach him, to help him. In New England, where I was from, we mixed with everyone, and this was very unusual to me.

The Army of Occupation took over, and the hospital train wasn't needed, so I worked in the Ninety-seventh General Hospital in Frankfurt, in the delivery room. The men were marrying local women and having babies, and I was much in demand.

General Patton was a patient in the hospital then, having been badly injured in an accident. His wife and son were always with him, according to my friend who was his special nurse. She said he wanted to make sure the driver didn't get any blame for the accident, which caused his death.

Americans were needed by the Army of Occupation to work as civilians, so I resigned from the army and was able to stay and work in Europe for six more months. The Americans there after the war were very idealistic. We had long discussions about how we would help the world and the poor countries. We were going to help Germany and others "stand on their own feet." We really wanted to help, but the Germans wanted us to leave. They used to write on the sidewalk, "Out Americans!" We could see the debris, the bombed cities, the people begging for food, and we talked about helping everyone and everything. We were quite altruistic.

I am really against wars, because they accomplish nothing. We saw the poverty and devastation and knew everything would have to be rebuilt. So what did everyone fight about?

Evangeline Bakke Fairall U.S. Army

After working almost a year and a half in England, nurses of the 250th were sent to the Continent in May 1945, as the war in Europe was winding down. The first week we were billeted in an eleventh century chateau in Mesnierres, France, where numerous other nurses were also awaiting further orders. The building was cold, damp, and musty, and many people became sick and were hospitalized. It was an unhappy time because volunteers were needed for CBI, and we knew we would be split up.

Most of our unit went to Verdun, where I saw my first French version of a toilet. The two toilets in the house we stayed in were simply two porcelain tiled squares on the floor with a hole in the middle and a couple of grooved spots simulating the shape of a pair of shoes. You were supposed to squat and hit the hole. Later, one of the men built a wooden one-seater over the hole, which helped. Our unit was split up constantly, as the war with Japan ended and everyone was being sent back to the States.

Regensburg, Germany, was our next assignment. A four-day train trip across the country showed the utter destruction brought on by the bombing. I thought I had seen a lot of damage in London, where buildings were badly blitzed, but there was no comparison with what we saw from the train. We passed other trains going in the opposite direction with signs chalked on the sides of the cars saying, "Headed for the U.S.A."

We took over a beautiful, modern hospital in Regensburg. Nuns lived on the top floor of the building where we were quartered, and we thought it very luxurious. There were three of us in a room, and finally I was warm. We couldn't get over the toilets and baths everywhere, modern lighting, tiled operating room, and marvelous kitchen equipment. A Messerschmidt airplane plant was in our backyard, and it was in shambles as a result of our bombers in 1942. How the hospital escaped damage was a mystery.

I met my future husband there, and he persuaded me to stay longer so we could marry in Germany, and perhaps go home together. He worked at the Nuremberg war crimes trials, which I was able to attend sometimes. Everyone was given earphones to hear the translations. I remember when Goering, the Nazi, was on trial he really played to the public. He was a charmer.

My father was a Lutheran minister, so I wanted to be married in the Lutheran church in Regensburg, though we also had a ceremony performed by the army chaplain. The nuns made a beautiful wedding dress for me and for my bridesmaids. We honeymooned in Switzerland, but they weren't used to married army couples, and someone was always trying to separate us. Bud had to constantly keep showing our marriage papers. We returned to the States in December 1945, though not together.

To this day, many still call me Bakke, instead of my first name. Part of the camaraderie we enjoyed included being called by a nickname, or the other nurses called each other by their last name.

Florence Viergutz U.S. Army

I returned from Europe and went back to Detroit, but so much had changed, and everything was a big adjustment from being overseas. I packed my bags and went to California to work in a veteran's hospital. A year later I went back home. The veterans were facing unemployment and a lot of rough times ahead. I was at loose ends for awhile, finding out what I wanted, but luckily, there was a shortage of nurses.

Helen Wenning U.S. Army

After I was discharged in 1946, I returned home to Michigan, but the adjustment to civilian life was not easy. Life in the service in wartime is unique, and though there are many hardships, the *esprit de corps* is tremendous. For two years I was too restless to remain in any job longer than a few months each, though I did appreciate being close to my family again.

The GI Bill had a great deal to do with my life, by giving me the opportunity to obtain a Bachelor of Science in Nursing Education degree from Wayne State University in Detroit, and studying a term at Mexico City College, in Mexico. The next twenty-five years were spent teaching nursing, during which time I was able to get a leave of absence and earn a master's degree. After many years on the faculty at Harper Hospital in Detroit, I became Director of Nursing Education, before retiring in 1975.

My army service provided me with educational opportunities I would not otherwise have had. It exposed me to many people from different walks of life, and gave me maturity as well as an opportunity to recognize my own stamina.

Marion Hein Burrell U.S. Army

In the spring of 1945, we rotated home from Italy by pulling names out of a hat, and I went home. Our chief nurse became a cloistered nun after the war. We always said, "What did we do to her, she wasn't even Catholic."

Rosemary O'Connell Smith U.S. Army

I sailed from Naples on a troop ship in the summer of 1945. It was said that if we passed the Straits of Gibraltar before the war ended in Japan, we would head for the Panama Canal. Then, if it had not ended before we entered the canal, we would go on to Manila. We were all happy when it ended while we were still in the Mediterranean and we returned to the States.

I could never have done this if I hadn't been young.

Lucille Rosedale Tubbs U.S. Army

When missions to land planes in Russia were discontinued, we were sent back to Europe. On V-E Day I was stationed near Paris, and there was

Homebound from Italy after V-E Day, the crowded deck of the *David C. Shanks* troop ship included the music of Les Brown's band, playing "Sentimental Journey."

a lot of celebrating. I can't express how great I felt. As soon as the war was over, I transferred to Air Force Headquarters in Weisbaden, but it was a dangerous time. Local people couldn't be trusted, so we weren't allowed to go out after dark. I was happy to leave.

Being back home was such a letdown. My mother would ask what I wanted to eat, and I'd have to give it some thought, because I wasn't used to making choices like that. I found it hard to settle down. A couple of times I went from my home in New Jersey to Washington, D.C., just to walk around with all the people in uniform. I would meet friends there, and we'd talk over old times, and that seemed to help. After living out of a footlocker and being on the move for three years, it was really hard to be in one place and figure out what you wanted to do with the rest of your life. That was a big question mark. Some people just went ahead, and others just floated for a while.

I attend reunions of the Eighth Air Force, and am included with the separate group of pilots who flew to Russia. Not many people know about us.

Clara Wynick White U.S. Army

My patients in the Philippines were upset with me on V-J Day because I wasn't very jubilant. I was sad, thinking of the thousands who wouldn't be going home. In New Guinea I often visited a military cemetery, and my heart ached for the families who would never see their loved ones again.

Pearl Will Haugland Bach U.S. Army

In the Philippines I carried a small radio with me on the ward when I was working, and the GIs loved listening to Armed Services Radio. One afternoon we heard the U.S. had dropped the atomic bomb on Hiroshima, and later, one on Nagasaki. After that, we heard the Japs had offered to surrender. What a day and night of celebration! The end of the war was something you never forget. Everyone had a bottle of booze they'd been saving. The navy ships out in the bay were shooting up in the air. That night, I tell you, was a celebration, and I mean it. On September 2nd, General MacArthur accepted the Japanese surrender on board the USS *Missouri*, and a bunch of happy people listened to it over my radio. It was very, very moving.

The 133rd General Hospital was closed down by September 15. Everything was inventoried, put in trucks and boats, and taken out in the bay and dumped. I mean everything. I guess they figured it would cost so much to ship it all back, that this was the best thing to do.

I had more than enough points for discharge but had to wait for transportation home. I waited from September 15 to November 14 without any work; just waiting and waiting. This was hard because my husband was discharged already, and was waiting too. I'll never forget November 14th, when they took us out to a Liberty ship in the bay for the trip home. There was a barge with a GI band playing "White Christmas" and "Sentimental Journcy." This music still brings tears to my eyes after all these years.

Audrey Lampier U.S. Army

August 8, 1945, was a wild night in Zamboango as we celebrated the war's end. Everyone was exhilarated, dashing around the island, yelling, singing, and drinking. It was difficult to come back down to earth later when we had to go on duty. Our unit went to Kure, Japan, to work with the Army of Occupation in a steam-heated school building that had been turned into a hospital. I remember it was an art to learn to use the hole in the floor that was the Japanese toilet. Strong legs helped.

I was home in Wisconsin in time for Christmas and looked forward to a reunion with a PT boat captain I met in New Guinea. However a letter soon came from him telling of his marriage to a girl in his hometown. The real world began to set in. My interest in art led me to use the GI Bill, and eventually I went to Paris to study.

Edith Vowell U.S. Army

In September 1945 our numbers thinned as nurses were being shipped back to the States, and suddenly, seventeen Australian war brides and their nineteen children arrived. They lived in the nurses' quarters with us until they, and we, could get shipped out. We closed the 153rd in December 1945, which by now was located out in the boondocks at an abandoned U.S. Infantry training camp, where we had at the most five patients. Called back to active duty in 1948, I retired in 1963.

Fran Knutson Menown U.S. Army   Twenty-second Station Hospital

Eight of Fran's classmates joined the army with her in 1945, and they were able to stay together during their assignment to Hawaii as the war ended.

By the time we arrived in Hawaii in June, the USS *Arizona* had been enshrined, and I remember nothing but the beauty of the islands. When the Japanese surrendered in August 1945, the Twenty-second closed, and all the equipment and appliances were pulled out and stockpiled for the navy's use. I was transferred to Schofield Barracks, which was almost completely a POW compound. The hospital had a Japanese ward, a ward of Koreans, a German ward, and a ward of Italians. They were pretty hostile and uncooperative, especially the Japanese.

One morning I came on the Japanese ward and nothing had been done. The patients were able enough and were supposed to serve breakfast and tasks like that. The prisoners were on strike. I was just a young second lieutenant, new to the army, and had no idea what to do. I had an interpreter, but all I knew was that they refused to work.

I called the ward surgeon, who came right away and wrote orders for them to get out of bed and go to the rock pile and break up rocks. He was able to get them out, and when they came back later that day, they were docile, and we had no more problems.

Some prisoners stand out, like the Japanese man who said he was a taxi driver in Tokyo. He had pictures in his wallet and on the wall by his bed of American movie stars. The Italians were most cooperative. One in particular, Giannini, had cancer and was sent back home to die after we did everything we could do for him.

One thing that was loud and clear was how well they were treated by us, and they realized the same treatment wasn't on the other side. The food was terrific, though the Japanese sent it back and just wanted rice. Sometimes we heard a siren in the night, which meant that one of them escaped. I never felt there was danger, personally. They were repatriated gradually, rather than all at once.

Hilda Riskedahl Cornelius U.S. Navy   USS *Benevolence*

From North Dakota, Hilda was a senior nursing student in Chicago when Pearl Harbor was bombed.

My father was from Norway, so when I heard about the bombing of Pearl Harbor, my Viking blood made me want to join the navy. After I graduated from nurse's training, I entered the Navy Nurse Corps at Great Lakes Naval Training Center near Chicago. My first assignment was Bethesda, Maryland, but I was always hoping to get sea duty.

In 1945 I was thrilled to be assigned to the hospital ship, USS *Benevolence*, and was in Brooklyn, New York, waiting for it to sail, on V-E Day. We all went to Times Square to celebrate because there were mobs of people, all cheering and dancing.

The ship sailed from New York, crossed through the Panama Canal and wound up on Eniwetok. This was a little group of islands where there was nothing. We didn't have anything to do, but each morning more and more ships appeared. It was fascinating to see how they multiplied overnight.

We heard later that there were somewhere between three hundred to four hundred ships altogether, and it was Admiral Halsey's Third Fleet assembling for the invasion of Japan.

Then they dropped the bomb. We weren't really aware of it, but heard about a big bomb that had mushroomed. Right away we were ordered to go to Japan, to process the American prisoners of war who were being released.

On the way we passed alongside a Japanese ship that was stopped and boarded by our navy. We all stood on the deck and watched, and I felt this was a historic time. The harbors had been heavily mined during the last months, so our ship slowly followed mine sweepers as we came closer to Japan.

Arrival at the Yokosuka harbor was truly exciting. At least three hundred ships were there as a show of force, and I felt a thrill as we maneuvered among these huge ships to get inside the breakwater. We never docked but stayed in place in the water. The former prisoners had been brought from land to other ships, then transferred to our hospital ship. We spent all that first night processing them. First they were taken down in the hold and de-loused, then given clean clothes and brought up to the various wards.

Two of the men died that night. Some had wounds where they had been beaten with bamboo sticks, and these sores had splinters that were festering. Several had to have IVs, and many were very emaciated. They were given all the food they wanted, like bacon and eggs and ice cream, but since these men had been starved, they couldn't keep anything down.

A lot of the men were dumbstruck when they saw us nurses, and I remember one man in particular, who was so very, very thin. When he walked in, he just looked at me, and I reached out my hand. He hesitated and started to say something, but couldn't even talk. Later, the corpsman told me the man said he hadn't seen a woman for so long.

All night and the next day we worked with the men, until some were sent to other ships, or flown to hospitals, or the States. Some just remained there overnight, but the majority of former prisoners were gone within a week. Marine Major "Pappy" Boyington was one of the former prisoners we treated. He was well-known and had the record for having shot down more Japanese planes than anyone else before he was shot down himself.

From then on we treated the sailors who were on the support ships in port. We were there from September to December and found those early days after the war interesting when we went out into the countryside. One time I was riding in a jeep, and it needed water. We found a large container along the road, and when it was opened, out poured human excrement. That's what was used to fertilize the fields. In the towns, I remember seeing little kids with terrible complexions and running sores from malnutrition. The people were very courteous to us, and most of us felt sorry for the civilians.

The admiral hosted two parties for us. All of us who weren't on duty were excited to attend, but it turned out to be just a bunch of wolves, and old ones at that. One of them was a prominent former governor who was there to help with the return of the American prisoners. He was playing up to me, and he would like to have gone to bed, so I said, "You are old enough to be my father, and anyway, I wasn't trained for that at Lutheran Deaconess Hospital." So, when we were invited to the second party, very few nurses went. By golly, they sent a boat back to our ship with an order from the captain that every nurse who wasn't on duty had to attend. We knew what to expect that time.

By now, our work wasn't terribly serious, the war was over, and we were enjoying ourselves. A pilot from the Fifth Fleet took me on a wonderful flying tour of Japan, and it was really exciting taking off and landing on the water in an aircraft equipped with pontoons.

An officer from the *New Jersey* invited me to Thanksgiving dinner on his ship, but when I came aboard, I was escorted to the captain's cabin. The captain had pulled rank, and I never saw my date. Thankfully, the captain was a gentleman. I remember his telling me that I should consider staying in the navy because there were so many old biddies around. I told him that if I stayed in twenty years, I'd become just another old biddy.

An eye-opener for me was something the pathologist on our ship told us. One evening, when we were standing on the deck watching the water and the lights, he told us he'd been ashore that day helping set up houses of prostitution. There was one for senior officers, another for junior officers, and others for the various enlisted ranks. When we protested, he said, "Regardless of what your feelings are about this, you know these men have not been home for years. At least the girls they have in these places are clean."

The combination of these experiences has always stayed with me. After treating our prisoners of war, I don't care to watch war movies or think too much about all that. It has affected how I think about the presidents who send men, and women now, to war. When my son was about to be drafted during Vietnam, I was very much against it. I fought for him and got him a deferment because of the asthma and allergies he had. I would do it again.

I met my future husband in Japan, where he was stationed on an aviation supply ship. It was kind of a game for us girls to try to tell who was married by calculating how many months they'd been in the navy and things like that. I knew he was really single, and we dated by usually having dinner on his ship or mine. We kept in touch, and after both of us were out of the navy, we married in 1947.

Esther Wallenga U.S. Navy

When the war ended, I was at Pearl Harbor, and it was wonderful being there. The people around me looked like they wanted to pray. During World War II, nurses never thought about adulation or thanks, though nurses on the *Refuge* were awarded ribbons for the American Defense, European Theater, Asiatic Theater, Pacific Theater, and Philippines Liberation. I just felt I was needed and stayed in the Navy Nurse Corps, retiring twenty-two years later.

Helen Wentz Miller U.S. Navy

After leaving the hospital ship, USS *Refuge*, I was stationed at the Brooklyn Navy Hospital in New York. On V-J Day, four of us girls went to Times Square in our uniforms. What bedlam! It was a mass of people, and the sailors were going around kissing and hugging everyone. There is a famous photograph that is printed year after year when they commemorate the end of World War II. In it a sailor has a nurse in a big clinch and is kissing her, and I always look to see if we are in the picture. We decided that things were getting a little rough and tried to go home. Finally, we worked our way over to a side street and found a cab. Before the four of us had our doors closed, there were sailors coming in both sides, saying they were going with us. We got them out, but WOW! That was a real celebration!

I couldn't get rid of my seablood when I got out of the navy after the war. I worked on a Moore-McCormick luxury liner, making five trips to South America, and on an army transport ship that brought back displaced persons from Europe. I met my husband on the ship when we went to Australia.

Even though it was a war, most of us try not to focus on the bad things, but on the friendships and lighter times we had. I know, though, what a rehabilitation period after the war means, because I couldn't watch war movies or listen to the "Star Spangled Banner." They just choked me up and still do.

Evelyn Hill Page U.S. Army Air Force

When the Japanese surrendered, I was on leave in Kashmir, India, and returned to a postwar Chabua, where the military was beginning to wind down its forces. Everyone was planning to leave, when I was called to the office and given a few hours to pack and be on my way in a plane over the Himalaya Mountains to Chungking, China, to pick up a patient.

I stayed in Chungking with WACS, who took me along to a tea given by Generalissimo and Madame Chiang Kai-shek. We gathered in a spacious, reception hall and waited for our host and hostess to arrive. The General strolled into the room, his wife following. He raised his hand in greeting and then sat on a throne-like chair, smiling the rest of the time.

Madame was dressed in the traditional Chinese dress and was very attractive and gracious, visiting with all of us. They both signed my "Short Snorter Bill." We were served tea and cookies, then given a tour of an orphanage, which was very dear to her heart.

General Patrick Hurley, Ambassador to China, was being recalled by President Truman, so along with my patient and a flight surgeon, I flew with him in his personal C-54. We were treated royally at each stop, and when we landed in Long Beach, California, my patient was let off, and we flew on to Memphis to refuel. I was able to call home, completing my circling the world, beginning in 1943. In India I had been as far from home as I could be.

Janet Kearsley Faubion U.S. Army Air Force

Janet became an army nurse in 1943 in Albany, New York.

Just three other flight nurses and I were stationed in Anchorage at the end of the war, flying patients from the end of the Aleutian chain to Anchorage and Seattle. I remember seeing hundreds of ships in the harbor at Adak, getting ready for the invasion of Japan, but we heard it was part of the "Lend-lease" program and they were being given to Russia.

It was quite a contrast when we heard about V-E Day and V-J Day. I was on a flight when V-E Day was announced, and everyone was very excited about it. Then when V-J Day came, it was a shock. After all those years, we couldn't believe it was ending all of a sudden.

Norma Harrison Crotty U.S. Navy Flight Nurse

I came back from the Pacific at the end of the war and went back to live with my parents and worked in a hospital. How I missed the other flight nurses and the strong bonds that I had with them! Old high school friends were almost strangers to me, and it was difficult to explain my experiences. My years in the navy taught me I could endure hardship and still enjoy life, that I could take care of myself and "weather the storm." Experiencing sorrow together gave us a strong bond, but our happier times are what we cherish now. I have always been glad I joined the navy.

Lenore Terrell Rickert U.S. Navy

I'd been at Pearl Harbor a year before the attack and saw interesting changes come about after the war started. Navy nurses did not have rank when I joined in 1939. In those days you were either a nurse or became a chief nurse, which meant you wore another stripe on your cap. It took the war to get us rank and uniforms. When the war started we couldn't go to Honolulu without a uniform, so we had to wear our white ward uniforms and carry gas masks at all times. We were really cute. Shortly afterward they issued uniforms similar to the men's, with rank on the collars and sleeves.

I stayed in Hawaii for a year after the Japanese attack, then was transferred to Long Beach, California, near my home, where I spent half my time giving talks about Pearl Harbor. I soon found it hard to see everyone hoarding food and doing things like that. People stood in line to buy cigarettes to hoard, even though they didn't smoke. I asked to be assigned overseas.

In 1943 I went to New Caledonia to a mobile hospital, where I was chief nurse. Our work there was very spasmodic. If a ship came in with injured, we worked around the clock just like at Pearl Harbor, but in between we didn't have patients at all. Ships would bring in some pretty badly wounded men from the Pacific battles. If they could be returned to duty they were, and if not they were sent back to the States. It was diffi-

In 1991, the 50th anniversary of the bombing, Lenore Terrell Rickert was a guest speaker, and introduced President George Bush at the ceremony in Honolulu honoring all who were present on that fateful day.

cult to get patients back to the States because there weren't enough ships.

On V-J Day, August 15, 1945, I arrived in Bremerton, Washington, for my next assignment. Everyone was celebrating, and everything was closed. No restaurants were open or anything.

Before the war, I'd been going with a marine, who was taken prisoner by the Japanese on Wake Island in December 1941. One of the first prisoners to be brought back, I was told he was coming to Bremerton. I was very worried about what he would be like and had a lot of reluctance about marrying him. If I thought it couldn't work, I planned to give him a week like he hadn't had and let it go at that. I had the places we'd go all picked out.

When he came off the plane I wouldn't have recognized him, but he walked right up to me and put his hands on my shoulders. He said, "We've got so much catching up to do, so much living to do." I knew right then there was nothing wrong with this guy.

There was a seven-day waiting period before we could marry, but we found a judge could waive that. At thc courthouse, the judge came in and asked, "What makes you think you got to get married?" I answered, "Nothing makes us, we just think it's time." He asked how long we'd known each other, and I told him, "Give and take, five years." Then he asked, "Why right now?" I said, "He was just released from a prison camp yesterday." The judge couldn't get the paperwork done fast enough, and the next day we were married by the chaplain, with my commanding officer standing up for us.

What I experienced at Pearl Harbor and the rest of my time in the navy has stayed with me during my whole life. In 1993 hillside fires burned hundreds of houses near my home in California. I knew what to do when the flames came close and I had to evacuate. I didn't panic but just took boxes of photos and left. I'd learned what is important and what isn't.

ABOUT THE AUTHOR

Diane Fessler began this book after discovering the letters of her aunt, who was a World War II army nurse. Attending reunions led to interviews with other nurses who served overseas between 1941 and 1946.

A graduate of the Walter Cronkite School of Journalism at Arizona State University, Tempe, Diane and her husband live in Phoenix, where she is an editor with Primer Publishers.

Additions to these reminiscences are welcomed.

A portion of the proceeds from this book will be donated by the author to the Women in Military Service for America Memorial Foundation, Washington, D.C.

Further Reading

Archard, Theresa. *G.I. Nightingale: The Story of an American Army Nurse.* New York: W. W. Norton & Co. Inc., 1945.

Aynes, Edith. *From Nightingale to Eagle.* Englewood Cliffs, NJ: Prentice Hall, 1973.

Berendsen, Dorothy M. *The Way It Was: An Air Force Nurse's Story.* New York: Carlton Press, Inc., 1988.

Blassingame, Wyatt. *Combat Nurses of World War II.* New York: Random House, 1967.

Buchanan, Margaret S. *Reminiscing: An Account of the 300th Army General Hospital in WWII.* Dickson, TN, 1988.

Cooper, Page. *Navy Nurse.* New York: McGraw-Hill Book Co., 1946.

Daly, H. C. *The U.S.S. Solace Was There.* San Anselmo, CA, 1991.

DeWitt, Gill. *The First Navy Flight Nurse on a Pacific Battlefield.* Fredericksburg, TX: Admiral Nimitz Foundation, 1983.

Farrell, Brenda McBryde. *Quiet Heroines.* London: Chatto & Windus, 1985.

Flikke, Julia O. *Nurses in Action: The Story of the Army Nurse Corps.* Philadelphia: J. B. Lippincott, 1943.

Glines, Edna L. *Heads in the Sand.* Los Angeles, 1990.

Hager, Alice Rogers. *Wings for the Dragon.* New York: Dodd, Mead & Co., 1945.

Hardison, Irene. *A Nightingale in the Jungle.* Philadelphia: Dorrance, 1954.

Haskell, Ruth. *Helmets and Lipstick.* New York: G. P. Putnam's sons, 1944.

Jopling, Lucy Wilson. *Warrior in White.* San Antonio, TX, 1990.

Kielar, Eugenia M. *Thank You, Uncle Sam: Letters of a WWII Army Nurse from North Africa and Italy.* Bryn Mawr, PA: Dorrance, 1987.

La Forte, Robert S., and Ronald E. Marcello, eds. *Remembering Pearl Harbor: Eyewitness Accounts by U.S. Military Men and Women.* New York: Ballantine Books, 1991.

Littoff, Judy Barrett, and David C. Smith. *We're in This War, Too.* New York: Oxford University Press, 1994.

Lutz, Alma, ed. *With Love, Jane.* New York: John Day Co., 1945.

Moseley, Esther Baer. *Lady Don't Stop Here: The True Story of a Young Woman's Adventures as an Air Evacuation Nurse in the Army Air Corp of WWII.* Peachtree City, GA, 1988.

Newcomb, Ellsworth. *Brave Nurse.* New York: Appleton Century Co., 1945.

Peto, Marjorie. *Women Were Not Expected.* West Englewood, NJ, 1947.

Ratledge, Abbie C. *Angels in Khaki.* San Antonio, TX: The Naylor Co., 1975.

Redmond, Juanita. *I Served on Bataan.* Philadelphia: J.B. Lippincott Co., 1943.

Russell, Maxine. *Jungle Angel: Bataan Remembered.* Brainerd, MN, 1988.

Sforza, Eula Awbrey. *A Nurse Remembers.* Batavia, IL, 1991.

Tayloe, Roberta Love. *Combat Nurse: A Journal of World War II.* Santa Barbara, CA: Fithian Press, 1988.

Thruelsen, Richard, and Elliott Arnold. *Mediterranean Sweep: Air Stories from El Alamein to Rome.* New York: Duell, Sloan and Pearce, 1944.

Treadwell, Mattie E. *The Women's Army Corps: Special Studies.* Washington: Department of the Army, 1954.

Wandrey, June. *Bedpan Commando: The Story of a Combat Nurse During World War II.* Elmore, OH, 1989.

Weatherford, Doris. *American Women and World War II.* New York: Facts On File, Inc., 1990.

Williams, Denny. *To the Angels.* Denson Press, 1985.

World War II Flight Nurses Assn. *The Story Of Air Evacuation: 1942-1989.* Dallas, 1989.

Inter-library loan will locate out-of-print books.

INDEX

A

abdominal, 133, 170, 208. *See also* belly, stomach

Acorn, Catherine, 37

Admiralty Islands, 51, 55-7

Africa: Liberia, 233-34; theater of war, 123-35; USS *Refuge*, 147

African American: blood designation, 41; experiences in U.S., 37, 154-56, 233; in England, 154-56; in Liberia, 233-34; in Pacific Theater, 37-41; marriage, 155-56, 237-38; struggle to be in Army Nurse Corps, 5; University of Minnesota, 39, 154. *See also* black, segregation

Air Corps, 138-39, 142-43, 193-97

Alameda CA: navy flight nurse training, 75

Alaska: army nurse, 235; flight nurse, 256-57; navy nurse, 240-41, Skagway, 235; Territory of, 2

Albania: crash landing and rescue, 136-46

Algeria: flights, 135; Goat Hill, 127, 129; Oran, 123, 129, 132; tent fire, 235

American Medical Association, 19

American Red Cross. *See* Red Cross

amtracs, 99-100, 102

anesthesia: operating room, 17, 59-60,

125, 180; promotions, 180; surgery without, 168; training, 7, 16, 125, 209

Angerer. *See* Wood, Dorothy

appendicitis: internment camp, 86-7

Arabs: impression of, 125, 127, 132

Arizona: Fort Huachuca, 37, 154-56, 233-34; Hyder, 55

Arkansas, 174-75

Armold. *See* Scholl, Dorothy

Army of Occupation: Germany, 229, 245-46; Japan, 230-31, 253-54

Aschaffenburg, Germany, 189

Atabrine: destination clue, 127; malaria despite use, 234; medicine in prison, 95; yellowing skin, 35, 106, 120

atom bomb: 58, 224, 250, 253

Atkinson. *See* Budway, Mary

Australia: African American nurses, 5, 37-41; Brisbane, 34, 39, 41, 70; escape to, 96; first flight nurses in, 70; harbor at Fremantle, 108; hospital in Queensland, 34, 42-3, 238; wedding, 69

Australian: African Americans and, 40-1; Kenny, Sister Elizabeth, 39; patients in Tunisia, 127; prisoners in Los Banos, 83; war brides, 251 autoclave: cooking in, 210; in prison camp, 86. *See also* sterilize

Azores: as an Atlantic route, 118, 161

B

B-17: in England, 161; in Russia, 193-94

B-24, 195

B-29: flight to bomb Tokyo, 76; in China 116-17

Baass, *See* Hutchison, Mildred

Babczak, Mary Catherine (Croyle), 21, 23

Bach, *See* Will Haugland, Pearl

Backinger, *See* Francis, Doris

Baer, Esther (Moseley), 4, 110

Bakke, Evangeline (Fairall), 151, 246-47

barbed wire: around barracks, 72, 87, 160; crawling under, 55

Baroniak, Anne, 117

barrage balloons, 160-1

Barron, *See* Matthews, Gelane

Barton, *See* Johnson, Hazel

bashas (straw huts), 106-8, 111, 114-15

Bataan, Philippines: army escape to, 86, 89, 94-6; Bataan Maizie, 37; survivors, 55, 58, 112, 118

Battle of the Bulge: close to combat, 171, 174, 187; patient loads, 170, 178, 185, 221

Behnke, Eleanor (Williams), 206, 215, 219-20, 222-23

Belgium, 171, 221, 226, 228

Bell, Margaret (Rasmussen), 228

belly: plaster cast exposing, 23; wounds, 46. *See also* abdominal, stomach

Benny, Jack, 19

beriberi, 83, 101

Bermuda, 118

Berry, Betty (Godin), 111

Bilibid Prison, 86, 94-5, 100, 102-3

blacks: in Burma, 110; patients, 126-27, 216, 233-34, 245; prejudice against, 127, 216; U.S. soldiers, 170. *See also* African American, segregation

Blagen, *See* Theobald, Betty

Blanchfield, Florence, 200

blind patients, 42-3, 160

blood: African American, 41; clotting, 109; description of wounds, 18, 20, 32, 133; transfusions, 57, 100, 174, 185

Borup, Laura (Wild), 213, 219-21, 223-24

Bougainville, 32

Bowman Field KY: army flight nurse training, 30, 34, 70, 109, 141-42, 239; navy nurse attends, 235

Boy *See* Gleason, Jeannette

Boyington, "Pappy", 253

Brandvold, Florence, 178-79

Brazil, 233-35

Breger, Private, (cartoon), 205

Brethouwer, Myrtle (Hoftiezer), 204, 210, 218-19, 222-24, 230

British: ex-prisoners, 171; in India, 105-7, 112; locals in England, 161; patients in Africa, 127; troops in Albania, 138-43

British Columbia, 236

Brown, Les, 249

Bruner, *See* Kasmer, Fannie

Budway, Mary (Atkinson), 213

Burford, England, 152, 157

Burma: theater, 105-120

burns: nurses, 71; patients, 12-3, 20, 46; smell, 13, 51; treatment 13, 132

Burns, Prudence (Burrell), 37-41, 237-38

Burrell. *See* Burns, Prudence

Burrell. *See* Hein, Marion

Bush, George, 258

buzz bombs, 148, 159

C

C-46: Curtis time bomb, 118; to Russia, 195

C-47: D Day invasion, 162; evacuation in CBI, 120; in Europe, 169; in Mediterranean, 136; in Pacific, 31

C-54: ambassador's plane, 256; civilian crews, 118; crash in Albania, 136, on Eniwetok, 71, in Pacific 75; evacuation in Atlantic theater, 161, in Pacific theater, 75

C rations, 114, 208

Cairo, Egypt, 119

California: Corona hospital, 30; desert training, 55; ex-prisoners in San Francisco, 98,101; fires, 259; Long Beach, 106, 256-57; navy flight evacuation training, 75; San Diego hospital, 30; training along the coast, 107

Camp McCoy WI: army nurse training, 141-42; letters from, 199-201

Camp McCoy WI: arm*See* Cavite Navy Yard

Cañacao Hospital, *See* Cavite Navy Yard

Carlson, Ethel (Cerasale), 161-63, 239-40

Carlson, Margaret (Larson), 53-4, 163-64, 237

Carollo *See* Godfrey, Monica

Carr *See* Phelps, Eunice

Carter, Dorothy (Morris), 23-5

Casablanca, Morroco, 117-19, 195, 233

cavalry, 94

Cavite Navy Yard, 79-80, 103

CBI: theater 104-20

Cerasale *See* Carlson, Ethel

Chambers, Beatrice, 93-5, 97

chaplain: crossing the equator, 49; on president's death, 220; scolding for gambling, 42; tours to villages, 35; wedding, 157, 223, 227, 247, 259

Chennault, Claire, 116-17

Cherbourg, France: 167th General Hospital, 178-83; German mines, 220; hospital train, 207

Chiang Kai-shek, 256

Chicago Tribune, 143, 158, 218

China: Chengtu, 116; Chungking, 116, 256; Kunming, 116; theater of war, 104-120; Yangtze River, 117

Chinese: language, 108, 112; patients, 108-11

Christmas: bombing, 185; carols, 43; celebrating, 35, 213-14; French home, 210; internment camp, 83, 92; letter from ship, 52

Churchill, Winston: December 7th speech, 19; on a Tunis street, 125; on the *Queen Mary*, 174

Clark, Mildred Irene (Woodman), xiii, xiv, 16-8, 240

Coast Guard, 230

Cobb, Laura, 88, 100

Coile. *See* Dial, Kathleen

Colona, Jerry, 130, 184

Comes, Rosanna (Jones), 45-7

concentration camps, 171, 189-90, 226

Coral Sea, 29-30, 34

Cornelius. *See* Riskedahl, Hilda

corpsmen: as prisoners, 86-7; crash landing, 75-6; non-nursing duties, 7; Pearl Harbor, 15, 18; training, 21, 134, 233; USS *Refuge*, 147-51; working, 15, 77, 81, 100, 154, 187. *See also* surgical technicians, wardboys

Corregidor, Philippines: captured by Japanese, 90, 95-6, 103; nurses escape from, 74, 96; nurses escape to, 81, 89

Creel, Mary, 71

Crotty. *See* Harrison, Norma

Croyle. *See* Babczak, Mary Catherine

D

D Day: first casualties, 159, 161-62; planes overhead, 152, 160, 162; preparation, 2. *See also* Omaha Beach, Utah Beach

D rations, 169, 177

Dachau, Germany. *See* concentration camps

Dana, Phyllis, 13, 22

Daniels. *See* Glembocki, Bessie

Danner. *See* Still, Dorothy

Davey. *See* Hess, Ernestine

Davey Jones, 48-9

Davidson, Maude, 91

Davis, Benjamin, 156

DC-3, 75

December 7, 1941: Hawaii, 11-21; Philippines, 79; reactions, 113, 119, 154. *See also* Pearl Harbor

DeGaulle, Charles, 125

Dellane *See* Green, Ellen

dengue fever, 82, 86, 90

dermatology, 241. *See also* skin disease

Dial, Kathleen (Coile), 68-70

Dietrich, Marlene, 167, 201

diphtheria, 61, 181, 218

Dixen, Georgia, 71

doctors: Austin Grant, 171; D Day, 2; work with nurses, 3, 7.

Dolan. *See* Doll, Jeanne

Doll, Jeanne (Dolan), 75

draft: nurses, 6, 203

Drennan, Aloha (Sanchez), 116-17

Dumond, Louise (Kopchak), 157

Dutch East Indies, 28, 42-4, 54, 70

dysentery: internment camps, 86, 91, 96-7; nurses, 33, 129, 138; patients, 33, 129, 138

E

earthquake, 43, 57, 231

edema, 108

Edginton, Esther (Kelly), 107,159

Edginton, Florence, 107-9, 159

Edwards, Esther, 131-35, 186-90

Eighth Air Force, 250

Eighth Field Hospital, 169-70, 190-91

Eighty-first Hospital Train, 244-45

Eighty-first Station Hospital, 126-31, 239

Eighty-second Airborne, 239

Eighty-fifth Evacuation Hospital, 223-24

801st Medical Air Evacuation Squadron, 30-4

802nd Medical Air Evacuation Squadron, 135

803rd Medical Air Evacuation Squadron, 109-11, 114, 119

804th Medical Air Evacuation

Squadron, 68-70
806th Medical Air Evacuation
    Squadron, 4, 161
807th Medical Air Evacuation
    Squadron, 136-46
811th Medical Air Evacuation
    Squadron, 161
821st Medical Air Evacuation
    Squadron, 111-17
825th Medical Air Evacuation
    Squadron, 117-19
828th Medical Air Evacuation
    Squadron, 70-4
829th Medical Air Evacuation
    Squadron, 74-5
Eisenhower, Dwight: German surren-
    der, 174; hospital visit, 156, 181;
    secret assignment, 195; Tunis, 125
Eleventh Airborne, 99-103
Emory, Lillie (Skinner), 155-56
England: African American nurses, 5,
    154-56; closing hospitals, 243-44;
    first popcorn, 158, 173; preparing
    for D Day, 2, 171; theater of war,
    151-165; trains, 207. *See also* Great
    Britain.
English Channel: crossing experiences
    167, 176, 203-4, 220; wearing class
    A uniforms, 179
English language: Albanians, 137-38,
    144; French, 181; Germans, 154,
    174, 180, 185; Italians, 138;
    Japanese, 81, 85, 90-1, 230
Eniwetok, 70-2, 252
Entrikin, Helen, 15-6; 249-41
Entrikin, Sara, 15-6
Equator, 47-50. *See also* International
    Date Line, Short Snorter
European Theater, 53, 122-229, 255.
    See also individual countries

F

Fairall. *See* Bakke, Evangeline
Faubion. *See* Kearsley, Janet
Faust, 182, 218
Ferrell, Mary, 160-61, 167-68
Fifth Fleet, 254
Fifth Station Hospital, 42
Fifty-second General Hospital, 244
Fifty-sixth General Hospital, 158-59,
    174
Fifty-eighth Evacuation Hospital, 55-8
Filipinos: during bombing, 80; helping
    internees, 84; language, 41
firearms: for protection, 58, 71, 112,
    115; issue to nurses, 4, 71; patient
    threatens nurse, 215; training, 57,
    70; wearing sidearms, 70
First Army, 171
First Cavalry, 93
First Troop Carrier Command, 109
Ford. *See* Shackelford, Wilma
Forty-first Infantry Division, 43, 238
Forty-third Station Hospital, 235
Forty-fifth Division, 189
Forty-ninth Field Hospital, 227
Forrestal, James, 46
Fort Bragg NC, 154-55, 233
Fort Shafter HI, 19, 21, 23
442nd Regimental Combat Team, x
Fourteenth Air Force, 116
Fox. *See* Steele, Anna
foxholes: GI's, 153, 159; nurse's, 32,
    44, 68
fractures, 12, 153, 170
France: Aubin, 226; Biarritz, 190;
    Caen, 207; Camp Philip Morris,
    225; Cherbourg, 178- 83, 207, 220;
    Enghien, 226; La Milesse, 207, 209;
    Le Bourget Airfield, 170; Le Havre,

224-5, 228; Le Mans, 205-26; L'Orient, 22; Marseilles 182, 184, 222-23; Mesnierres, 246; Mirecourt, 185-86; Normandy, 2, 162, 167, 176; Reims, 174-75; St. Avold, 187; St. Lo, 174; St. Mere-Egliese, 208; southern, 147, 185-86, 227; Strasbourg, 186; theater of war, 167-87; Verdun, 160, 246. *See also* Omaha Beach, Paris, Utah Beach

Francis, Doris (Backinger), 19-20, 22

French: African home, 130; German speaking, 186; language, 181, 213, 216, 156, 177, 229; patients, 127, 186; perfume, 219, 226; rubble cleanup, 218, 231; toilet, 246; women, 180, 187, 206, 219

fungus, 43, 83

G

Gallagher. *See* Jevaraus, Mary

gas: chamber, 158, 201, 222; masks, 204, 257

Geneva Convention, 16, 51, 70, 112, 135

Georgetown University, 148

Gerlach, Marian (Hanifan), 228

German: artillery, 159, 187; baby farms, 222; battles, 133-35, 167, 171, 174; bombings, 185, 193-95; in Albania, 137, 139, 141, 143-44; former prisoners of, 214-16, 218, 290; language, 154, 186, 215; mines, 180, 220; nurse taken prisoner, 240; occupation by, 195, 220; patients, 147-48, 154, 158, 162, 179-82, 189-90, 215-16, 222; pillboxes, 124,212; prisoners, 5,

158, 185-87, 189-90, 202, 222; surrender, 174

Germany: at war's end, 189-92, 244-46, 249; Bertchesgaden, 222-23; Bielefeld, 190; Dachau and prison camps, 171, 175, 189-90; Frankfurt, 228, 244-45; Nuremburg War Trials, 247; Regensburg, 168, 246-47; Rhine River, 171, 185, 190, 219; River Elbe, 171; Weisbaden, 223, 228

GI Bill, 7, 58, 228, 238, 248, 251

Gibeau. *See* Lamson, Ruby

Gibraltar, 243, 248

Gibson-Girl radio, 195, 197

Gilbert Islands, 70

Gleason, Jeannette (Boy), 4

Glembocki, Bessie (Daniels), 47-51, 146-49

Godfrey, Monica (Carollo), 228-29

Godin *See* Berry, Betty

Goering, Hermann, 247

Golden Gate Bridge, 30, 236

Gordon. *See* MacLeod, Janet

Goumiers, 126, 127

Grabowski, Virginia (Shannon), 123-26; 185-86

Grant, Austin R., 171

Green, Ellen (Dellane), 61-5, 238, 241

Greenfield. *See* Whitlow, Evelyn

Grim's Ditch, England, 152

Guadalcanal, 30, 31

Guam, ex-prisoners, 101; Fleet hospital, 45-7, 79; flight nurses, 75-78; nurses captured, 1, 4

gut, 170 *See also* abdominal, belly, stomach

H

Haddon, Janet (Hoffmann), 178-85

Halsey, William, 253-54

Hanifan. *See* Gerlach, Marian

Harriman, Averill, 196

Harrington, Mary Rose (Nelson), 87-8, 102-3

Harrison, Norma (Crotty), 77-8, 257

Harvard University, 54

Haugland Bach. *See* Will, Pearl

Hauser, Ernest, 168

Hawaii: bombing and afterward, 11-27, 257; island of Hawaii, 23; Kauai, 22; Lei Day, 60; Maui, 22,25; nurses return from prison, 98; territory of, 2; training, 59; war ends, 25, 251. *See also,* Hickam Field, Pearl Harbor, Schofield Barracks, Tripler Hospital

Hawkins. *See* Van Hoorebeck, Rosedith

Hayes, Harold, 136, 143-44

head wounds, 32, 67

headquarters: Air Force, 195, 249; British in Cairo, 138, 143; carrier pigeons, 134; Casablanca, 117; Eisenhower, 174, 245; MacArthur, 89, 99, 231; Nimitz, 46; Vervier, 228

Heermance, Florence (Wiechman), 176-78

Heifetz, Yasha, 228

Hein, Marion (Burrell), 126-28, 248

helmet: for bathing, 35, 62, 66, 183, 206, 209, 211; for protection, 134, 151, 187, 203; with uniforms, 132

hepatitis, 43, 117

Hess, Ernestine (Davey), 47-50, 146-47

Hesson *See* Weltzien, Gladys

Hickam Field, HI, 14-16, 19, 21

Hill, Evelyn (Page), 119-21, 256

Himalayan Mountains, 111, 256

Hiroshima, Japan, 61, 250

Hitler, Adolph, 171, 182, 186, 220, 222

Hoffmann. *See* Haddon, Janet

Hoftiezer, *See* Brethouwer, Myrtle

Holland, 123, 171, 210

Hollandia, New Guinea, 50-2, 66

Honolulu: 12-25, 101, 240, 257-58. *See also* Hawaii

Hope, Bob, 130, 184

hospital ships: USS *Benevolence*, 252-55; USS *Comfort*, 4; USS *Dogwood*, 53-4, 163-65; USS *Refuge*, 47-52, 146-49, 255; USS *Solace*, 11-2; 29-30

hospital trains, 177-78, 207, 244-45

Howard, *See* Tremper, Frances

Hungarian, 144

Hurley, Patrick, 256

Hutchison, Mildred Vorpahl (Baass) 128

I

Iceland, 161, 236

Ie Shima, 68

Ile de France, 108, 161

Illinois: Camp Ellis, 199, 202; Great Lakes Naval Training Center, 252; POW camp, 151, 199, 202

impetigo, 58

India: Calcutta, 114; Chabua, 109-11, 119, 256; Ganges River, 108; Karachi, 109, 115, 118, 256; Ledo, 106, 108; Margarita, 106; Myitkyina, 110; Shimbuyung, 108; theater of war, 104-12

Indio, CA, 55

Inouye, Daniel K., ix-xi
International Date Line, 70. *See also* equator
internment: army nurses, 89-99; camps, 79-103; liberation, 93, 95, 97-103; navy nurses, 79-88, 99-103
Iran, 118, 195
Iraq, 118, 195
Italian: air force, 129-30; army, 138, language, 181; prisoners, 5, 118, 251-52
Italy: Anzio, 4, 134-35, 147; Aulla, x; Bari, 137, 140-41, 143, 146; Capua, 134; Caserta, 133-34; Cassino, 134; Livorno (Leghorn), 127, 130-31, 239; Mt. Vesuvius, 130, 134; Naples, 125-7, 134, 147-48, 185, 197, 248; nurses killed, 4; Rome, 123, 126, 135, 148-9, theater, 123-49
IV (intravenous transfusion): anesthesia, 16; carelessness, 127; first time, 57, 59, 117, 174, 185; patient drinking, 35-36; prisoners refuse, 189
Iwo Jima, 1, 29, 46, 59, 70, 75-77, 101

J

Jacobs, Florence, 195-97
James, Theresa, 154
Japan: Kure, 251; Nagoya, 230-31; Nagasaki, 250; Tokyo, 76, 231; Yokosuka, 253
Japanese: air battle, 74; bombing of Burma, 110-11, of Biak, 44, of India, 110-11, of Pearl Harbor, 11-21, 119, of Owi, 44, of Saipan, 64; CBI, 105; countryside, 254; distrust of, 12, 21; internment camps, 79-103; patients, 42, 112, 251-52; prisoners, 36, 78, 200, 251; ship boarded, 253; soldier

holdouts, 72, 230, 240; surrender, 68, 250-51, 256; toilets, 231, 251
Javanese, 41
Jensen, Agnes (Mangerich), 136-41
Jevaraus, Mary (Gallagher), 243-46
Jews, 171, 187, 226
Johns Hopkins Hospital, 158
Johnson, Hazel (Barton), 67-8, 238
Johnson *See* Yunker, Jean
Johnson Islands, 70
Jones, *See* Nelson, Leviatha
Jones, *See* Comes, Rosanna
Jouvenat, *See* Lonergan, Dorothy

K

K rations, 58, 177, 179
Kansas, 19, 179
Kasmer, Fannie (Bruner), 203, 215-16, 226
Kastelanetz, Andre, 218
Kau Kau Korners, 24-25
Kearsley, Janet (Faubion), 256-57
Kelly, *See* Edginton, Esther
Kennedy, Imogene (Schmidt), 95, 98
Kenney, George 70
Kenny, Sister Elizabeth, 39
Kentucky: *See* Bowman Field
Kinkaid, Thomas, 101
King Neptune, 47-9
Knutson, Fran (Menown), 251-52
Kolczak, Jean (Sciora), 203-4, 215, 227
Kopchak, *See* Dumond, Louise
Koreans, 251
Kotex, 106-7, 127, 148, 183
Krause, Lorraine (Taylor): at sea, 229-30; France, 199-206, 211-15, 217-22, 229; Japan, 230-31
Kwajelein, 76, 78
Kyser, Kay, 37

L

Lady Don't Stop Here, 4
Lampier, Audrey, 34-8, 251
Lamson, Ruby (Gibeau), 236
Langford, Frances, 130
Lapham, *See* Yungblut, Eva
Larson *See* Carlson, Margaret
Latrine: 5-holer, 233; 12-holer, 177; bomb hit, 44; diarrhea, 33, 129; distance away, 33, 152, 233; Latrinogram, 153; privacy, 77, 177; train, 184; trench, 176, 211; unsanitary, 129. *See also* toilets
Lawrence, Ruth (Little), 164-65
Le May, Curtis, 116, 117
Ledo Road, 105, 112. *See also* India
leukemia, 58
Liberia, 5, 233-34
Life, 239
life vests: 41,44, 204. *See* also Mae West
Liquor, 35, 178, 182, 206, 212, 226, 230
Lithuania, 181, 243
Little, *See* Lawrence, Ruth
Liverpool, England, 151
Lizards, 35, 56, 233
London, 154, 156, 159, 195-97
Lonergan, Dorothy (Jouvenat), 135
Loomis, Verna (Rodd), 44-5
Los Baños prison camp, 82-8, 99, 102-3
Los Negros, 55, 56
Louisiana, Camp Livingston, 154-55; Camp Polk, 54; New Orleans, 54, 127
Louisville KY, *See* Bowman Field
Luxembourg, 123, 171
Lytle, Wilma, 145

M

M*A*S*H, 37, 127
MacArthur, Douglas: escape from Philippines, 37, 86, 95; evacuation of Baguio, 94; hospital inspection, 37; in Manila, 89, 237; in Tokyo 231; Japanese surrender, 29, 250; Los Baños rescue, 99; nurses praised, 97
MacLeod, Janet (Gordon), 208-9, 213
Mae West, 137, 163. *See also* life vest
Makar, Stella (Smith), 76
malaria: fatal to staff, 43; further study, 58; in internment camps, 90, 96-7; nurses ill from, 234; nurses not taking Atabrine, 35, 106, 120; patients, 55, 134, 159, 233-34
Mallon, *See* McFall, Charlotte
Malnutrition: German prisoners, 157, 190; in internment camps, 83, 90, 94; Japanese children, 254; starvation, 92, 96
Malvern Wells, England, 158
Mandot, *See* Ott, Elsie
Maness, Ava, 136, 144-46
Mangerich, *See* Jensen, Agnes
Manila, Philippines: assist prisoner release, 66, 74; Manila Bay, 230, 237; occupation, 79- 82, 86-93, 95-7; patients from, 53; war's end, 41, 230; wedding in, 238
Markowitz, Ann, 143
Married, 6, 7, 22-3, 25, 54, 61, 68-9, 78, 88, 98, 99, 101, 117, 119, 127, 142, 156, 157, 160, 182, 216, 217, 226-27, 230, 236, 238-39, 245, 247, 255, 258-59
Massachusetts: Camp Miles Standish, 163; Fort Devens, 158

Matthews, Gelane (Barron), 18, 21
Mayo Clinic, 16, 113
McCarthy, *See* Shikoski, Dorothy
McDonald, *See* Rodgers, Audrey
McFall, Charlotte (Mallon), xv, 70-4
McGlory, *See* Simpson, Phyllis
McKenzie, *See* Watson, Lois
Malinta Tunnel, 89-91, 95
Menown, *See* Knutson, Fran
Merrill's Marauders, 113, 118
Messerschmidt, 247
Michigan: Clio, 161; Detroit, 41, 136,
    160, 247-48; Marlette, 201; nurse's
    training, 61, 70, 203; University of,
    xiv, 202
Miller, *See* Wentz, Helen
Miller, Bertha, 132
Minnesota, University of, 39, 154
Missouri: Kansas City, 37; St. Louis,
    154, 239; St. Louis U., 125
Molloy, Viola, 158-59, 174
monkey, 233
monsoon, 106, 111, 120
morphine, 12-13, 18, 71, 76, 80, 112,
    236
Morris, *See* Carter, Dorothy
Moseley, *See* Baer, Esther
mosquito net, 35, 43, 54, 56, 127, 233
mosquitoes, 31, 43, 82
mud: Camp Kilmer NJ, 203-4; Capua
    Italy, 134; cow pasture in France,
    176, 207-8, 210; Fenschafen, 36;
    Grim's Ditch, 153; Guam, 75;
    Leyte, 57; Malvern Wells, 159;
    Margarita, 106; Saipan, 64; south-
    ern France, 186; "*up to knees*" at
    Le Mans, 2, 211- 13
Mussolini, Benito, 125, 220
mutiny, 45, 229
Myitkyina, Burma, 110

N

Nash, Margaret, 79-85, 99-102
Navy Nurse, 4
Nazi, 156, 202, 222, 244, 247
Nelson, *See* Harrington, Mary Rose
Nelson, Leviatha (Jones), 178-85
New Caledonia, 29-33, 257
New Guinea: African American units,
    5, 37-41; Finschafen, 36, 39, 55;
    Hollandia, 50; Lae, 43, 68; Milne
    Bay, 35, 39, 41; Oro Bay, 35, 42;
    Port Moresby, 34, 69. *See also* Biak,
    Owi
New Hebrides, 32
New Jersey: Camp Kilmer, 202, 204,
    209, 238, 220, 238; Hoboken, 58,
    233; Kearney, 47, 126, 149
New Mexico, 178, 181
New York: Camp Shanks, 126; New
    York City, 220; St Albans, 101;
    Times Square, 252, 255
New Zealand, 29, 30, 33, 106, 238
Newfoundland, 118, 161
Nimitz, Chester, 46
Ninetieth General Hospital, 193
Ninety-second Evacuation Hospital,
    43-5
Ninety-second Infantry, 37
Ninety-third Infantry, 37
Ninety-seventh General Hospital, 245-
    46
Norine, June (Norlin), 178, 182-84
Norlin, *See* Norine, June
Notre Dame Cathedral, 219, 244

O

O'Connell, Rosemary (Smith), 129-31
Ohio, 117, 160-61
Okinawa: invasion, 29, 46, 74-6;
    President Roosevelt's death, 78;
    typhoon, 68
Omaha Beach: first casualties, 161;
    invasion of, 167; nurses land, 171,
    207-8; white crosses, 174, 207, 220.
    See also D day
100th Evacuation Hospital, 171-73
101st Evacuation Hospital, 160-61, 167-
    68
103rd Fleet Hospital, 45-7
111th Fleet Hospital, 45-7
112th General Hospital, 243-46
114th Station Hospital, 123-26, 185-86,
    235
119th Station Hospital, 34-7, 251
128th General Hospital, 158
132nd Evacuation Hospital, 223
132nd General Hospital, 44
133rd General Hospital, 66-67, 250
147th Station Hospital, 23-25
148th General Hospital, 23
153rd Station Hospital, 34, 251
156th Station Hospital, 67-8
166th General Hospital, 199-231
167th General Hospital, 178-85
168th General Hospital, 174-75
168th Station Hospital, 154-56
170th General Hospital, 225
178th General Hospital, 244
187th General Hospital, 107, 159
195th General Hospital, 244
196th General Hospital, 226
OSS, 139-40, 144, 146
Osterlund, Nellie, 19-22
Ott, Elsie (Mandot), 109
Ouija board, 200, 202

Owi, 44-45, 54

P

P-38, 139, 169
P-47, 224
Pacific Theater, 28-78 237, 255
Page, *See* Hill, Evelyn
Page, *See* Robinson, Ellen
Panama Canal: shop for uniforms, 34;
    stuck for days, 229
parachute: drop mines, 194, notes,
    173, supplies, 138; not enough,
    137; nurse in China, 4; patients,
    133; wedding dress, 61, 223, 238
Paris: after the war, 224, 244, 251;
    American Hospital, 217, 220-1, 236;
    LeBourget Airfield, 170; liberation,
    170, 178; opera house, 170, 182,
    218; passes, 187, 217-19; Pigalle,
    244; subway, 221; tropical medi-
    cine training, 168; wedding, 216,
    227. *See also* Notre Dame
Patton, George, 162, 167, 216, 246
Payne, Shirley (Sweet), 199, 201-2,
    204, 207, 217, 224
Pearl Harbor: bombs dropped, 11-21,
    26; frightening announcement, 79,
    113, 119, 252; nurse status
    changes, 257; quota for African
    American nurses, 5; war declared,
    19
penicillin, 43, 58, 67, 100, 108, 194
Pennsylvania, University of, 15, 105
Peterson, Grace G., 169-70, 190-91
Phelps, Eunice (Carr), 218, 226,
Philippine Islands: African American
    nurses in, 41; Baguio, 93-95; Fort
    McKinley, 95; Fort Stotsenberg, 89;
    internment camps, 79-103, 239;

Leyte, 43, 57-8, 66-7, 96-7, 100; Mindanao, 36-7, 96; Mindoro, 42; Samar, 66, 101; San Fernando North, 55; Tongatabu, 29; World War I nurses, 5; Zamboanga, 36, 79. *See also* Bataan, Corregidor, Manila

plague, 83

Polchlopek, Julia (Scott), 58-61

polio, 39

Polish: guards, 158; invasion, 123, 243; patients, 126-27; 190, 214, 216

Polliwogs, 47-50

Pons, Lily, 218

Pope Pius XII, 126, 135, 148-49

Porter, Helen, 145

Pravda, 196

prayer, ix, 17, 57, 149, 200, 213, 219, 255

Price, *See* Whitlow, Elizabeth, 98, 239

Pride of the Yankees, 25

prison camps: German, 171, 189-90, 218, 240; Japanese, 79-103, 112, 239, 253, 258

prisoners: American, 74-5, 112, 118, 157, 175, 221, 240, 244, 253, 258; British, 171, 221; German, 5, 127, 147-48, 151, 154, 157-58, 179-82, 185-86, 189, 202, 215, 218-19, 221, 224, 251; Italian, 5, 129, 118, 251-52; Japanese, 5, 36, 42, 78, 112, 115, 200, 251-52; Korean, 251; nurses, 1, 17-8, 66, 74, 79-103, 239-40; Polish, 127, 190; Russian, 190, 218

prostitutes, 13, 19, 82, 219, 230, 244, 254

psychiatric patients: Chinese, 111; during battle, 124; hospital, 158; in camp, 43, 120; in plane crash, 68; on ship, 163; German prisoners, 179; with gun, 215-216

Puerto Rico, 5, 113

Q

Queen Elizabeth, 199, 204, 220, 225, 230

Queen Mary, 108, 157, 163, 174

Quezon, Manuel, 89

Quonset huts, 61, 63, 75, 77, 160, 181, 224

R

Raffa, *See* Richey, Margaret

Raiche, Violet, 203

RAMPS, 221

rank, 5-7, 101, 180, 224, 239, 257

Rasmussen, *See* Bell, Margaret

rats: dead bodies, 92; hepatitis, 117; in barracks, 35, 43, 233; in New Guinea hospital, 35, 43; mouse, 172

Red Cross: African American nurses recruited, 37; blood bank, 126; bridesmaid dresses, 223; feed patients, 46, 118; French lessons, 213; mail for prisoners, 98, 103; meet trains, 151, 228; poems, 128, 208-9; recruit nurses for military, 6, 34; send off ships, 205, workers, 3

Richey, Margaret (Raffa), 30-33

Rickert, *See* Terrell, Lenore

Riskedahl, Hilda (Cornelius), 252-55

Robertson, Mary, 36

Robinson, Ellen (Page), 233-34

Rodd, *See* Loomis, Verna

Rodgers, Audrey (McDonald), 110-11

romance: fiancé killed, 186; getting dates, 173; long distance, 68; in prison camps, 98-9, 101; on ship, 255; with enlisted, 7, 25, 54, 217, 224, 227; with married men, 127, 133, 245, 255

Romanian patients, 181

Rommel, Erwin, 129, 243

Roosevelt, Eleanor: and African American nurses, 5; visits to bases, 46

Roosevelt, Franklin: death, 78, 149, 159, 220; December 7 speech, 19, 146; Russian bases, 97, 195; son on Ulithi, 67

Rosedale, Lucile (Tubbs), 193-94, 248-50

Ross, Roberta, 113

RUSPS, 221

Russia: Eastern Command nurses, 193-97; ex-prisoner patients, 156, 171, 190, 214, 218; language, 216; lend lease, 256; Mirgorod, 195-97; Moscow, 196; Piryatin, 193-94; Poltava, 193-95

S

Saipan, 58-65, 71, 73-4

Sanchez, *See* Drennan, Aloha

Santa Scholastica, Philippines, 81, 86, 87

Santo Tomás Prison, 66, 82-6, 88, 91-3, 95-101

Saturday Evening Post, 168

Schmidt, *See* Kennedy, Imogene

Schofield Barracks HI, 16-7, 25, 67, 251-52

Scholl, Dorothy (Arnold) 96, 98

Sciora, *See* Kolczak, Jean

Scott, *See* Polchlopek, Julia

Seabees, 32, 56

Seagraves, Gordon, 113

Second Field Hospital, 34-7, 251

segregation, x, 5, 37-41, 154-56, 233-34. *See also* African American, Blacks

Senegalese, 126-27

Seventh Army, 189

Seventh Fleet, 56

Seventy-third Evacuation Hospital, 107-9

Shackelford, Wilma (Ford), 117-19

Shannon, *See* Grabowski, Virginia

Shea *See* Vinsant, Wilma

Shellbacks, 48-50

Shikoski, Dorothy (McCarthy), 33-4

Short Snorter, 70, 256

Shurr, Agnes, 11-2, 29-30

Sicily, 123, 129, 133, 135-37

Silva, *See* Simons, Jane

Simons, Jane (Silva), 74-5

Simpson, Phyllis (McGlory), 41-2

Sixtieth Field Hospital, 222-23

Sixty-first General Hospital, 157

Sixty-second General Hospital, 226

Skinner, *See* Emory, Lillie

smell, 13, 47, 51-2, 90, 163-64, 218

Smith, *See* Makar, Stella

Smith, *See* O'Connell, Rosemary

Smith, Maude, 26, 235

snakes, 55-7, 108-9, 111, 120

songs: *A Pretty Girl*, 205; *Alouette*, 178; *Anchors Aweigh*, 82; *Bless Them All*, 178; *Glory, Glory Halleluja*, 65; *Here Comes The Bride*, 223; *Lili Marlene*, 167; *Mademoiselle From Armentiers*, 178; *Nearer My God To Thee*, 51; *Notre Dame Fight Song*, 66; *Oh, Johnny*, 114; *Oh Holy Night*, 43; *Pistol Packin Mama*, 205; *Roll Me Over*, 168, 178; *Sentimental*

Journey, 250; *Spring Will Be A Little Late*, 168; *Star Spangled Banner*, 41; *The Boys In The Back Room*, 167; *Till We Meet Again*, 65; *When The Lights Come On Again*, 57; *White Christmas,* 250

Sours, Elsie, 105-7

South African patients, 127

Spam, 47, 68, 103, 133

Spanish-American War, 5, 93

Spanish language, 41, 89, 181

SS *Tabinta*, 67-8

Staats, *See* Torrance, Betty

Stahovich, Irina, 209-10, 227-28

Steele, Anna (Fox), 158

sterilize, 17, 83, 86, 132. *See also* autoclave

Sternberg Hospital, Philippines, 80-1, 89, 95-6

Still, Dorothy (Danner), 86, 103

Stockport, England, 161

stomach, 170, 173. *See also* abdominal, belly

Stonehenge, 152

Sudanese patients, 127

surgical technician, 69, 117-18, 136, 143. *See also* corpsmen, wardboys

Sweet, *See* Payne, Shirley

Swindon, England, 152, 158

Switzerland honeymoon, 247

T

XII Corps, 167

XX Corps, 167

Tagalog, 41

Tarawa, 29, 70

Taylor, *See* Krause, Lorraine

Tennessee: Knoxville, 155-56; Memphis, 119, 256

Tenth Field Hospital, 131-35, 186-87, 189-90

Terrell, Lenore (Rickert), 14-15, 257-59

tetanus, 13, 18, 80, 200

Texas, xi, 30, 136, 154-55

Thanksgiving, 211, 254

Theobald, Betty (Blagen), 161

Third Army, 113, 167, 171

Third Combat Cargo, 115

Third Fleet, 253

Third Station Hospital, 195

Thirteenth Station Hospital, 42

Thirty-third Surgical Hospital, 41-2

Thirty-fifth Evacuation Hospital, 167

Thirty-fifth General Hospital, 42-3, 54

Thorp, Frances, 113-15

Tidwell, England, 159, 195

Tilton, Martha, 37

Times Square, New York, 252, 255

Tinian, 70-1

Todd, Carrie Edwina, 85, 88, 99, 102

Toilets: 2-holer, 61-2; 5-holer, 233; 8-holer, 61; boxes, 106; broken, 97; foot holders, 132, 246; fur covered, 124; "head," 67; hole in floor, 231, 246; "inside," 145; plentiful, 247; portable in airplane, 120; public, 204; trenches, 94; whizzers, 77. *See also* latrine

Tokyo, Japan, 231

Tongatabu, Philippines, 29

Torrance, Betty (Staats), 47-52, 146-49

trains, 177, 183

Tremper, Frances (Howard), 210

Tripler Hospital HI, 16, 18-21, 67

Truman, Harry, 149, 220, 224, 256

Tubbs, *See* Rosedale, Lucille

tuberculosis, 30, 79, 83, 101, 190, 218

Tunisia: Bizerte, 124, 127, 129;

Casbah, 124; Ferryville, 124, 133; Mateur, 124-25, 132-33
Tuskegee Air Field AL, 233
Twentieth General Hospital, 105-8, 111
Twenty-first General Hospital, 123-26
Twenty-second Station Hospital, 23, 25, 251-52
Twenty-fifth Station Hospital, 233-4
Twenty-sixth Station Hospital, 228
216th General Hospital, 160
217th General Hospital, 176-78
218th Hospital Ship, 53-54, 163-65, 237
250th Station Hospital, 151-54
268th Station Hospital, 37-41, 237-38
286th General Hospital, 228
327th Station Hospital, 157
362nd Station Hospital, 34-6, 41-2
369th Station Hospital, 58-66
typhoid, 83, 218
typhoon, 31, 43, 68
typhus, 44, 189

207; wraparound dress, 24, 60, 106
USS *Arizona*, 251
USS *Benevolence*, 252-55
USS *Comfort*, 4
USS *Cristobal*, 126-27
USS *David Shanks*, 249
USS *Dogwood*, 53-4, 163-65, 237
USS *General Aultman*, 229-30
USS *General Bundy*, 68
USS *George Washington Carver*, 163
USS *Holbrook*, 66
USS *Lurline*, 41, 43
USS *Missouri*, 29, 68, 250
USS *Monterey*, 37-9
USS *Monticello*, 106
USS *Nevada*, 21
USS *New Jersey*, 254
USS *Randall*, 111
USS *Refuge*, 47-52, 146-49, 255
USS *Sea Perch*, 225
USS *Solace*, 11-2, 29-31
USS Solace Was There, 30
Utah Beach, 167, 169, 176

U

Ullom, Madeline, 89-93, 97-8
uniforms: army blue, 24, 60, 201; army dress, 22; army fatigue, 60, 64; army flight, 71-72, 115, 135, 137, 146; used for dressings, 86; changes, 6, 24, 257; class A, 127, 129, 152, 172, 179, 193; dress pink, 60, 201, 219; ex-internees', 74; list of supplies, 131-32; mismatched, 34; navy dress, 35, 75, 101; navy duty, 51, 147; navy flight, 73; olive drab, 24, 60, 201, 219; order by mail, 200; *Seersucker*, 24, 60, 106, 201; supplemental, 202,

V

V-E Day: Germany, 168, 171; LeMans, 225-26; Paris, 221, 248-49; Scotland, 243; Times Square, 252
V-J Day: at sea, 229, Bremerton, 258; Kau Kau Korners, Honolulu, 25; LeHavre, 184; Marseilles, 184; Philippines, 250; Times Square, 255
Van Gorp, Dymphna, 234-5
Van Hoorebeck, Rosedith (Hawkins), 54-5
Vaubel, Valera (Wiskerson), 12-13
venereal disease, 37, 58, 126, 194, 231, 244, 254
veterinarian, 91

Viergutz, Florence, 160, 247
Vinsant, Wilma (Shea), 4
Vowell, Edith, 34, 251
Vroeman, Martha, 174-75

W

Wake Island, 258
Wallenga, Esther, 47-51, 146-47, 255
wardboys, 3, 153, 216. *See also* corpsmen, surgical technicians
Warrington, England, 154-56
washing machine, 31, 56, 77, 196. *See also* helmets
Watson, Lois (McKenzie), 136, 140-43
weddings, 22-3, 25, 54, 61, 69, 119, 142, 182, 216, 223, 227, 237, 247, 259
Wedemeyer, Albert, 116
Weltzien, Gladys (Hesson), 207-8, 222
Wenning, Helen, 202, 208, 213, 225, 248
Wentz, Helen (Miller), 47-53, 146-49, 255-56

White, *See* Wynick, Clara
Whitlow, Elizabeth (Reith Price), 98, 239
Whitlow, Evelyn (Greenfield), 96-8, 239
Whittle, Reba, 240
Wiechman, *See* Heermance, Florence
Wild, *See* Borup, Laura
Will, Pearl (Haugland Bach): Alaska, 235; Philippines, 66, 250
Williams, Althea, 43-4, 238
Williams, *See* Behnke, Eleanor
Wisconsin: Madison, 178, 180; Milwaukee, 34, 126, 207, 228. *See also* Camp McCoy
Wiskerson, *See* Vaubel, Valera
Wood, Dorothy (Angerer), 55-8
Woodman, *See* Clark, Mildred Irene
Wynick, Clara,(White), 42-3, 250

Y

Yungblut, Eva (Lapham), 216
Yunker, Jean (Johnson), 111-12